The Dog Lovers Companion to Los Angeles

1ST EDITION

Maria Goodavage

LASSIE

AVALON
TRAVEL

THE DOG LOVER'S COMPANION TO LOS ANGELES
INCLUDING VENTURA, L.A., ORANGE, SAN BERNARDINO, AND RIVERSIDE COUNTIES

Published by
Avalon Travel Publishing
1400 65th Street, Suite 250
Emeryville, CA 94608, USA

AVALON Avalon Travel Publishing
publishing group incorporated An Imprint of Avalon Publishing Group, Inc.

Printing History
1st edition—October 2005
5 4 3 2 1

ISBN-10: 1-56691-923-1
ISBN-13: 978-1-56691-923-4
ISSN: 1555-9394

Editor and Series Manager: Kathryn Ettinger
Acquisitions Manager: Rebecca K. Browning
Copy Editor: Deana Shields
Designer: Jacob Goolkasian
Graphics Coordinator: Tabitha Lahr
Production Coordinator: Amber Pirker
Layout Artist: Mary Gilliana
Map Editor: Kevin Anglin
Cartographers: Sheryle Veverka, Kat Kalamaras
Indexer: May Hasso

Cover and Interior Illustrations by Phil Frank

Printed in the United States by Worzalla

ABOUT THE AUTHOR

© Laura Altair

Jake the Yellow-Lab-Sort-of-Dog has traveled throughout Southern California to check out some of the most dog-friendly parks, beaches, lodgings, and restaurants in the world. As part of his research, he's ridden on ferries, gondolas, and steam trains. He's visited drive-in movies, kitschy tourist attractions, and dog-friendly wineries. He's eaten at restaurants where dogs are treated almost like people (except they never get the bill). He's stayed at the best hotels, the worst motels, and everything in between. His favorite saying: "You're not really gonna leave the house *without* me, are ya?" (This is usually accompanied by all his extra folds of neck skin drooping forward into his face, his floppy ears hanging especially low, his tail sagging dejectedly, and his big brown eyes looking remarkably tearful.)

Since Jake is a dog without a driver's license (his furry feet don't reach the pedals), he relies on Maria Goodavage, former longtime *USA Today* correspondent, to be his chauffeur. Maria is well qualified. She started chauffeuring dogs in 1989, when her pooches joined her during some of her statewide travels for the newspaper. The results: Her book *The Dog Lover's Companion to California* is a best-seller, now in its fifth edition. Maria is also the author of the popular book *The Dog Lover's Companion to the Bay Area,* in its fifth edition as well.

Although Jake lives near the beach in San Francisco with Maria, her husband, and her daughter, he spends so much time in Southern California that he's considering buying a second home there.

To get more information or offer a suggestion about dog-friendly travel in California, visit Maria's website, www.caldogtravel.com.

CONTENTS

LOS ANGELES

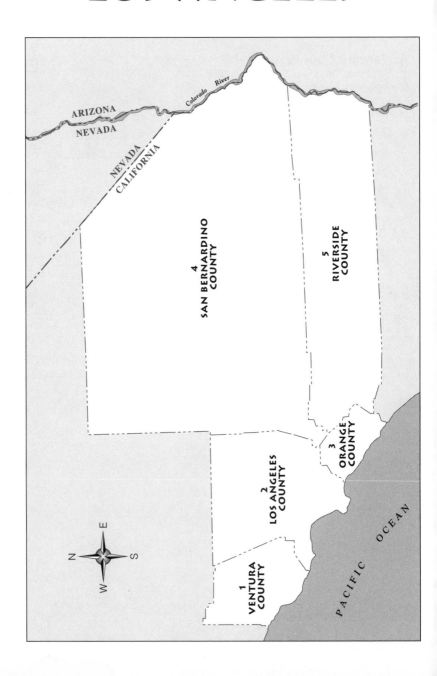

MAPS

Introduction

Now, Charley is a mind-reading dog. There have been many trips in his lifetime, and often he has to be left at home. He knows we are going long before the suitcases come out, and he paces and worries and whines and goes into a state of mild hysteria, old as he is.

John Steinbeck, *Travels with Charley*

There was a time when dogs could go just about anywhere they pleased. Well-dressed dogs with embarrassing names attended afternoon teas, while their less-kempt counterparts sauntered into saloons without anyone's blinking a bloodshot eye.

No one thought it strange to see a pug-nosed little snookum-wookums of a dog snuggled on his mistress's lap on a long train journey. Equally accepted were dogs prancing through fine hotels, dogs at dining establishments, and dogs in almost any park they cared to visit.

But then there came a time (a period perhaps best referred to as the Doggy Dark Ages) when dogs came to be seen as beasts not fit for hotels, restaurants, or even many parks. The world was getting more crowded, patience grew thinner, there was only so much room, and—dang it—four-legged varmints weren't going to be sharing it. They were just *dogs* after all—animals who eat from bowls on the floor and lick their heinies at unfortunate moments. Dogs were for the house, the backyard, sidewalks (with canines being "curbed"), and some tolerant parks. So we got used to leaving our dogs behind when we took off for an afternoon or a road trip. It hurt, oh, how it hurt, but what could you do?

Many of us know that guilt too well. The guilt that stabs at you as you push your dog's struggling body back inside the house and tug the door shut can be so painful that sometimes you just can't look back. Even a trip to the grocery store can become a heart-wrenching tale of woe. The most recent survey by the American Animal Hospital Association shows that the vast majority of us feel guilty when leaving pets at home. Thirty-nine percent of pet people call to talk to their pets when they're away. I've tried that, but it always made me feel even worse.

Joe, the Airedale terrier who inspired not only this book but the entire *Dog Lover's Companion* series, was born with an unparalleled gift for knowing how to make people feel guilty—and not your ordinary, run-of-the-mill guilt where you smart for a couple of hours after seeing your dog's moping eyes follow your car as you speed away. It's that deep-in-the-gut-for-days guilt, where the sight of that pouting snout, those drooping ears, and that tail lowered to half-mast hangs with you until you return home.

John Steinbeck's blue poodle, Charley, was a master of powerful pleas that were carefully designed to allow him to accompany his people on trips. Eventually, his hard work paid off and he won himself a seat in Steinbeck's brand-new truck/house on their epic journey across America. They sought and found the heart of this country in their adventures across 34 states.

Joe's guilt-inducing expertise won him a spot in my rusty, beat-up, hiccupping pickup truck in our sporadic little journeys around the L.A. area and, in fact, the whole state. We sought and found thousands of dog-friendly places in our adventures and misadventures.

Joe and I were frequently joined by two other experts in the field of rating parks and sniffing out good dog attractions. Nisha, our old-lady springer spaniel, insisted on standing in the back of the truck, under the camper top, madly wagging her tail for hours on end as we drove and drove and drove. She was a real asset to have around when it came to checking out beaches, lakes, rivers, and ponds—any area with water. (Joe hated to get his paws wet, so he couldn't be impartial in his rating of watery attractions.)

Bill, a big, lovable galoot of a dog, was my other original canine researcher. I found him partway through my travels. He was trembling in the middle of a semi-rural road (a trailer-park-festooned one, actually), with a big chain tight around his neck. He'd evidently broken loose, because the last link of the thick chain was mauled. I came to find out that his owner beat him regularly. Bill went back home with me that afternoon. During the months when I was looking for the perfect home for him (oh, and did he ever get the perfect home!), he became one of the friendliest, most outgoing dogs I've ever had the pleasure to meet. His presence during my journeys was invaluable. He lifted my spirits when I was tired, and his 85 pounds of muscle kept away bad spirits when we visited questionable areas.

Time moves on. All journeys have to end someday. Bill is the only remaining dog from the original crew. Gregarious, lovable Nisha departed for Dog Heaven years ago. There, she can chew rocks and chase sticks to her heart's content.

And Joe, my most wonderful furry friend and constant traveling buddy for 13 years, joined her just a couple of years ago. He is dearly missed, but his legacy—that of helping other dogs lead better lives by sniffing out places they're allowed to go with their humans—lives on. I'm pretty sure that now he's chasing—and finally catching—cats (in Dog Heaven, in case you didn't know, all cats are slow) and eating all the horse manure he wants. And he *always* gets to go for rides in the car.

Before I choke up, I'd like to introduce you to a dog you'll be seeing plenty of throughout this book. His name is Jake, and we figure he's about 97 percent yellow Lab, leaving 3 percent for hound or Great Dane or some other big thing with short fur. When he was about six months old, we were asked to foster him for a week. That was well over a year ago. (We hear this happens when you foster a dog.)

Jake now weighs in at Bill's weight—85 pounds—and is one of the sweetest, most noodley dogs I've ever met. When we're home, he can usually be found reposing on the couch (despite our best attempts to keep him off it, the couch is now referred to as "Jake's couch"), jowls sprawled over the windowsill (which is half chewed away from his younger days, a very attractive sight), big brown eyes staring off into the distance as if longing for another road trip.

We've had some terrific trips together so far. Since traveling with a giant furry termite is a bad idea, I waited until his penchant for chewing furniture, windowsills, and floorboards had disappeared. Then we hit the road, enjoying dog-friendly lodgings, restaurants, and parks around Southern California.

As a water dog, he's wonderful at checking out liquid attractions, from wading pools at dog parks to ponds, lakes, and beaches. Fortunately, I never have to worry about him going after ducks, per his breed's instinct. For some reason, when swimming ducks see him dog-paddling, they make a beeline right for him. This gives Jake the creeps, and he swims away, with the ducks fast on his tail. It's a sight that would make a duck hunter cry.

On a similar note, he's always glad when we visit a dog park that has a separate section for small dogs. Tiny dogs become giants with Jake, yapping a couple of times while giving him the chase. He tucks his tail between his

legs and runs away, glancing nervously behind him to make sure he's escaped before relaxing enough to be his big doggy self again.

You'll be meeting up with Jake throughout this book, and Joe is still a big part of it, too. I think you'll find them, together with Nisha and Bill, excellent representatives of dogs in the L.A. area.

We've tried to sniff out the very best of everything you can do with your dog in these parts, so you'll never again have to face the prospect of shutting the door on your dog's nose. This book is crammed with descriptions of hundreds of dog-friendly parks, restaurants with outdoor tables, and lodgings.

The Dog Lover's Companion to Los Angeles finds the Doggy Dark Ages far behind. L.A.-area dogs are lucky dogs indeed: Dog parks are sprouting from the earth as if some giant fairy dog has planted fast-growing dog-park seeds. Dog parks are a huge trend, one that shows no signs of slowing. These parks run the gamut from very basic (often just bones city governments provide to appease their dog-bearing constituents) to gorgeous, perfectly manicured, custom-designed doggy playgrounds. If you don't like fenced pooch parks, try the millions of acres of wilder land set aside to keep life from being over-run by developments. Our favorites are managed by the U.S. Forest Service, the Santa Monica Mountains National Recreation Area and the Santa Monica Mountains Conservancy.

The book also describes myriad unusual adventures you and your dog can share. You can ride on ferries, stagecoaches, and miniature trains. You can sip chardonnay at wineries that welcome dogs, go to dog camp in Malibu, march in pet parades, shop at high-fashion stores, and play tourist by visiting various walks of fame and their ilk.

If you know of any great places that should be included in the book but aren't, please see the last paragraph in this introduction for information on how to contact us. We're always looking for new places to sniff out.

Beyond L.A.

Dog travel is scorching hot—a big difference from its chilly state when I started writing on the topic of dog travel in the early 1990s. Everyone's getting in on it. For many reasons, dogs have become a real part of our families, and businesses have seen the golden opportunities.

Pet-focused travel agencies are starting to pop up. A pet-centered airline that transports dogs alongside their humans (Companion Air; www.companionair.com) is getting off the ground, with hopes business will soon take off. Iams pet food is producing handy little Travel Meals for "pets on the run" (www.travelmeals.com).

The hospitality industry, which has been lagging for a few years, is opening doors to dogs as never before. Motel 6, the first chain to allow dogs, has eliminated its policy of allowing only small dogs, and now most of its motel managers give the thumbs-up to any size good dog. Many upscale chains have taken the dog-friendly policy a step further. Loews has its "Loews Loves Pets" program. Kimpton hotels all welcome dogs, and most provide them some sort of VIP package. And most recently, Starwood Hotels, one of the leading hotel companies in the world, started its Starwood LTD (Love That Dog) program in its Sheraton, Westin, and W hotels in the United States and Canada.

"Dog owners are a market niche that's been underserved by the travel industry," a Starwood press release announced. And Barry Sternlicht, Starwood's chairman and CEO, has lofty goals for Starwood: "We intend to become the most dog-friendly hotel company in the land, and not just allow dogs to stay, but actually pamper and spoil them," says Barry, who has two dogs of his own.

Many other lodgings, from the humblest cabins to the most regal luxury suites and chichi vacation rentals, are now allowing dog guests. "If we have a house that doesn't permit dogs, they're just not going to do very well," a vacation rental agent told me.

The vacation industry is truly going to the dogs.

(Reflecting these trends, the comic strip *Cathy* devoted a week to its namesake character planning a vacation with her little dog, Electra. "Look, Electra!" exclaimed Cathy, who had been poring over dog-travel literature. "Hotels that allow dogs! Restaurants that allow dogs! Beaches that allow dogs! Museums that allow dogs! People can finally take a real vacation with their dogs!" Deadpanned Electra, "We don't have a dog.")

If you want to travel beyond the L.A. area with your dog, you'll find a state full of dog-friendly places to visit. You just have to know where to look. I've included a chapter at the end of this book with some great ideas for dog-friendly getaways. But that's just the beginning. If you'd like to explore the state with your dog, you'll want to get my 1,000-page tome, *The Dog Lover's*

Companion to California. It's essential reading for anyone interested in going beyond their backyard with their dog. (If I do say so myself.)

The California book provided a springboard for the entire series of *Dog Lover's Companions*, popular around the United States, so if you want to go beyond the borders of California, you now have some wonderful companions (besides your dog) to join you. My website, www.caldogtravel.com, lists them all, as does my publisher's, www.dogloverscompanion.com.

The Paws Scale

At some point, we've got to face the facts: Humans and dogs have different tastes. We like eating oranges and smelling lilacs and covering our bodies with soft clothes. They like eating roadkill and smelling each other's unmentionables and covering their bodies with horse manure.

The parks, beaches, and recreation areas in this book are rated with a dog in mind. Maybe your favorite park has lush gardens, a duck pond, a few acres of perfectly manicured lawns, and sweeping views of a nearby skyline. But unless your dog can run leash-free, swim in the pond, and roll in the grass, that park doesn't deserve a very high rating.

The very lowest rating you'll come across in this book is the fire hydrant symbol 🐾. This means the park is merely "worth a squat." Visit one of these parks only if your dog just can't hold it any longer. These parks have virtually no other redeeming qualities for canines.

Beyond that, the paws scale starts at one paw 🐾 and goes up to four paws 🐾🐾🐾🐾. A one-paw park isn't a dog's idea of a great time. Maybe it's a tiny park with few trees and too many kids running around. Or perhaps it's a magnificent-for-people park that bans dogs from every inch of land except paved roads and a few campsites. Four-paw parks, on the other hand, are places your dog will drag you to visit. Some of these areas come as close to dog heaven as you can imagine. Many have lakes for swimming or zillions of acres for hiking. Some are small, fenced-in areas where leash-free dogs can tear around without danger of running into the road.

This book is *not* a comprehensive guide to all of the parks in the L.A. area. If I included every single park, it would be ridiculously unportable. Instead, I tried to find the best, largest, and most convenient parks—and especially parks that allow dogs off leash. Some locales have so many wonderful parks that I had to make some tough choices in deciding which to include and which to leave out. Others have such a limited supply of parks that, for the sake of dogs living and visiting there, I ended up listing parks that wouldn't otherwise be worth mentioning.

I've provided specific directions to the major parks and parks near highways. Other parks are listed by their cross streets. I highly recommend checking an Internet map site such as Mapquest.com or picking up detailed street maps from the AAA—California State Automobile Association (maps are free for members)—before you and your dog set out on your adventures.

He, She, It

In this book, whether neutered, spayed, or au naturel, dogs are never referred to as "it." They are either "he" or "she." I alternate pronouns so no dog reading this book will feel left out.

To Leash or Not to Leash...

This is not a question that plagues dogs' minds. Ask just about any normal, red-blooded American dog whether she'd prefer to visit a park and be on leash or off, and she'll say, "Arf!" No question about it, most dogs would give their canine teeth to frolic about without a cumbersome leash.

Whenever you see the running dog symbol 🐕 in this book, you'll know that under certain circumstances, your dog can run around in leash-free bliss. Fortunately, the L.A. area is home to dozens of such parks. The rest of the parks demand leashes. I wish I could write about the parks where dogs get away with being scofflaws. Unfortunately, those would be the first parks the animal control patrols would hit. I don't advocate breaking the law, but if you're going to, please follow your conscience and use common sense.

Also, just because dogs are permitted off leash in certain areas doesn't necessarily mean you should let your dog run free. In large tracts of wild land, unless you're sure your dog will come back when you call or will never stray more than a few yards from your side, you should probably keep her leashed.

An otherwise docile homebody can turn into a savage hunter if the right prey is near. Or your curious dog could perturb a rattlesnake or dig up a rodent whose fleas carry bubonic plague. In pursuit of a strange scent, your dog could easily get lost in an unfamiliar area. (Some forest rangers recommend having your dog wear a bright orange collar, vest, or backpack when out in the wilderness.)

There's No Business Like Dog Business

There's nothing appealing about bending down with a plastic bag or a piece of newspaper on a chilly morning and grabbing the steaming remnants of what your dog ate for dinner the night before. It's disgusting. Worse yet, you have to hang onto it until you can find a trash can. And how about when the newspaper doesn't endure before you can dispose of it? Yuck! It's enough to make you wish your dog could wear diapers. But as gross as it can be to scoop the poop, it's worse to step in it. It's really bad if a child falls in it, or—*gasp!*—starts eating it. And have you ever walked into a park where few people clean up after their dogs? The stench could make a hog want to hibernate.

Unscooped poop is one of a dog's worst enemies. Public policies banning dogs from parks are enacted because of it. And not all poop woes are outside. A dog-loving concierge at an upscale hotel told us that a guest came up to her and said there was some dirt beside the elevator. The concierge sent someone to clean it up. The dirt turned out to be dog poop. The hotel, which used to be one of the most elegant dog-friendly hotels around (it even had a Pampered Pet Program), now bans dogs. (There were other reasons, including a new boss, but the poop was the last straw.)

Just be responsible and clean up after your dog everywhere you go. (And obviously, if there's even a remote chance he'll relieve himself inside, don't even bring him into hotels or stores that permit dogs!) Anytime you take your dog out, stuff plastic bags in your jacket, purse, car, pants pockets—anywhere you might be able to pull one out when needed. Or, if plastic isn't your bag, newspapers will do the trick. If it makes it more palatable, bring along a paper bag, too, and put the used newspaper or plastic bag in it. That way you don't have to walk around with dripping paper or a plastic bag whose contents are visible to the world. If you don't enjoy the squishy sensation, try one of those cardboard or plastic bag pooper-scoopers sold at pet stores. If you don't feel like bending down, buy a long-handled scooper. There's a scooper for every taste.

This is the only lecture you'll get on scooping in this entire book. To help keep parks alive, I should harp on it in every park description, but that would take another 100 pages—and you'd start to ignore it anyway. And, if I mentioned it in some park listings but not others, it might imply that you don't have to clean up after your dog in the parks where it's not mentioned.

A final note: Don't pretend not to see your dog while he's doing his bit. Don't pretend to look for it without success. And don't fake scooping it up when you're really just covering it with sand. I know these tricks because I've been guilty of them myself—but no more. I've seen the light. I've been saved. I've been delivered from the depths of dog-doo depravity.

Etiquette Rex: The Well-Mannered Mutt

While cleaning up after your dog is your responsibility, a dog in a public place has his own responsibilities. Of course, it really boils down to your responsibility again, but the burden of action is on your dog. Etiquette for restaurants and hotels is covered in other sections of this chapter. What follows are some fundamental rules of dog etiquette. I'll go through it quickly, but if your dog's a slow reader, he can read it again: no vicious dogs; no jumping on people; no incessant barking; no leg lifts on surfboards, backpacks, human legs, or any other personal objects you'll find hanging around beaches and parks; dogs should come when they're called; dogs should stay on command.

Joe Dog managed to violate all but the first of these rules at one point or another. (Jake has followed in his pawsteps to an amazing extent, considering he never even met Joe.) Do your best to remedy any problems. It takes patience, and it's not always easy. For instance, there was a time during Joe's youth when he seemed to think that human legs were tree trunks. Rather than pretending I didn't know the beast, I strongly reprimanded him, apologized to the victim from the depths of my heart, and offered money for dry cleaning. Joe learned his lesson—many dry-cleaning bills later.

Safety First

A few essentials will keep your traveling dog happy and healthy.

Heat: If you must leave your dog alone in the car for a few minutes, do so only if it's cool out and if you can park in the shade. *Never, ever, ever* leave a dog in a car with the windows rolled up all the way. Even if it seems cool, the sun's heat passing through the window can kill a dog in a matter of minutes. Roll down the window enough so your dog gets air, but also so there's no danger of your dog's getting out or someone breaking in. Make sure your dog has plenty of water.

You also have to watch out for heat exposure when your car is in motion. Certain cars, such as hatchbacks, can make a dog in the backseat extra hot, even while you feel OK in the driver's seat.

Try to time your vacation so you don't visit a place when it's extremely warm. Dogs and heat don't get along, especially if the dog isn't used to heat. The opposite is also true. If your dog lives in a hot climate and you take him to a freezing place, it may not be a healthy shift. Check with your vet if you have any doubts. Spring and fall are usually the best times to travel.

Water: Water your dog frequently. Dogs on the road may drink even more than they do at home. Take regular water breaks, or bring a heavy bowl (the thick clay ones do nicely) and set it on the floor so your dog always has access to water. I use a non-spill bowl, which comes in really handy on curvy roads. When hiking, be sure to carry enough for you *and* a thirsty dog.

Rest Stops: Stop and unwater your dog. There's nothing more miserable than being stuck in a car when you can't find a rest stop. No matter how tightly you cross your legs and try to think of the desert, you're certain you'll burst within the next minute… so imagine how a dog feels when the urge strikes, and he can't tell you the problem. There are plenty of rest stops along the major California freeways. I've also included many parks close to freeways for dogs who need a good stretch with their bathroom break.

How frequently you stop depends on your dog's bladder. If your dog is constantly running out the doggy door at home to relieve himself, you may want to stop every hour. Others can go significantly longer without being uncomfortable. Watch for any signs of restlessness and gauge it for yourself.

Car Safety: Even the experts differ on how a dog should travel in a car. Some suggest doggy safety belts, available at pet-supply stores. Others firmly believe in keeping a dog kenneled. They say it's safer for the dog if there's an accident, and it's safer for the driver because there's no dog underfoot. Still others say you should just let your dog hang out without straps and boxes. They believe that if there's an accident, at least the dog isn't trapped in a cage. They say that dogs enjoy this more, anyway.

I'm a follower of the last school of thought. Jake loves sticking his snout out of the windows to smell the world go by. The danger is that if the car kicks up a pebble or angers a bee, his nose and eyes could be injured. So far, he's been OK, as has every other dog who has explored the Golden State with us, but I've seen dogs who needed to be treated for bee stings to the nose because of this practice. If in doubt, try opening the window just enough so your dog can't stick out much snout.

Whatever travel style you choose, your pet will be more comfortable if he has his own blanket with him. A veterinarian acquaintance brings a faux-sheepskin blanket for his dogs. At night in the hotel, the sheepskin doubles as the dog's bed.

Planes: Air travel is even more controversial. Personally, unless my dogs can fly with me in the passenger section (which very tiny dogs are sometimes allowed to do), I'd rather find a way to drive the distance or leave them at home with a friend. I've heard too many horror stories of dogs suffocating in what was supposed to be a pressurized cargo section, dying of heat exposure, or ending up in Miami while their people go to Seattle. There's just something unappealing about the idea of a dog's flying in the cargo hold, as if he's nothing more than a piece of luggage. Of course, many dogs survive just fine, but I'm not willing to take the chance. (That said, an airline called Companion Air is hoping to be the first to offer a way for humans and any size dog to be together during plane travel—and not in the cargo section! It's still in the planning stages, but you can visit the website at www.companionair.com for updates.)

If you need to transport your dog by plane, try to fly nonstop, and make sure you schedule takeoff and arrival times when the temperature is below 80°F (but not bitterly cold in winter). Consult the airline about regulations, required certificates, and fees. Be sure to check with your vet to make sure your pooch is healthy enough to fly.

The question of tranquilizing a dog for a plane journey is very controversial. Some vets think it's insane to give a dog a sedative before flying. They say a dog will be calmer and less fearful without a disorienting drug. Others think it's crazy not to afford your dog the little relaxation he might not otherwise get without a tranquilizer. Discuss the issue with your vet, who will take into account the trip length and your dog's personality.

Many websites deal with air-bound pooches. I highly recommend checking them out for further info on safe air travel with your dog. Most of the web pages have long and cumbersome names, so you're best off searching for keywords such as "Traveling Airlines Pets."

The Ultimate Doggy Bag

Your dog can't pack his own bags, and even if he could, he'd probably fill them with dog biscuits and chew toys. It's important to stash some of those in your dog's vacation kit, but here are other handy items to bring along: bowls, bedding, a brush, towels (for those muddy days), a first-aid kit, pooper-scoopers, water, food, prescription drugs, tags, treats, toys, and—of course—this book.

Make sure your dog is wearing his license, identification tag, and rabies tag. Bringing along your dog's up-to-date vaccination records is a good idea, too. If you should find yourself at a park or campground that requires the actual rabies certificate, you'll be set. In addition, you may unexpectedly end up needing to leave your dog in a doggy day care for a few hours so you can go somewhere you just can't bring your dog. A record of his shots is imperative. (You'll also have to get him a kennel-cough shot if boarding is a possibility.)

It's a good idea to snap a disposable ID on your dog's collar, too, showing a cell phone number or the name, address, and phone number either of where you'll be vacationing or of a friend who'll be home to field calls. That way, if your dog should get lost, at least the finder won't be calling your empty house. Paper key-chain tags you buy at hardware stores offer a cheap way to change your dog's contact info as often as needed when on vacation. Dog-book author and pet columnist Gina Spadafori advises always listing a local number on the tag. "You'd be surprised how many people don't want to make a long-distance phone call," she writes in her book *Dogs for Dummies.*

Some people think dogs should drink only water brought from home, so their bodies don't have to get used to too many new things. I've never had a problem giving my dogs tap water from other parts of the state, nor has anyone else I know. Most vets think your dog will be fine drinking tap water in most U.S. cities.

"Think of it this way," says Pete Beeman, a longtime veterinarian with a sage view of the world. "Your dog's probably going to eat poop if he can get hold of some, and even that's probably not going to harm him. I really don't think that drinking water that's OK for people is going to be bad for dogs." (Jake can attest to the poop part. But let's not talk about that.)

Bone Appétit

In some European countries, dogs enter restaurants and dine alongside their folks as if they were people, too. (Or at least they sit and watch and drool while their people dine.) Not so in the United States. Rightly or wrongly, dogs are considered a health threat here. But many health inspectors I've spoken with say they see no reason why clean, well-behaved dogs shouldn't be permitted inside a restaurant. "Aesthetically, it may not appeal to Americans," an environmental specialist with the state Department of Health told me. "But the truth is, there's no harm in this practice."

Ernest Hemingway made an expatriate of his dog, Black Dog (a.k.a. Blackie), partly because of America's restrictive views on dogs in dining establishments. In "The Christmas Gift," a story published in *Look* magazine in 1954, he describes how he made the decision to take Black Dog to Cuba, rather than leave him behind in Ketchum, Idaho.

> This was a town where a man was once not regarded as respectable unless he was accompanied by his dog. But a reform movement had set in, led by several local religionists, and gambling had been abolished and there was even a movement on foot to forbid a dog from entering a public eating place with his master. Blackie had always tugged me by the trouser leg as we passed a combination gambling and eating place called the Alpine where they served the finest sizzling steak in the West. Blackie wanted me to order the giant sizzling steak and it was difficult to pass the Alpine.... We decided to make a command decision and take Blackie to Cuba.

Fortunately, you don't have to take your dog to a foreign country to eat together at a restaurant. The L.A. area is full of restaurants with outdoor tables, and hundreds of them welcome dogs to join their people for an alfresco experience. The law on outdoor dining is somewhat vague, and each county has different versions of it. In general, as long as your dog doesn't go inside a restaurant (even to get to outdoor tables in the back) and isn't near the food

DIVERSION

Ch-Ch-Chains: An increasing number of stores permit pooches these days, including many within chains such as Borders, Saks Fifth Avenue, REI, Nordstrom, Big Dogs Sportwear, and Restoration Hardware. Not all stores within these chains welcome dogs, but most do. If your dog is longing to do more than just window shop, she'll likely be in luck if one of these stores is on your shopping list.

preparation areas, it's probably legal. The decision is then up to the restaurant proprietor.

The restaurants listed in this book have given us permission to tout them as dog-friendly eateries. But keep in mind that rules can change and restaurants can close, so I highly recommend phoning before you set your stomach on a particular kind of cuisine. Since some restaurants close during colder months, phoning ahead is a doubly wise thing to do. (Of course, you can assume that where there's snow or ultra-cold temperatures, the outdoor tables will move indoors for a while each year.) If you can't call first, be sure to ask the manager of the restaurant for permission before you sit down with your sidekick. Remember, it's the restaurant proprietor, not you, who will be in trouble if someone complains to the health department.

Some basic rules of restaurant etiquette: Dogs shouldn't beg from other diners, no matter how delicious their steaks look. They should not attempt to get their snouts (or their entire bodies) up on the table. They should be clean, quiet, and as unobtrusive as possible. If your dog leaves a good impression with the management and other customers, it will help pave the way for all the other dogs who want to dine alongside their best friends in the future.

A Room at the Inn

Good dogs make great hotel guests. They don't steal towels, and they don't get drunk and keep the neighbors up all night. The Los Angeles area is full of lodgings whose owners welcome dogs. This book lists dog-friendly accommodations of all types, from motels to bed-and-breakfast inns to elegant hotels—but the basic dog etiquette rules are the same everywhere.

Dogs should never be left alone in your room. Leaving a dog alone in a strange place invites serious trouble. Scared, nervous dogs may tear apart drapes, carpeting, and furniture. They may even injure themselves. They might also bark nonstop and scare the daylights out of the housekeeper. Just don't do it.

Bring only a house-trained dog to a lodging. How would you like a house-guest to go to the bathroom in the middle of your bedroom?

Make sure your pooch is flea-free. Otherwise, future guests will be itching to leave.

It helps to bring your dog's bed or blanket along for the night. Your dog will feel more at home and won't be tempted to jump on the hotel bed. If your dog sleeps on the bed with you at home (as 47 percent do, according to the American Animal Hospital Association survey), bring a sheet and put it on top of the bed so the hotel's bedspread won't get furry or dirty.

Don't wash your dog in the hotel tub. "It's very yucky," I was told by one motel manager who has seen so many furry tubs that she's thinking about banning dogs.

Likewise, refrain from using the ice bucket as a water or food bowl. Bring your own bowls, or stay in a hotel that provides them, as many of the nicer ones do these days.

After a few days in a hotel, some dogs come to think of it as home. They get territorial. When another hotel guest walks by, it's "Bark! Bark!" When the housekeeper knocks, it's "Bark! Snarl! Bark! Gnash!" Keep your dog quiet, or you'll find yourselves looking for a new home away from home.

For some strange reason, many lodgings prefer small dogs as guests. All I can say is, "Yip! Yap!" It's really ridiculous. Large dogs are often much calmer and quieter than their tiny, high-energy cousins.

If you're in a location where you can't find a hotel that will accept you and your big brute (a growing rarity these days), it's time to try a sell job. Let the manager know how good and quiet your dog is (if he is). Promise he won't eat the bathtub or run around and shake all over the hotel. Offer a deposit or

sign a waiver, even if they're not required for small dogs. It helps if your sweet, soppy-eyed dog is at your side to convince the decision-maker.

I've sneaked dogs into hotels, but I don't recommend it. The lodging might have a good reason for its rules. Besides, you always feel as if you're going to be caught and thrown out on your hindquarters. You race in and out of your room with your dog as if ducking sniper fire. It's better to avoid feeling like a criminal and move on to a more dog-friendly location. With the number of lodgings that welcome dogs these days, you won't have to go far.

The lodgings described in this book are for dogs who obey all the rules. I list a range of rates for each lodging, from the least expensive room during low season to the priciest room during high season. Most of the rooms are doubles, so there's not usually a huge variation. But when a room price gets into the thousands of dollars, you know we're looking at royal suites.

Many lodgings charge extra for your dog. If you see "Dogs are $10 (or whatever amount) extra," that means $10 extra per night. Some charge a fee for the length of a dog's stay, and others ask for a deposit. These details are also noted in the lodging description. A few places still ask for nothing more than your dog's promise that she'll be on her best behavior. So, if no extra charge is mentioned in a listing, it means your dog can stay with you for free.

Natural Troubles

Chances are your adventuring will go without a hitch, but you should always be prepared to deal with trouble. Make sure you know the basics of animal first aid before you embark on a long journey with your dog.

The more common woes—ticks, foxtails, poison oak, and skunks—can make life with a traveling dog a somewhat trying experience. Ticks are hard to avoid in many parts of Southern California. They can carry Lyme disease, so you should always check yourself and your dog all over after a day in tick country. Don't forget to check ears and between the toes. If you see a tick, just pull it straight out with tweezers, not with your bare hands.

The tiny deer ticks that carry Lyme disease are difficult to find. Consult your veterinarian if your dog is lethargic for a few days, has a fever, loses her appetite, or becomes lame. These symptoms could indicate Lyme disease. Some vets recommend a new vaccine that is supposed to prevent the onset of the disease.

Foxtails—those arrow-shaped pieces of dry grass that attach to your socks, your sweater, and your dog—are an everyday annoyance. In certain cases, they can also be lethal. They may stick in your dog's eyes, nose, ears, or mouth and work their way in. Check every nook and cranny of your dog after a walk if you've been anywhere near dry grass. Despite my constant effort to find these things in Joe's curly tan fur, I missed several and they beat a path through his foot and into his leg. Be vigilant.

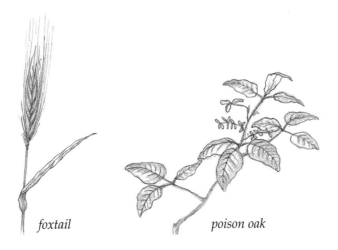

foxtail   *poison oak*

Poison oak is also a common California menace. Get familiar with it through a friend who knows nature or through a guided nature walk. Dogs don't generally have reactions to poison oak, but they can easily pass its oils on to people. If you think your dog has made contact with some poison oak, avoid petting her until you can get home and bathe her (preferably with rubber gloves). If you do pet her before you can wash her, don't touch your eyes and be sure to wash your hands immediately.

If your dog loses a contest with a skunk (and she *always* will), rinse her eyes first with plain warm water and then forget the old tomato-juice remedy. All that does is make a dog itchy—and if she starts out white, she can turn a creepy shade of orange.

I've had the fortune of being handed the best-ever recipe for de-skunking by Jamie Ray, an expert in the field. She's the founder of an urban wildlife rescue group. And it just so happens that some of the urban wildlife her group rescues is black and white and furry and occasionally whiffy, if you get my drift.

I phoned her one day after Jake had a much-too-close encounter of the skunky kind. The fumes were so bad I could barely breathe. Tomato juice wasn't an option, as it had never worked for our other dogs. I figured if anyone could help, Jamie could. And did she ever. Jake was left with barely any eau d'skunk, and you had to get very close to smell it. On two subsequent occasions, the recipe also worked magic.

I suggest you write down the recipe and keep it handy. You may also want to keep an extra bottle or two of hydrogen peroxide around so you'll always be ready. The other ingredients are in just about any household.

Make a mixture with the ratio of one cup hydrogen peroxide, two tablespoons of baking soda, and one tablespoon of dishwashing soap—Dawn works best. (For Jake, we multiplied this recipe times six, since he is so big and was so stinky.) Stir, then apply it all over your dog. Don't hold back. Use plenty, being careful to keep it away from the eyes. Rub it in, wait a couple of minutes, and rinse. You may need to do it again to really eradicate the stink. Rinse well. I've followed up each de-skunking with some gentle dog shampoo.

Ruffing It Together

Whenever we went camping, Joe insisted on sleeping in the tent. He sprawled out and wouldn't budge. At the first hint of dawn, he'd tiptoe outside (sometimes right through the bug screen) as if he'd been standing vigil all night. He tried not to look shamefaced, but under all that curly hair lurked an embarrassed grin.

Actually, Joe might have had the right idea. Some outdoor experts say it's dangerous to leave even a tethered dog outside your tent at night. The dog can escape or become a late dinner for some hungry creature.

All state parks require dogs to be kept in a tent or vehicle at night. Some county parks follow suit. Other policies are more lenient. Use good judgment.

If you're camping with your dog, chances are you're also hiking with him. Even if you're not hiking for long, watch out for your dog's paws, especially the paws of those who are fair of foot. Rough terrain can cause a dog's pads to become raw and painful, making it almost impossible for him to walk. Several types of dog boots are available for such feet. It's easier to carry the booties than to carry your dog home.

Be sure to bring plenty of water for you and your pooch. Stop frequently to wet your whistles. Some veterinarians warn against letting your dog drink out of a stream because of the chance of ingesting giardia and other internal parasites, but it's not always easy to stop a thirsty dog.

A Dog in Need

If you don't have a dog but could provide a good home for one, I'd like to make a plea on behalf of all the unwanted dogs who will be euthanized tomorrow—and the day after that and the day after that. Animal shelters and humane organizations are overflowing with dogs who would devote their lives to being your best buddy, your faithful traveling companion, and a dedicated listener to all your tales of bliss and woe.

Need a nudge? Remember the oft-quoted words of Samuel Butler:

> "The great pleasure of a dog is that you may make a fool of yourself with him and not only will he not scold you, but he will make a fool of himself, too."

Keep in Touch

Our readers mean everything to us. We explore the Los Angeles area so you and your dogs can spend true quality time together. Your input to this book is very important. In the last few years, we've heard from many wonderful dogs and their people about new dog-friendly places or old dog-friendly places we didn't know about. If you have any suggestions or insights to offer, please contact us using the information listed in the front of this book or via my website, www.caldogtravel.com.

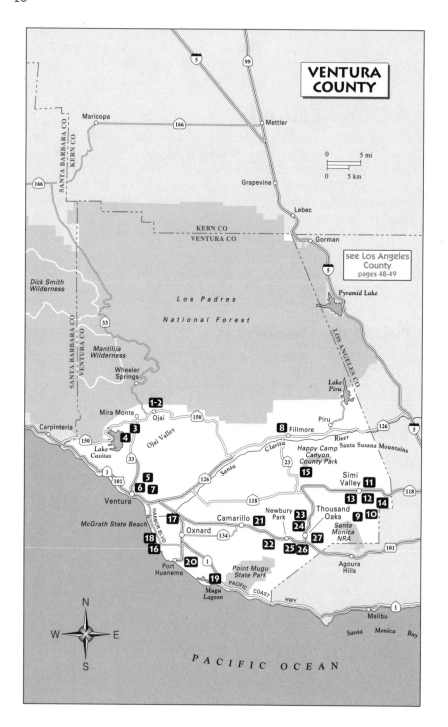

VENTURA
COUNTY

see Los Angeles
County
pages 48-49

CHAPTER 1

Ventura County

This diverse coastal county is not a place to bring a dog who is seriously obsessed with swimming. All but a handful of beaches along the 42 miles of coastline here ban dogs, although a few allow them in their camping or picnicking areas.

Even the big and bassy Lake Casitas makes sure dogs stay more than 50 feet from the lake's edge. We've seen water dogs tremble with genetic anticipation as they try to pull their owners close enough to dip a paw. A ranger told us about a dog who got so frustrated at not being able to swim that when he got back to the motel that night, he ran straight past the manager and into the swimming pool.

Try not to let your dog visit Dog Hell here. You enter Dog Hell when you drive miles and miles to get to a county park, only to find Sir Ranger shaking his head at you, hands on hips, ready to do battle. County parks ban dogs from every inch of their terrain except campgrounds, which are generally not the most scenic spots in the world.

PICK OF THE LITTER—VENTURA COUNTY

COOLEST TRAIL
Ojai Valley Trail, Ojai (page 23)

MOST DIVERSE HIKE POSSIBILITIES
Happy Camp Canyon Regional Park, Moorpark (page 34)

BEST DOG PARK
Arroyo Verde Dog Park, Ventura (page 27)

BEST PARK FOR BOB HOPE FANS
Rocky Peak Park/Runkle Ranch, Simi Valley (page 31)

BEST PARK FOR WESTERN FANS
Corriganville Park, Simi Valley (page 32)

BEST BEACHES
Hollywood Beach, Oxnard (page 36)
Sycamore Cove Beach, Port Hueneme (page 38)

COOLEST PLACE TO EAT
Deer Lodge, Ojai (page 24)

MOST DOG-FRIENDLY PLACE TO EAT
Ojai Brew Pub, Ojai (page 25)

BEST RIDE
Channel Islands Water Taxi, Oxnard (page 35)

FRIENDLIEST DOG CLUB
Star Canine Social Club, Oxnard (page 37)

Fortunately, between the Santa Monica Mountains National Recreation Area and the Santa Monica Mountains Conservancy, there's plenty of terrific land to explore. (For specific parks in Ventura County run by these entities, see below. For more details on these park entities themselves, see Los Angeles County.)

NATIONAL FORESTS

The National Forests and Wilderness Areas resource at the back of this book has important information and safety tips on visiting national forests with your dog and has more information on Los Padres National Forest.

Los Padres National Forest

Ojai

Dogs enjoy a visit to this friendly, pleasant community, whose name is derived from a Chumash Indian word, *a'hwai,* which means both "nest" and "moon," according to town officials. Agriculture, nature, artists, and business live in fairly decent harmony here.

For a fun mini road trip, take your dog to the top of Dennison Grade (locals will point you in the right direction) and show him the view that was portrayed as Shangri-La in the film *Lost Horizon*—not the 1967 musical version (whose pop-music score by Burt Bacharach apparently I alone in the world happen to enjoy), but the 1937 classic. If you make a point to be there toward day's end, you may also be able to see the area's "pink moment," when the nearby mountains become a remarkable, unearthly shade of pink. Your dog may not appreciate this sight, especially if dogs really see only in black and white (I don't think this is the prevailing wisdom anymore), but he'll still enjoy being at the top of the world with you.

PARKS, BEACHES, AND RECREATION AREAS

1 Libbey Park
🐾🐾🐾 (See Ventura County map on page 20)

This attractive seven-acre park can get mighty crowded if there's a big event going on at its 1,500-person-capacity bowl. At those times, the city asks dogs and their people to sniff out other venues, or at least the more far-flung reaches of the park. Ditto for events like "The Ojai," the oldest ongoing amateur tennis tournament in the nation. (It was 100 in 2000.) But most of the time, this park is a swell place to take a leashed pooch, especially one who likes trees: Oaks, sycamores, and eucalypti figure heavily in the park's natural feel.

The park is at Signal Street and East Ojai Avenue. 805/640-2560.

2 Ojai Valley Trail
🐾🐾🐾 (See Ventura County map on page 20)

You and your leashed dog may have to share this 9.5-mile trail with a few fast bicycles and sweet-smelling horses, but don't let that stop you. It's a great way to get from Ojai to Ventura. Although most people start at the southern end and work their way northeast, it's an uphill climb that can get mighty toasty certain times of year. We recommend starting from Ojai. As they say, Go Southwest, young dog! (You can always meet up with a friend at the end who will drive you home.)

The trail is a "rails-to-trails" conversion of a more than century-old railroad line that hauled oranges and other goodies from local orchards to far-flung markets. It takes you and your leashed dog through little forested areas and quiet neighborhoods, past rolling hills and Christmas tree farms. Views of the surrounding mountains at times are to drool for. For the fair of paw, there are plenty of shaded, tranquil resting spots along the way. About midway there's a market and some fast-food-type restaurants—nothing you'd normally care to see on a nature hike, but a welcome oasis if you've worked up an appetite, or if you're crossing your legs for a pit stop. (There are no public restroom facilities on the trail at this point.)

Even if you walk only one segment of the trail, it's worth the trip. When the trail first opened, dogs were banned (it's a county parks thing), but the rule was so difficult to enforce that eventually pooches were given the OK. Take advantage of this! Rejoice! Take a hike!

The trail runs parallel to Highway 33. Its easternmost end just brushes Soule Park, but it's not well marked or as easy to access as it is just a few blocks to the west, on Fox Street, east of Libbey Park. Park at the Park & Ride lot at East Ojai Avenue and Fox Street and walk down Fox to the trail. There's also limited parking on residential streets. 805/654-3951.

PLACES TO EAT

Deer Lodge: This wood and stone landmark restaurant is one of the most cool, fun eateries where you can bring a doggy. You feel like you're at an old-West outpost, albeit a most civilized and attractive one, when you dine here. Deer figure prominently on the signage, decor (heads on old wooden walls), and the menu. You can get a venison salad, sample venison barley soup, or go for broke and try the "World Famous Deer Lodge Game Plate," which can include a selection of deer, wild boar, elk, antelope, kangaroo (oh god, no, say it's not true! Not cousins of Kanga and little Roo!), alligator, and pheasant. Your dog wants you to order this plate. Your dog is getting your car keys right now.

For those whose palates prefer animals of the more farmy variety, the apricot cashew chicken, Buffalo Bill burger, and cowboy's tri-tip offer less wild alternatives. Vegetarians can even make a meal here, with a hearty salad, some slowly roasted garlic, and a big plate of deer-free pasta.

Best of all, the cowboy-hat-clad waitresses are mighty dog friendly, and dogs and their people have a choice of two patios. We prefer the lower patio, which is bigger, prettier, bamboo-covered, and warmed on cool evenings by an outdoor fireplace. 2261 Maricopa Highway; 805/646-4256.

Friends Ice Cream: The folks here live up to the restaurant's namesake: "We're very dog friendly at Friends!" said a friendly manager. Your best friend can join you at the sidewalk seating or in the courtyard patio next to big oak trees. (Guess which one dogs prefer.) Thirsty dogs get water while you eat yummy sandwiches and delectable ice cream treats. 323 East Matilija Street; 805/646-5038.

Jim & Rob's Fresh Grill: Even though this sweet little eatery has only two outdoor tables, it gets a fair number of canine customers, according to servers (who will happily supply your dog with a bowl of water). 805/640-1301.

Ojai Brew Pub: If you like tasty brews and your dog likes free biscuits and water, you're in luck. The Ojai Brew Pub serves up all this and then some at its oft-shaded outdoor tables. You can chow down on some beer-battered onion rings, delicious salads, pizzas, and sandwiches, including an oven-roasted turkey sandwich made from house-roasted turkey breast and topped with caramelized onions and provolone cheese. (Be prepared from some hard staring from your dog if you order that one. Ditto for the shaved tri-tip sandwich with melted jack cheese.) 423 East Ojai Avenue; 805/646-8837.

PLACES TO STAY

Best Western Casa Ojai: Enjoy this motel's heated outdoor pool and whirlpool (without your dog; sorry) and free continental breakfast (ditto about the dog). Room rates are $85–200. Dogs are $10 extra. 1302 East Ojai Avenue 93023; 805/646-8175.

Blue Iguana Inn: This old mission-style inn is "hip and stylish," according to *Sunset* magazine, which can now add the description, "dog friendly." The arched entrances, the ivy-covered trellises, the beautiful tilework and artwork, and the attractive pool make the Blue Iguana eye candy from the exterior. The rooms and suites themselves are just as wonderful, with a warm, cozy, sometimes colorful, sometimes muted natural ambience. Rates are $95–205. You can also rent a lovely bungalow for $179–209. 11794 North Ventura Avenue 93023; 805/646-5277; www.blueiguanainn.com.

Ventura

This seaside community has always had a wealth of parks for leashed dogs to sniff out. But thanks to some hard-working dog people, it's now home to two parks where dogs can throw their leashes to the wind. It's also home to the ninth—and last—mission founded by Father Junípero Serra. Dogs can't go inside, but they're more than happy to smile at the camera for an exterior shot.

PARKS, BEACHES, AND RECREATION AREAS

🐾 Ojai Valley Trail

🐾🐾🐾 (See Ventura County map on page 20)

Please see the listing in Ojai for details about this 9.5-mile trail that goes from Ojai to Ventura. In case you want to go from Ventura to Ojai (if you like a vigorous uphill hike that leads you away from the ocean), Foster County Park (see Places to Stay) is the trail's staging area. But keep in mind that dogs are allowed at that park only at the trailhead and the campsites. Exit Highway 33 at Casitas Vista Road and follow the signs. As you head northeast on the trail, you can also access it from points such as San Antonio Creek, Santa Ana Boulevard, Barbara Street, and Baldwin Avenue. 805/654-3951.

🐾 Lake Casitas Recreation Area

🐾🐾🐾 (See Ventura County map on page 20)

Don't bring a water dog here. She'll just stare at the water and weep. Dogs have to be kept 50 feet away from the lake, meaning they can't even go on a boat with you. With 50,000 people who rely on this lake for water, it's understandable that they wouldn't want a bunch of flea-bitten beasts floating around in their drink. But that's a hard one to explain to a quivering, frothing Labrador retriever. Actually, people aren't permitted to swim here either, but that news probably won't do much to console your dog-paddling pooch.

Once you enter this 6,200-acre park, your best bet is to bear to the right and follow the road to a dense, lush, oak-filled campground. Park wherever you can and walk with your leashed dog as far back as possible. You'll find some short trails winding through this part of the park and some excellent places to

relax and get away from the bulk of the people who visit here. (They're all at the water, like most normal folks.)

The day-use fee is $6.50. Dogs are $1. Sites at the 480 campsites are $16. Camping dogs cost $2. Reservations are not necessary. From the heart of Ventura, drive 11 miles north on Highway 33. Turn left on Highway 150 and drive about four miles to the main entrance. 805/649-2233.

5 Arroyo Verde Dog Park

😊😊😊😊 🐕 (See Ventura County map on page 20)

Early-rising canines have it good here: They've got eight acres of grassy, shady land to frisk about on without leashes in the early morning. The dog area is unfenced, full of trees, and features a drinking fountain for dogs and their people, Mutt Mitts, and restrooms (for people—dogs can use the grass).

I've been told three different things by three different park department employees about the hours and days the park is open to off-leash dogs. The schedule has been in flux for a while because of some conflicts between dog people and other park users, so be sure to check the signs at the park before you set your dog free, or call before you visit. The hours given me by the park supervisor who probably knows the most and latest about the situation: The dog area is open for off-leash fun Tuesday–Friday 6–9 A.M., Saturday 6–8 A.M., and Sunday 6–9 A.M. It's closed Monday for maintenance, and it's also closed on city holidays and for special events.

The dog area is right at the entrance of the rugged 129-acre Arroyo Verde Park. It's clearly marked. Most of the park is pretty much impassable by anyone except creatures of nature, but you and your leashed dog can take a short trail or two to get you a little closer to the wilds.

There's a $1 fee per vehicle on Sundays and holidays. (You probably won't be coming here on a holiday, since you can't bring your leash-free dog.) Be sure to leash up from the parking lot to the off-leash area. Exit U.S. 101 at Victoria Avenue and drive north on Victoria for about two miles. Where it ends, turn left on Foothill Road. In about two-thirds of a mile, the park will be on your right, at the corner of Foothill and Day Roads. 805/652-4550.

6 Grant Memorial Park

😊😊😊 (See Ventura County map on page 20)

In 1782, Father Junipero Serra raised a wooden cross on the mountain overlooking his newly built Mission San Buenaventura. That mountain is now part of this 107-acre park. A cross still sticks out of the top of the park, and if you go anywhere near it, you'll find wonderful views of the city, the Pacific, and the Channel Islands.

Surrounding the cross is a little grassy area where you can unwind, take in the views, or eat a picnic. But if you want to be kind to your dog, before you sit down to ooh and aah at the scenery, turn around. On the other side of the parking lot you'll see a dirt trail heading up the adjacent hill. It's not shady, so your leashed dog won't be able to ooh and aah at the trees, but it's a great way for you to get away from the park's never-ending trickle of visitors.

From Cedar Street (two blocks east of Ventura Avenue), turn east on Ferro Drive and follow it to the top of the park. 805/652-4550.

7 Annie Dransfeldt Dog Park

🐾🐾🐾🐕 (See Ventura County map on page 20)

Annie Dransfeldt is a great local dog advocate. So great, in fact, that they named this terrific little park after her. It's about two fenced grassy acres, with trees, double gates, a separate area for small dogs, a drinking fountain for dogs and their humans, and poop bags. Since the park is named after her, she asks people to please scoop the poop. (You could even pick up an "orphan" poop while you're at it. Apparently there have been too many of these little lovelies hanging around.)

The park is within Camino Real Park, a 38-acre complex with lots of playing fields and courts and a refreshing eucalyptus smell. It's closed on city holidays. Unlike the other city dog park, this one's open 6 A.M.–dusk every day except Wednesday, when it opens at 9 A.M. because of park maintenance. It's at Dean Drive and Varsity Street. 805/652-4550.

PLACES TO EAT

Ventura restaurants are generous with doggy water bowls. As one server recently told us, "A dog can't order food. The least we can do is give them a free drink." A big thank-you to Colby and Dane Dogs, and their person, Annie Dransfeldt (who has a dog park named after her), for helping us sniff out a few of these eateries.

Andria's Seafood: The middle name here should be "& chips." You can get halibut & chips, Alaskan cod & chips, shrimp & chips, oysters & chips, ostrich burger & chips, krabby cake sandwich & chips, and really almost anything with chips. But wait! There's healthful stuff here, too. You can even get a veggie stir-fry or a charbroiled garlic sandwich. If that's just too virtuous, you can order a big side of chips. Dine with doggy at tables at the water's edge. 1449 Spinnaker Drive; 805/654-0546.

Café Nouveau: Enjoy tasty California cuisine with your dog at the outdoor tables. Thirsty dogs get water. 1497 East Thompson Boulevard; 805/648-1422.

The Coastal Cone Company: Dine on frosty treats at one of three patio tables. Thirsty dogs can get water on request. 1583 Spinnaker Drive; 805/658-2837.

Duke's Griddle 'n' Grill: Your dog just might get a special treat from a waiter while you dine on the good grilled grub served at the outdoor tables here. At the very least, she'll get a bowl of water if she asks for one. 1124 South Seaward Avenue; 805/653-0707.

The Greek at the Harbor: The traditional Greek food here is scrumptious. Your dog would surely say *"Opa!"* if her little snouty mouth allowed. Even vegetarians delight in this lovely harborside restaurant. Dine at the patio tables with your dog. If she's thirsty, she can get a bowl of water. 1583 Spinnaker Drive; 805/650-5350.

The Habit: Dogs and their people rave about this hamburger haven. There's a reason it's called the habit. "I can't get enough of this place," writes Melvin Dog, who visits every time he's passing through town. "It's the best hamburger place we've ever eaten at and that's a lot of hamburger places. Oh, and the milk shakes are to die for." Dine with doggy at the outside tables. Thirsty dogs always get water. 487 East Thompson Boulevard; 805/667-2065.

Top Hat Burger Palace: You don't have to be of royal blood to enjoy this fast-food palace. All of the seating is outdoors; you just go to an order window to get your food and then dine in leisure with your mutt. Thirsty dogs can order a bowl of water. 299 East Main Street; 805/643-9696.

PLACES TO STAY

For a city of this size, there's a disappointing dearth of decent doggy digs. We don't even list the one upscale hotel, the Marriott Ventura Beach Hotel, because only dogs under 15 pounds can stay, and we don't want to disappoint dogs whose only crime is that they're bigger than cats.

Foster County Park Campground: Some of the sites here are near oaks, but that's about the best thing we can say about this place, except that the park is the local staging area for the Ojai Valley Trail (see above). Dogs are banned from the day-use area of the park. The 48 sites here are $22–35. 805/654-3951.

Hobson County Park Campground: You're so close to the water here (you're actually at the ocean's edge), yet so very far away. Dogs aren't allowed on the beach, and that can be a bummer with a capital B. This is not beach camping at its most peaceful. In fact, before you come, open a can of sardines to get an idea of how tight the campers, RVs, and tents can be packed. The campground is small and has 31 oceanside sites. Rates are $22–35. Dogs are $1 extra. From Ventura, drive northwest on U.S. 101 and exit at the State Beaches exit. Drive north on West Pacific Highway for five miles. The campground is on the left. For park info or campsite reservations, call 805/654-3951.

Lake Casitas Recreation Area: See Lake Casitas Recreation Area, above, for camping information.

La Quinta Inn: This inn has had all sorts of nonhuman visitors—even birds and rabbits. Dogs are welcome here, as long as they're under 40 pounds and they stay out of the outdoor pool and whirlpool. Rates are $83–103. 5818 Valentine Road 93003; 805/658-6200.

McGrath State Beach Campsites: Your dog can't go on the beach with you here, but the camping area is pretty enough that it's not such a bad fate to hang out here together and read a good book. There are 174 sites. Rates are $10–12. From U.S. 101, take the Seaward Avenue/Harbor Boulevard exit and drive four miles west on Harbor Boulevard to the beach. For reservations, phone 800/444-7275. For park info, call 805/968-1033.

Motel 6: Rates are $48–70 for the first adult, $6 for the second. 2145 East Harbor Boulevard 93001; 805/643-5100.

Vagabond Inn: There's a decent grassy area on the premises dogs like to sniff out. This is where many Kennel Club Fair attendees stay with their humans when in town. Rates are $69–99. (That's a hefty price for vagabonds.) Dogs are $5 extra. 756 East Thompson Boulevard 93001; 805/648-5371.

Fillmore

This historic little city, nestled in the midst of flourishing citrus groves and with an attractive old downtown, was named one of "The West's Best Cities" by *Sunset* magazine. Fillmore, whose citrus was portrayed so elegantly on labels for wooden crates of fruit, is a fun place to sniff out with a doggy. Some downtown stores permit well-behaved pooches, but on a case-by-case basis, so we won't list them here. Unfortunately, dogs aren't allowed to ride the historic Fillmore & Western railroad cars ("Home of the Hollywood Movie Trains"), which are one of the city's biggest attractions.

PARKS, BEACHES, AND RECREATION AREAS

🐾 Shiells Park

🐾🐾🐾 (See Ventura County map on page 20)

At just over eight acres, this park isn't huge, but it's a fairly attractive one, adjacent to Sespe Creek. Leashed dogs enjoy walking around the grass, picnicking, and watching kids play ball. But most of all, dogs (especially dogs of the male persuasion) enjoy the large trees.

When we're in the mood for a good walk, we leave the park (which has no real paths to speak of) and take a stroll on the paved bike path that runs adjacent to the creek. The path is about two miles long, so your dog should get all the exercise he needs. The park is at Old Telegraph Road and C Street. 805/524-1500.

PLACES TO EAT

Margaret's Cocina Drive-In: The dog-friendly people here will give a thirsty canine customer a big bowl of water while she joins you for a bite on the patio. 446 Ventura Street; 805/524-3638.

Simi Valley

PARKS, BEACHES, AND RECREATION AREAS

🟅 Ahmanson Ranch/Upper Las Virgenes Canyon Open Space Preserve

🐾🐾🐾🐾 (See Ventura County map on page 20)

Every acre of this spectacular 3,000-acre park is in Ventura County, but the only access is from Los Angeles County, so that's where you'll find its description in this book. See the Calabasas section.

🔟 Sage Ranch Park

🐾🐾🐾🐾 (See Ventura County map on page 20)

The 652 acres of wild parkland at Sage Ranch have the kind of diversity most parks can only dream of. Coastal sage scrub, the park's namesake, dominates, but along the park's 2.6-mile loop trail you'll also find grasslands, wildflowers (in spring), oak woodlands, an old orange grove, and a riparian area with sycamores, walnut trees, and ferns. The ferny fauna isn't far from some rocky outcroppings that look like they belong in an old Western flick. The contrast of environments makes for intriguing hikes. Even dogs seem to dig the varying scenery.

Exit U.S. 101 at Valley Circle Drive/Mulholland Drive. Drive north on Valley Circle Drive for about six miles. You'll come to a three-way stop at Woolsey Canyon Road. Go left and follow Woolsey Canyon Road to the end, where you'll head right on Black Canyon Road. The entrance to the park is about 200 yards north of the intersection. 1 Black Canyon Road; 818/999-3753 or 310/589-3200.

🔢 Rocky Peak Park

🐾🐾🐾🐾 (See Ventura County map on page 20)

If you and your dog want to pay homage to Bob Hope, watch some of his Road flicks one evening, then the next morning venture out to this sprawling 4,815-acre park. Hope once owned the 4,400 acres of this land. Back then it was known as Runkle Ranch. Today it's an amazing place to hike through wide-open grasslands, oak savannahs, and gigantic sandstone boulder formations. If you visit in the spring, you'll be wowed by the wildflowers here. There's abundant wildlife, in addition to mountain bikes and equestrians, so leashes are the law.

Several trails that start at various points on the park's perimeter take you to vastly different parts of this huge park. Go to www.smmc.ca.gov if you want to make hiking plans before going, or just check out the trail map near the park entrance when you get here. A trail leading to a couple of popular trails

starts here. The park entrance is across Highway 118 from Corriganville Park (see below). From the east, exit Highway 118 at Rocky Peak Road. The park is on the north side of the off ramp. From the west, exit Highway 118 at Kuehner Drive. Turn right and follow it to the top of the pass (it will become Santa Susana Pass Road) and to the park entrance. 310/589-3200.

12 Rancho Simi Community Park

🐾🐾 (See Ventura County map on page 20)

This park is pretty much one big field of green turf with some trees and shaded picnic tables. It's quite an attractive, decent-sized area for a community park, and it has Mutt Mitts to boot. Despite a few sports courts and a playground, you can usually find some seclusion here. Just go to the back section of the park. You'll know it when you see it.

Dogs would like to tear around chasing Frisbees and softballs, but alas, they have to be leashed. The park is on Royal Avenue, about a block east of Erringer Road. 805/584-4400.

13 Corriganville Park

🐾🐾🐾🐾 (See Ventura County map on page 20)

If you're a fan of old Westerns, stop your stagecoach right here, pardner. And if you have a penchant for old jungle flicks, you also need to swing into this big park, which is named after actor and stuntman Ray "Crash" Corrigan, who bought the property in the 1930s.

Hundreds of movies were shot here from the 1930s and into the 1960s. Back then, the property was as large as 2,000 acres, but now it's 220. That's OK.

There's still plenty of room for you and your leashed little doggy (or big doggy) to git along and see some fun old movie backdrops. A few of the films that were shot here: *Fort Apache, Trail of the Vigilante, Mule Train, Rogues of Sherwood Forest, Escape from Fort Bravo, Skipalong Rosenbloom, Tarzan Escapes,* and even *The Inspector General.*

A stream cuts through an empty concrete-lined pool that was filled during Corriganville's movie days. It has windows in the side where cameramen were stationed to get underwater shots of the good guys fighting the bad guys in the "lake," or in the case of the Jungle Jim movies (also shot here), wrestling an alligator.

If you're interested in more information about Corriganville, there's a marvelous website about Corriganville, with a biography of its colorful namesake, information on all the former sets and present sites, and tons of old photos. The site name is a long and clunky one, with lots of slashes, so it's easier to just type "Corriganville" into a search engine. It will come up immediately. One piece of news it won't tell you is that the park has poop bag dispensers; this is something dogs with forgetful humans (the kind who leave the poop bags at home) like to know.

(A huge thank you to Sheryl Smith and her dear English springer spaniel Gracie—who is now galloping around leash-free in Dog Heaven—for their heads-up about Corriganville and for their contribution to our description of this wonderful park.)

From I-5 or I-405, head west on Highway 118 (the Ronald Reagan/Simi Valley Freeway), exit at Kuehner Drive (you'll be coming down out of the Santa Susana Mountains), and turn left. In about a mile, turn left at the signal at Smith Road. The entrance to Corriganville Park is at the end of the street. (Shortly before that entrance on the left you'll see the original entrance to the property.) 805/584-4400.

14 Rancho Santa Susana Community Park

😺😺 (See Ventura County map on page 20)

Now *this* is suburbia. Parents in swollen SUVs pull into the parking lot and out of the car pop a few little soccer demons raring to clobber whatever team they happen to be opposing. Neighbors greet each other with compliments about how fine their lawns look this year. Parents push strollers up and down the walkway. Then they push them up and down again.

But when the talcum powder has cleared and it's just you and your leashed dog, you can actually have a decent time here. Between strolling on the path, checking out the bushes, and running on the playing fields, your dog might even enjoy himself. The park is at Stearns Street and Los Angeles Avenue. 805/584-4400.

PLACES TO EAT

Pasta and Salads Company: You'll enjoy eating healthful foods at the outdoor tables with your pooch at your side. 464 Madera Road; 805/520-4649.

PLACES TO STAY

Motel 6: Rates are $60–70 for the first adult, $6 for the second. 2566 North Erringer Road 93065; 805/526-3533.

Oak County Park Campground: This county campground is directly below some railroad tracks in what looks like a dirt parking lot with a few trees. It's not what you'd call a hot spot for getting back to nature, but it is popular with scout troops and their ilk, so there's definitely some habitat worth sniffing out. There are 55 sites. Rates are $5 per adult for tent sites, $2 per child, and $1 per dog. (The minimum charge for tent sites is $10, so if it's just you and your dog, you'll still have to fork over a tenner.) RV sites start at $25 per RV. Dogs are $1 extra, and more than two humans will cost you a little extra, too. This being a county park, dogs are not allowed on the park's trails or anywhere but the campground.

About halfway between Moorpark and Simi Valley on Highway 118, exit onto Los Angeles Avenue and drive southeast about 1.5 miles. The park entrance will be on your left, directly across from a really big, ugly contractor's storage facility. 901 Quimisa Drive; 805/654-3644.

Moorpark

PARKS, BEACHES, AND RECREATION AREAS

🐾 Happy Camp Canyon Regional Park

🐾🐾🐾🐾 (See Ventura County map on page 20)

This 3,000-acre wonderland of lush forests, colorful shale outcroppings, and wide-open grasslands is a great place for a dog to bring a human. People love the splendid geological formations and the seasonal wildflowers. Dogs adore the variety of hiking possibilities in this vast wilderness area. The park has more than 12 miles of trails, but only some permit pooches. Signs will let you know what's OK and what's not. Dogs need to be on leash here; the park is home to sensitive wildlife habitats.

Exit U.S. 101 at Highway 23 and drive north to New Los Angeles Avenue. Go left (west) and at the third signal, Moorpark Avenue, turn right. Drive 2.6 miles (Moorpark Avenue will turn into Walnut Canyon Road) past the railroad crossing. You'll see a sharp 30 mph left curve at that point, but do not go left; continue straight and you'll almost immediately come to Broadway Avenue, where you'll make a right. Continue to the park, which has plenty of parking. 14105 Broadway; 310/589-3200.

Oxnard

What this city lacks in the appealing name department (you just can't say "Oxnard" so it sounds like anything remotely attractive) it makes up for with a couple of beaches that allow dogs, and a twice-monthly dog gathering that's a real gas.

PARKS, BEACHES, AND RECREATION AREAS

I had a scintillating conversation with a parks department employee about the subject of dog doo-doo. He quoted from the scriptures (city code): "It says right here—'No person shall permit any dog to defecate on public property... without the consent of the person owning it.' That's the law."

"OK, so you have to fax the park commissioners, tell them your dog ate a whopper of a supper last night, and that you might be needing the use of their parks the next morning?" asked I. It took him a few minutes before he figured out that maybe there was more to this law than meets the eye. "Oh, right here it says that if you clean it up right away, you don't have to get permission," said he. "Whew!" said I. "Whew!" breathed Joe Dog.

Another city law says that you must always carry a pooper-scooper when with your dog. If you don't have one on hand, you could be fined. But what if your dog already did his business and you threw it out? "You'd better carry a spare just for show," another city employee told me.

DIVERSION

Be Harbor Hounds: The best way to see the sights of Channel Islands Harbor is from the water, and thanks to the **Channel Islands Water Taxi,** you don't have to rich or an angler to do the boat thing. You and your salty dog can hitch a ride on this 22-foot enclosed boat, which motors to five stops around the harbor, and it will barely make a dent in your dog food budget. The cost: $6 for a round-trip cruise (about 40 minutes), or $1–2 per hop. Dogs are free. During summer, the taxi runs most days noon–6 P.M. or 7 P.M. During the off-season, the taxi usually sets sail on weekends only. If you want to rent the boat for a private to-do, it will cost you $100 an hour, and you can bring up to 22 guests. (The captain is included with the fee.)

Our favorite place to catch the water cab is at Fisherman's Wharf. The wharf is at 2741 South Victoria Avenue, Oxnard. (That's also where you'll find the Channel Islands Visitors Center, where you can pick up water taxi schedules and fun info about the area.) For other stops or more information, call 805/985-4677 or 805/985-4852.

The biggest park in the city, College Park, doesn't permit pooches because it's actually a county park. (And we know how dog friendly those are.) Fortunately, there are two beaches dogs can visit on leash and a terrific free dog club that welcomes any decent dog to cavort around leash-free every couple of weeks. (See the Diversion Run, Spot, Run!)

16 Hollywood Beach
🐾🐾🐾 (See Ventura County map on page 20)

You may not see silver-screen stars at Hollywood Beach, but your dog will still be dazzled as she joins you on a leashed walk on this beautiful chunk of sand and sea. Many dogs drag their humans here for a walk, and you may find some naked ones (sans leash) running around, but leashes are the rule. It's off Harbor Boulevard, at the corner of La Brea Street and Ocean Drive. 805/382-3007.

17 Orchard Park
🐾🐾 (See Ventura County map on page 20)

It's not a large park, but it's attractive for its size. Even dogs seem to think the park is OK, but only early in the morning when less traffic is whizzing by. And there are plenty of trees.

The park is at Edelweiss Street and Erica Place, a few blocks west of Highway 1 and north of Gonzales Road. 805/385-7950.

18 Oxnard Beach Park
🐾🐾🐾 (See Ventura County map on page 20)

This is a state park, but don't let that scare you off: It's run by the city of Oxnard, and dogs are welcome on leash. The park is less developed than many other beaches in the area. It covers about 62 acres and features dune trails and a picnic area. The beach is an extra wide one, and dogs really dig it here, even though they have to be attached to people.

The parking fee is $5 for the day. The beach is west of Harbor Boulevard, between Beach Way and Falkirk Avenue. 805/385-7950.

PLACES TO EAT

Big Daddy O's Beach BBQ: This meat-lover's paradise is a block from Silver Strand, an isolated beach dotted with surfers. Dogs can join you at the outdoor tables here while you dine on Big Daddy O's popular tri-tip sandwich, killer cheeseburger, or great barbecued chicken. Dogs love the alluring flame-cooked-meat scent of this place and have been known to pull their people for blocks in some cave-dog like urge to eat meat cooked on a fire. 2333 Roosevelt Boulevard; 805/984-0014.

Buon Appetito: The food here is *delizioso*, the atmosphere charming. The

DIVERSION

Run, Spot, Run!: The **Star Canine Social Club** has to be the most fun, relaxed dog club in California. Any well-behaved dog can attend its lively off-leash gatherings in Oxnard two Saturday afternoons a month. Nothing is breed-specific, as is the case in most dog clubs. "If it vaguely resembles a dog, it's welcome here," says Becky, who is a vertebra in the club's backbone. There are no competitions, no membership fees. "We're a nonprofit organization," she says. "Extremely nonprofitable." (Donations will be accepted but are not solicited.)

Socialization and leash-free running on six areas of totally fenced open space are the biggest draws, but the gatherings offer much more, including: agility equipment, Frisbees, tennis balls, sticks, toys, a doggy pool, refreshing sprinklers, and fun events like egg-on-spoon walks for dogs, bobbing for hot dogs, obedience practice, and birthday parties. Small and timid dogs get their own fenced area. (They'll even work with dogs who have social problems, but you have to make prior arrangements.)

For location and schedule, phone 805/389-6149.

---

cuisine leans heavily toward Italian, but you can also get some great seafood dishes. (After all, it the restaurant *is* on Fisherman's Wharf.) We've heard the salmon in puff pastry is delectable, but we were more in the mood for a giant, drippy calzone when we visited. Dine with your dog at the 10 attractive patio tables. If you bring your pooch's water bowl, they'll be happy to pour her some fresh water. 2721 South Victoria; 805/984-8437.

Fisherman's Wharf: This is a thoroughly charming, dog-friendly collection of old-fashioned shops and good restaurants. Little benches abound, but many of the restaurants have their own outdoor seating. We see at least a couple of dogs here each time we visit, and we figure they're dogs of the nautical persuasion. They're in great shape, but their leashes seem to be boating line and their owners have tan, leathery skin and a hint of salt on the hair. 2721 South Victoria Avenue.

H. C. Seafood & Co.: Choose from a variety of fresh seafood dishes here, and eat them at the waterfront patio with your dog. You can also select from various live shellfish and crustaceans who would rather you choose something else. 3900 Channel Islands Boulevard; 805/382-8171.

Popeye's Famous Fried Chicken and Biscuits: This one isn't at the wharf, despite its namesake sailor man. Eat at the outdoor tables here. (There's no spinach on the menu, in case your dog was wondering.) 1900 North Ventura Road; 805/983-7790.

PLACES TO STAY

Best Western Oxnard Inn: The rooms here are comfortable and attractive, and the expanded continental breakfast will fill you up for a day of exploring the area. You'll have use of a pool, a Jacuzzi, and a little exercise room, too. Sounds great, but hold the phone if you have a large dog. "We prefer dogs to be under 35 pounds," a front-desk person said sweetly when I checked out the place. She didn't say firmly that "Dogs *must* be under 35 pounds," so maybe there's some leverage for larger beasts. Rates are $90–129. Dogs are $20 extra. 1156 South Oxnard Boulevard 93030; 805/483-9581.

Residence Inn by Marriott: This is a convenient place to park it when traveling with a pooch. All the rooms are studios or apartments, and all come with full kitchens. Rates are $119–159 and include a full breakfast and complimentary afternoon beverages. They're experienced in the world of dog travel here: If you forgot your dog's bowl or leash, you can get a loaner.

Here's the long list of dog fees: Dogs pay a $100 fee for the length of their stay (dogs usually stay a while here to make it worth their money), and they're $5 extra per night. In addition, there's a $250 deposit. 2101 West Vineyard Avenue 93030; 805/278-2200; www.residenceinn.com.

Vagabond Inn: There's a decent little neighborhood park across the street, should your dog want to stretch her legs upon arrival. Room rates are $81–84. Dogs are $5 extra. 1245 North Oxnard Boulevard 93030; 805/983-0251.

Port Hueneme

PARKS, BEACHES, AND RECREATION AREAS

Dogs are not allowed at this navy city's beaches, but they can peruse the parks here, in addition to one terrific beach down the coast just a bit in Point Mugu State Park territory. (See Sycamore Cove Beach.)

19 Sycamore Cove Beach

🐾🐾🐾🐾 (See Ventura County map on page 20)

This big, beautiful beach welcomes leashed dogs to stroll on the sand, wade in the surf, and sniff around a grassy picnic area. It's the most dog-friendly part of the 15,000-acre Point Mugu State Park, which bans dogs from trails. You can even camp here; across the highway is a 55-site campground. See Places to Stay for more details on camping at Point Mugu.

The day-use fee is a steep $10 per vehicle. The beach is about 11 miles south of Port Hueneme (about six miles north of the Los Angeles County line) on Highway 1/Pacific Coast Highway. 818/880-0350.

20 Moranda/Bubbling Springs Park

🐾🐾 (See Ventura County map on page 20)

A stream runs through much of this park, and in the summer dogs love to dip their hot little toes in it to cool off. The park is actually two connected parks. Most of the Bubbling Springs Park, to the north, is a greenbelt area. Moranda Park is a chunk of green with trees, green grass, shaded picnic areas, and playgrounds.

Many people and their leashed dogs hike from one end of the adjoining parks to the other. Going north to south (toward the beach), begin your walk at Bard Road and Park Avenue and follow the park as it winds south, crossing a few streets along the way. Your hike will end around Seawind Way. 805/986-6542.

PLACES TO EAT

Anacappuccino: "We're dog friendly!" exclaims a server who loves dogs. Dine on traditional café food with your pooch at the four umbrella-topped tables outside. Thirsty dogs get water. 289 East Port Hueneme Road; 805/488-9580.

Italian Villa: There's only one table for dogs and their people here, but it's worth grabbing. The Italian food is yummy, and your dog will get a bowl of *acqua*. 301 West Channel Islands Boulevard; 805/985-8663.

Three Rockies Pizzeria: This strip mall eatery serves up yummy pizza to happy dogs and their people at its sidewalk tables. Dogs who are thirsty get their whistles wetted with bowls of water. 307 East Hueneme Road; 805/488-7777.

PLACES TO STAY

Point Mugu State Park Campgrounds: Dogs aren't permitted on the magical trails in this spectacular park, even with a leash. "They're a hazard to wildlife and other park visitors," a young ranger told me in a monotone, robotic voice. Creepy! But there are a few paved roads you can walk them on, if tar's your cup of tea.

At least dogs are allowed to help you pitch a tent at one of the 131 campsites. One of our favorite camping areas is at Thornhill Broome Beach. Dogs love camping beachside. (They can't visit the beach here, but they're welcome at Point Mugu's Sycamore Cove Beach. See listing above.) Rates are $20. The park is about nine miles south of Port Hueneme Road, on Highway 1. For park info, call 818/880-0350. Call 800/444-7275 to reserve a site.

Camarillo

PARKS, BEACHES, AND RECREATION AREAS

21 Camarillo Dog Park

🐾🐾🐾🦮 (See Ventura County map on page 20)

If only dogs could see in color (and maybe they can, but that's another story): The fire hydrant and drinking fountain in this one-acre, fenced dog park are so dazzling you almost need sunglasses to look at them. The hydrant is a bright fire-engine red, the fountain a brilliant green. They look especially colorful when surrounded by white dogs, black dogs, and Dalmatians.

The park has plenty of trees, which provide welcome shade in the warmer months. Dogs and their humans also have water fountains, benches, and a picnic table. It's a fun place to visit for a little relaxation and a lot of leash-free dog fun.

The dog park is in Camarillo Grove Park. There's a $3 fee to enter this park, but if you have a dog with you, it's free. (Dogs are like a bulky coupon.) You're relegated to the dog park, so don't go wandering off anywhere else once you're in. Exit U.S. 101 at Camarillo Springs Road. If you're coming from the north, go left at the stop sign at the bottom of the off-ramp and continue to the park. If you're coming from the south, keep heading straight from the off-ramp and you'll hit the park. The park is off Camarillo Springs Road at the base of the Conejo grade. 805/482-1996.

Newbury Park

PARKS, BEACHES, AND RECREATION AREAS

22 Rancho Sierra Vista/Satwiwa

🐾🐾🐾🐾 (See Ventura County map on page 20)

This 760-acre park is the westernmost parcel of the Santa Monica Mountains National Recreation Area. (See Los Angeles County for more on this terrific entity of the National Parks system.) Its Satwiwa Native American Indian Culture Center and Chumash Demonstration Village are excellent places for learning about the history of the Chumash culture, whose people have lived in this area for thousands of years.

Dogs can't go in any buildings, but they're welcome on the park's four trails. Depending on which trail you take, you'll find yourself strolling on gentle hills, sweet-smelling grasslands, or possibly, if you go far enough, into a canyon shaded by sycamores and oaks. But don't go too far: Rancho Sierra Vista/Satwiwa provides easy access to Point Mugu State Park and Boney Mountain State Wilderness—both of which ban dogs from their trails. Jake's favorite, because of its ban on horses and bikes, and its lack of connections to off-limits parks, is the Satwiwa Loop Trail, an easy 1.5-mile hike that takes you through the Satwiwa Native American Indian Natural Area. He's not much interested in the historical aspect of the area, but the apparently all-too-fascinating scents on the chaparral keep him from getting too bored.

Exit Highway 101 at Lynn Road and drive south 5.25 miles to Via Goleta. The park entrance is on your left. To get to the Satwiwa Native American Indian Culture Center, drive to the main parking area (you'll pass a couple of smaller ones) and walk a third of a mile up a gravel road to the brown wooden building. The Satwiwa Loop Trail is a bone's throw away. 805/370-2301.

Thousand Oaks

PARKS, BEACHES, AND RECREATION AREAS

Zounds! The Thousand Oaks area is home to 13,000 acres of open space you can peruse with a leashed dog. Most of these areas are difficult to access, but if you can find them, they're well worth the visit. We describe a couple of open-space areas below. The Conejo Open Space Conservation Agency, which oversees these areas, can provide you with a general map and directions to other open space parks. 805/495-6471.

The city now even has its very own dog park. Conejo Creek Dog Park has proven very popular with the pooch set.

The Thousand Oaks area is also home to some of the Santa Monica Mountains National Recreation Area (see the National Recreation Areas section of the Los Angeles County chapter). Dogs dig Thousand Oaks. As one very helpful local reader, Carolyn Greene, put it: "Although I enjoy living here myself, it's even better for dogs." Her beautiful 85-pound German shepherd, Jasmine, couldn't agree more.

23 Conejo Creek Dog Park

🐾 🐾 🐾 🐕 (See Ventura County map on page 20)

Dogs who like to socialize dig this park. Every afternoon, dogs of all shapes, sizes, and backgrounds gather to sniff and chase around the three grassy acres here. (It's grassy in part because the park closes whenever it rains.) The dog park is divided into two sections: a smaller section for small or shy dogs and a bigger chunk for everyone else. There are three drinking fountains for dogs and their people, Mutt Mitt stations galore, and a few double-gated entries. But there's not much as far as trees: Lots of horses pass very close to the dog park to access popular trails, and trees could obscure their ability to see the dogs, which could lead to a startled horse and an injured rider. That said, all's not lost for dogs who like shade: By the time you read this, hot dogs (of the furry variety) and their humans should have some shade structures to hide out under.

The dog park is across the street from Waverly Park, a nice little community park, at 1350 Avenida de las Flores; 805/495-6471. A hotline for the dog park will tell you whether it's open or closed because of maintenance or mud; 805/381-1299.

24 Wildwood Park

🐾 🐾 🐾 🐾 (See Ventura County map on page 20)

It's not every day you and your dog get to hike to a 60-foot waterfall, so take advantage of this amazing 1,700-acre park, run by the Conejo Open Space Conservation Agency. Joe Dog liked to walk to the waterfall and stand there in awe that such waterworks can actually exist in what is otherwise dry land.

Several trails wind through the coastal sage and xeric scrub-covered hills that make up most of the park. In the spring, the wildflowers go wild in a burst of intoxicating color and scent.

You'll have to keep your dog leashed as you hike the many miles of trails. The wildlife appreciates it. After all, there's not much habitat around here for these animals anymore. If you need more convincing, see the plea made by a park official in the Los Robles Open Space description.

From U.S. 101, exit at Thousand Oaks Freeway/Highway 23 and drive north about 2.5 miles to Avenida de los Arboles. Turn left and follow the road all the way to the end (about three miles). The parking area is on the left, next to the entry kiosk that holds maps and brochures of the park. 805/495-6471.

25 Borchard Community Park
🐾🐾 (See Ventura County map on page 20)

Pooches prefer this park's pretty paved path to plenty of places in the proximity. Say that 10 times fast and you'll have something to occupy your time as you stroll through this attractive green park. There's not too much else here to occupy your attention, but boy dogs will give their attention to the many trees.

From U.S. 101, exit at Borchard Road/Rancho Conejo Road and follow Borchard Road southwest about a mile. The park will be on your right, at Reino Road. 805/495-6471.

26 Los Robles Open Space
🐾🐾🐾 (See Ventura County map on page 20)

If it's trails you want, it's trails you'll get at this terrific swatch of open space land run by the Conejo Open Space Conservation Agency (COSCA). The total trail system here is 15 miles! That's a lot of trail for you and your leashed, outdoors-loving pooch to peruse. Some of the trails are killer, with very steep grades, so avoid these for the sake of your dog's paws. The trail system is going to be a real wonder one day—there are plans to join the trails in Los Robles with trails in the Santa Monica Mountains National Recreation Area (see the National Recreation Areas section of the Los Angeles County chapter) to form a 40-mile trail system from Malibu to Point Mugu.

Before I continue, I promised COSCA coordinator Mark Towne that I'd make a plea for dogs to be leashed here. Since he said it so well, I'll put it in his words:

> We have a lot of problems with dogs off leash. It impacts the wildlife, and it could impact the dogs, too.... We've had dogs chasing rabbits, ground squirrels, and other wildlife. For a dog's sake, leashes are important because there are rattlesnakes and ticks.

Got it? It's tempting, but leashes are the law here, and apparently for good reason.

The trails at Los Robles are actually wide fire access roads, winding through chaparral country and coast live oaks. They're very well marked. If you start at the parking area at the end of Moorpark Road, you can connect to the Los Robles Trail. Take the trail west to the Spring Canyon Trail and follow it to Lynn Oaks Park and back for an easy three-mile round-trip hike. If you're in the mood for food, pack a lunch and take the Los Robles Trail due south (from Moorpark) for about a mile. You'll come to a pleasant little picnic area where you and your leashed beast can have a feast. If you continue on that trail, it gets extremely steep, with lots of switchbacks and mountain bikes careening blindly down. The views become splendid, but it's not worth it unless you're very tough of paw.

Dogs who like nature love the half-mile Oak Creek Canyon Loop. This is a self-serve nature trail detailing the area's indigenous plant life. You can get here by hiking from the Moorpark entrance, but you can also drive to this trail by following Green Meadow Avenue to the end.

JoAnna Downey and her gorgeous George Dog checked out this park for me on a recent visit and provided me with great info on the park. I don't usually rely on others to visit parks for me, but JoAnna and George are highly qualified dog park explorers: They're the co-authors of the wonderful *Dog Lover's Companion to New England.*

From U.S. 101, take Moorpark Road south to the end (about a mile). The parking lot is on the right. 805/495-6471.

27 North Ranch Open Space

🐾🐾🐾🐾 (See Ventura County map on page 20)

If you and your dog really want to get away from it all and have a rugged hike to boot, this 2,614-acre open space parcel is for you. North Ranch is one of the least-used open space lands around, in part because it's so doggone hard to find, and partly because the trail isn't for tenderpaws.

A quarter-mile trail takes you to the top of the ridge, where instead of a maintained trail, you follow an old fire break up and down the hills—not always an easy feat, since fire breaks are meant for stopping a blaze in its tracks, not for helping you make tracks. You'll hike through grassland and sage scrub, and past the occasional black walnut grove. The views along the ridge are quite spectacular, as is birdlife. As always, be sure to bring plenty of water for you and your dog.

Finding the open space from city streets can be rather difficult. Many (including Jake and I) have tried and failed. Your best bet is to go to North Ranch Playfield, at 952 Rockfield Street at Bowfield Street. If you want to find trail access nearby, look for obvious breaks between housing and obvious signs of a trail. (People have been known to visit residents' backyards in pursuit of the trail. If in doubt, stay out.) 805/381-2741.

PLACES TO EAT

Jamba Juice: You and your thirsty dog can down all kinds of tasty, healthful concoctions here. (Jake recommends avoiding the green ones, though.) Share your fruit shake at one of many tables at the plaza. (Jamba Juice shares its tables with the likes of Starbucks and Noah's Bagels, so there's something for every taste here.) 33 North Moorpark Road; 805/449-1300.

PLACES TO STAY

Motel 6: Rates are $40–45. 1516 Newbury Road 91320; 805/499-0711.

Thousand Oaks Inn: Stay here and you're next to Borders Books, which is great for literary dogs. You'll also get use of the hotel's free video library, which is great for couch potato dogs. Your room comes with use of the hotel's heated pool and Jacuzzi, complimentary passes to a local workout joint, and a continental breakfast. Rates are $130–250. There's a $75 pooch fee per visit. 75 West Thousand Oaks Boulevard; 805/497-3701 or 800/600-6878; www .thousandoaksinn.com.

CHAPTER 2

Los Angeles County

Slowly but surely, Los Angeles County is going to the dogs, in the best sense of the phrase. This is a wonderful development if you're a dog or just someone who knows a dog.

When I started researching parks for *The Dog Lover's Companion to California* back in the early 1990s, there were only a couple of leash-free areas in the whole county. Today, there are 21, and counting. Most are fenced dog parks, but one is a spectacular 1,500-acre swatch of wilderness. (See Westridge-Canyonback Wilderness Park in the Encino section.) Go ahead, dogs: Wag your tails, pant, let it all hang out. Look for the running dog symbol 🐕 in the pages that follow, and take your humans to a doggone great park.

Of course, there needs to be a much larger increase in the number of leash-free areas if L.A. County's estimated 300,000 dogs are going to get the running room they deserve. If dogs had opposable fingers, they'd be crossing them hard for more places where they could just be their good old doggy selves and trot around naked. Many cities and park departments are working hand in paw with dogs and their people to help accomplish this mission. Jake

PICK OF THE LITTER—LOS ANGELES COUNTY

BEST BACKDROP
The Paramount Ranch, Agoura Hills (page 73)

BIGGEST VICTORY FOR NATURE
Ahmanson Ranch/Upper Las Virgenes Canyon Open Space Preserve, Calabasas (page 75)

MOST SURPRISING OFF-LEASH HIKE
Westridge-Canyonback Wilderness Park, Encino (page 76)

BIGGEST DOG PARK
Laurel Canyon Park, Studio City (page 79)

BEST LEASH-FREE BEACH (ONLY LEASH-FREE BEACH)
Dog Beach Zone, Long Beach (page 128)

BEST ARCHITECTURAL KITSCH
Tail O' the Pup, West Hollywood (page 86)

MOST DOG-FRIENDLY PLACES TO EAT
All India Cafe, Pasadena (page 66)
Java Man, Hermosa Beach (page 122)
Fleur de Lis, Long Beach (page 130)

MOST DOG-FRIENDLY PLACES TO STAY
Sheraton Universal Hotel, Universal City (page 81)
L'Ermitage, Beverly Hills (page 91)
W Los Angeles, Westwood (page 112)
Loews Santa Monica Beach Hotel, Santa Monica (page 115)

COOLEST CANINE CAMP
Iron Dogs Training Camp, Malibu (page 106)

BEST RIDES
Griffith Park miniature trains, Los Angeles (page 97)
Catalina Express **ferry,** mainland–Catalina Island (page 136)

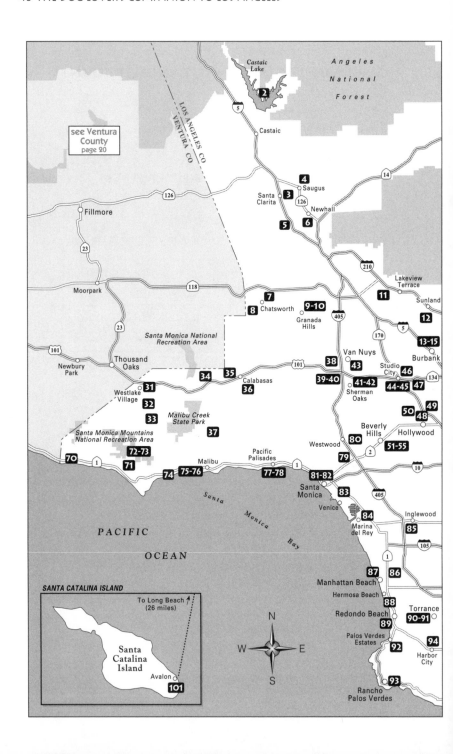

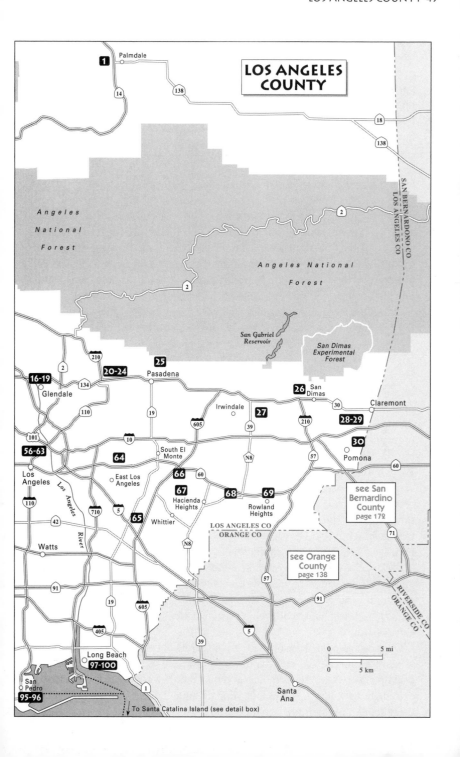

LOS ANGELES COUNTY

1 Palmdale
14
138
18
138

San Bernardino Co
Los Angeles Co

Angeles
National
Forest
2

Angeles National
Forest
2

San Gabriel
Reservoir

San Dimas
Experimental
Forest

2
210
20-24
25 Pasadena
16-19
Glendale
134
110
19
Irwindale
26 San Dimas
30 Claremont
27
28-29
101
56-63
10
64
605
39
210
57
30 Pomona
60
Los
Angeles
Los
Angeles
East Los
Angeles
South El
Monte
N8
66
60
110
710
5
67
68
69
65
Hacienda
Heights
Whittier
Rowland
Heights
42
Watts
N8
LOS ANGELES CO
ORANGE CO
see San
Bernardino
County
page 172
71
91
19
605
N8
see Orange
County
page 138
57
91
405
39
5
Riverside Co
Orange Co

0   5 mi
0   5 km

Long Beach
97-100
San
Pedro
95-96
1

Santa
Ana

To Santa Catalina Island (see detail box)

and I hope we'll be sniffing out many more leash-free havens for the book's next edition.

The Los Angeles County Parks system is a good one, with dozens of large parks dotting the county. Most allow leashed pooches. So do most of the huge, wonderful parklands within the Santa Monica Mountains National Recreation Area (see below) and just about every inch of land operated by the Santa Monica Mountains Conservancy.

But not everything is to a dog's liking here. Dogs are still banned from all beaches except one in the Malibu area and one in Long Beach. (Dogs can run leash free at the Long Beach one, but it's only in the testing stages; nothing is set in stone yet.) The rest of the county's 74 miles of shoreline are off-limits, verboten, badlands. But that may soon come to an end if a couple of active dog groups get their way: A group called Unleash the Beach is working to get a chunk of Santa Monica Beach OK'd for off-leash use, and the long-entrenched group Freeplay is striving for the same thing at El Segundo's Dockweiler Beach. Jake and I applaud both groups for going beyond setting their sights only on leashed use. See www.unleashthebeach.org and www.freeplay.org.

One of the best deals going for L.A.'s well-behaved dogs is the Sierra Club's K-9 Hiking Section, which encourages dogs on outings. Its stated purpose is "to explore and enjoy the trails and remote areas of the great outdoors with our canine friends and promote responsible dog ownership and behavior in pursuit of these goals." Outings include hikes in pristine national forest land, camping trips, and full-moon doggy hikes. "It's admirable to see a Pomeranian do a 10- to 12-mile hike cross-country, agilely dodging chollas (most of the time), fending off ticks, bounding over boulders in order to contemplate the fantastic views from the summit," a K-9 Committee chair writes me. For information on the K-9 Hiking Committee and its entertaining newsletter, *Waggin' Trails,* contact the Angeles chapter of the Sierra Club at 213/387-4287; www.angeles.sierraclub.org/k9.

Another terrific group to consider joining for awe-inspiring (and sometimes sweat-inspiring) hikes is California Canine Hikers (CCH). These fun folks hold about 50 hikes per year. For more information or an online application, see the website www.caninehikers.com.

Back in civilization, you can take a train ride with your dog at Griffith Park and even take your extremely well-behaved poochum-woochums shopping at certain exclusive Beverly Hills stores. You can spend the night at some of the world's finest hotels with your dog or take him to some super dog-friendly eateries around town.

Dogs can compare paw prints with the prints of Hollywood's biggest stars at Mann's Chinese Theatre. If you want a little exercise with your stargazing, pick up a map of the stars' homes and take a little walk around town. It's an extremely hackneyed, sometimes rude pastime, but most of the homes on these tours have long since changed hands, so you're often just staring at a home where the star lived many moons ago. Anyway, it's a great excuse to walk your dog.

Anthony Shipp, a Beverly Hills veterinarian to the stars, says celebrities often feel that their dogs are the only ones who really love them for who they are. "So many people like them only for what they can get from them, or for the dazzle," says Shipp, who has ministered to the dogs of Frank Sinatra, Kirk Douglas, Pierce Brosnan, and Richard Simmons, to drop a few names. (He recounts how, many years ago, he helped Sinatra's and Douglas's disinterested dogs to mate, but the dogs would do it only after they put on a tape of the crooner's hits. "It seems even dogs get romantic to Sinatra's voice," he says.)

Ah, doggy love.... But we must move on to the practical—the nuts and bolts of this section. This chapter separates some of the districts in the city of Los Angeles into their own sections. For instance, instead of listing Hollywood under "Los Angeles," it has its own heading. The city is too huge to lump all its districts together. Now, git along little doggy, and start sniffing out the tens of thousands of acres of urban and wild parks that welcome you and your ilk.

NATIONAL FORESTS

The National Forests and Wilderness Areas resource at the back of this book has important information and safety tips on visiting national forests with your dog and has more information on the Angeles National Forest.

Angeles National Forest

NATIONAL RECREATION AREAS

Santa Monica Mountains National Recreation Area
🐾🐾🐾🐾

Attention smog-coated dogs and city-weary people: You can breathe a sigh of relief. Nature is only a stick's throw away from the crowded freeways and urban sprawl of one of the largest cities in the world.

Contrary to what some local dog people have heard, leashed dogs really are allowed to explore portions of this 65,000-acre wonderland of mountains, canyons, woods, and fern glens. This national recreation area is a patchwork of county, state, and federal lands throughout the Santa Monica Mountains. While dogs are banned from trails on all state park lands and from most beaches within the recreation area, the majority of the recreation area's parks and open spaces welcome leashed dogs. Dogs need to wear a leash no longer than six feet (if it's retractable, measure carefully!) and be under control. (It seems like a redundant rule, but apparently the parks have had their share of out-of-control leashed dogs.) The most dog-friendly of the national recreation area's lands are managed by the Santa Monica Mountains Conservancy. We describe many of these gems throughout this chapter and the Ventura County chapter.

The Mountain Parks Information Service provides a free map showing all the parks, delineating which permit dogs. You can also get free brochures of many of the dog-friendly parks, which show trailheads and give descriptions and directions. They're essential for planning any enchanting back-to-nature outing with your dog. Call 800/533-PARK (800/533-7275) to get your maps and brochures. For a map of the entire recreation area, go to www.nps.gov/samo. In a hard-to-navigate-to page within that site (www.nps.gov/samo/brochure/dogleash.htm), you'll also find a list of parks within the recreation area that allow dogs, along with the detailed dog rules. The people at the National Park Service Visitor Center can be very helpful in answering questions about the recreation area. You can reach them at 805/370-2301.

Spring is a terrific time to explore these lands. Wildflowers blossom white, yellow, orange, blue, red, and every other color your dog might not be able to see if he's as color-blind as scientists claim. Birds sing their hearts out. The grasslands, normally a dead tan-brown color, become as green as green gets.

But watch out in the warmer months: "A lot of people bring their dogs hiking in the 90-degree heat and don't give them as much water as they need," says Walt Young, chief ranger for the Santa Monica Mountains Conservancy. "The dogs get heat stroke and we have to be called in to help out." Take his advice and leave your dog at home if it's hot. If you must take your dog during the hot months, bring only a fit, non-senior-citizen dog, and be sure to offer her water very frequently, even if she recently turned down a snootful.

Palmdale

PARKS, BEACHES, AND RECREATION AREAS

🐾 Ritter Ranch/Sierra Pelona Open Space

🐾 🐾 🐾 🐾 (See Los Angeles County map on pages 48–49)

You and your dog can hike forever when you start hoofing it at this 4,200-acre open space. The park itself has many miles of trails, which take you and your leashed dog through beautiful open land, rolling hills, sage-covered expanses, and desert-like territory on the east end of the Sierra Pelonas. You won't find much shade here, so it's best to come in winter and early spring, when your dog won't bake in her coat like a potato in its jacket.

A variety of trails in the eastern portion of the park will take you to the Sierra Pelona Trail, which leads to the Angeles National Forest. Here, if your dog is under voice control, you may let her off leash. (Of course, by the time you get here, your dog may be too well-exercised to really care about romping about all naked.)

Exit Highway 14 at Sierra Highway and drive north for about a mile until you get to Shannondale Road. Go right (north) on Shannondale, then right on Shannon Valley Road, driving east to Via Farnero Drive, where you'll go left and drive ever so briefly, going right on Shannon View Road (who is this Shannon, anyway?). Shannon View Road becomes Telephone Road. Follow it to the park entrance. 310/858-7272.

PLACES TO STAY

E-Z 8 Motel: We learned about this dog-friendly motel from Flint Dog and Serena Dog and their translator, Suzanne Stewart. They walked into the office and popped the question about whether or not dogs are allowed here, and the front-desk clerk smilingly told them, "We are a dog-friendly company." She says the first-floor room was very comfortable, with its own access to a landscaped area. At the time, there was a field of several acres next door for general dog romping, but this may not be the case when you visit. Time and developers march on. Rates are $44–81. Dogs require a $25 deposit. 430 West Palmdale Boulevard 93551; 661/273-6400.

Castaic

PARKS, BEACHES, AND RECREATION AREAS

🐾 Castaic Lake

🐾🐾🐾 (See Los Angeles County map on pages 48–49)

At 9,000 acres, this is the largest of Los Angeles County's recreation areas. But before your dog starts drooling with excitement, you should be warned that there's not much for a dog to do around here.

Hiking trails are virtually nonexistent. Dogs must be leashed everywhere. They're never allowed in either large Castaic Lake or the 180-acre Afterbay Lagoon, no matter how many trout or bass they see. (But humans can once again go swimming at the lake now that a bacteria problem is gone.)

Because there are no trails around Castaic Lake, it's pretty much impossible to hike its perimeter. The Afterbay Lagoon is a good sight easier for a dog jaunt, since it's developed. It has plenty of grassy areas, some trees, picnic tables, and a couple of playgrounds.

If you and your dog aren't anglers, but you're with someone who is, it's a fine place to spend the day. But it's not the kind of destination you'd want to visit just to walk your dog.

There's a $10 fee per car in summer, $8 in winter. Boat launching is an additional $8. The lake's 60 campsites cost $15–18 nightly. From I-5, exit at Lake Hughes Road and follow it to the lake. 661/257-4050.

PLACES TO STAY

Castaic Lake: See Castaic Lake, above, for camping information.

Comfort Inn: The lake is down the road a bit. Rates are $50–110. Dogs can stay only in smoking rooms. Dogs under 25 pounds are $5 extra. Over that size, they're $10. 31558 Castaic Road 91384; 661/295-1100 or 800/228-5150.

Santa Clarita

PARKS, BEACHES, AND RECREATION AREAS

I've listed the Santa Clarita Woodlands Park under Santa Clarita because it's the closest real city to the park. While you're in the area, be sure to check out the former oil boomtown of Mentryville (see Newhall).

🖪 Santa Clarita Woodlands Park

🐾🐾🐾🐾 (See Los Angeles County map on pages 48–49)

Come here on a spring day and you and your leashed dog will swear you're nowhere near Los Angeles County. That's because this park is huge, with deep green (OK, seasonally green) hills of oaks and grasslands, hidden meadows, and a long, gurgling stream with banks of lush flora. We enjoy hiking here in the rain. After a long day in the valley, it's a refreshing way to wash away the dirt and stress of urban life.

The park, with its miles of trails and splendid views of the surrounding canyons and forests, opened to the public in 1997 after more than 100 years in the hands of the oil industry. It was actually the oil industry that kept this large swatch of land from succumbing to the rampant development of neighboring communities. Fortunately, the Santa Monica Mountains Conservancy got hold of the property before developers could. The result awaits the pitter-patter of your dog's paws.

Exit I-5 at Calgrove Boulevard and drive west a short jog to The Old Road; drive south until you see signs for the park, then head west again. The main entrance is at Ed Davis Park. 310/589-3200.

Saugus

PARKS, BEACHES, AND RECREATION AREAS

🖪 Vasquez Rocks Natural Area Park

🐾🐾🐾 (See Los Angeles County map on pages 48–49)

This is Los Angeles County? It looks more like another planet. The slanted, jagged rocks and hidden caves are among the state's most famous geological wonders. They're so unusually beautiful that film crews routinely use them as a backdrop. When you call the park, chances are the answering machine will tell you how to get permission to make movies here. It's probably not the kind of information you and your dog need to know, but that's entertainment.

This smog-free 745-acre park, in the high desert near Agua Dulce, also features Tataviam Indian archaeological sites. Many trails branch off through chaparral and riparian plant communities. Make sure you bring drinking water; there's none in the park and you can work up a mighty thirst.

Dogs must be leashed, but back in the days of the bandit Tiburicio Vasquez, there were no such rules. If there had been, Vasquez, the park's namesake, would have found a way to break them. In the mid-1800s, Vasquez was a sort of Robin Hood character, robbing from the wealthy and giving the money to poor Mexicans. He used the caves and rocks as a hideaway from the sheriff's posses and vigilantes who were always on his trail. When you visit the park, stop at the entry kiosk and read about Vasquez's dramatic final days here. Then take your dog for a hike on the very trails Vasquez may have fled on, and let your imagination take you back to the days of the Wild West.

Exit Highway 14 at Agua Dulce Canyon Road and follow the signs to the park. 661/268-0840.

Newhall

PARKS, BEACHES, AND RECREATION AREAS

5 Mentryville

🐾🐾🐾 (See Los Angeles County map on pages 48–49)

Once upon a time, there was oil in these hills. Mentryville was home to what's claimed to be the longest continually operating oil well in the world, running from the 1880s until 1990. The little town housed more than 100 families from its inception to about 1930, and some of it has been preserved and turned into a very cool park. You can see a handful of historic buildings and landmarks here, including a one-room schoolhouse, an old barn, the site of the famed oil well, and founder Charles Mentry's big old mansion.

Dogs can't go in the buildings, but they can check them out with you from the outside, as long as they're leashed. If this disappoints your dog, tell her that there's something even better for visiting pooches: They can join you on a wonderful hike through Pico Canyon, in the north end of Santa Clarita Woodlands Park. The trail takes you from Mentryville through chaparral-covered slopes and into a shaded, lush, riparian area near the headwaters of Pico Canyon and the Santa Susana Mountains. The trail continues but gets very rugged, so be prepared to turn around when your dog is tired. This isn't a loop trail.

From the San Fernando Valley, go north on I-5 and take the Lyons Road/Pico Canyon Road exit. Turn left at the off-ramp's stop sign (this will be Pico Canyon Road), cross over the freeway, and continue straight until you come to a Y intersection near the end of the road. Go left at the Y and continue to the end of that road, where you'll find a parking lot. 27201 Pico Canyon Road; 310/589-3200.

6 William S. Hart Regional Park

🐾🐾🐾 (See Los Angeles County map on pages 48–49)

If you and your dog are fans of the Old West, you must amble on down here. Coming to this park is like getting a personal invitation to the house and ranch of the silent Western movie hero William S. Hart. Unfortunately, Hart isn't around anymore to give you a personal tour, but feel free to peruse the property via a couple of trails. If you get a hankering to check out his hacienda, you can leave your dog at the shaded picnic area with your traveling pardner and take a guided tour.

Dogs have to be leashed at the park. Hart, a cowboy himself, might not have liked that rule, but it's a small price to pay to enjoy the hospitality of the ghost of these here hills. Besides, the property houses a little zoo with farm animals and a compost demonstration site. You don't want your pooch meddling with either.

Exit Highway 14 at San Fernando Road and follow the signs west to the park. 661/259-0855.

Chatsworth

PARKS, BEACHES, AND RECREATION AREAS

7 Garden of the Gods

🐾🐾🐾 (See Los Angeles County map on pages 48–49)

The huge sandstone rock formations at this 23-acre park have provided a dramatic background for many an old film. The Garden of the Gods is one of the last undeveloped remnants of the once thriving Iverson Movie Ranch, used by dozens of directors during its reign from the earliest days of film in 1912 all the way up through 1976. Movies and shows shot at the ranch include *Stagecoach, The Lone Ranger, Bonanza, Superman, Batman and Robin, Tarzan the Apeman, Little Bighorn,* and *The Fighting Seabees.* Even Laurel & Hardy and Shirley Temple filmed some scenes here.

If your dog's nose is very keen, he just might be able to sniff out where Rin Tin Tin once performed some scenes. We're not sure if the famous dog ever actually ventured to the Garden of the Gods during his time at Iverson, but he was definitely nearby.

A short trail takes you to some jaw-dropping rock formations. Exit Highway 118 at Topanga Canyon Boulevard and in less than a half mile make a right at Santa Susana Pass Road. In about another half mile you'll come to Redmesa Drive. Go right and follow it a few hundred feet to the park's entrance. (Redmesa bisects the park.) 310/589-3200.

8 Chatsworth Park South

🐾🐾🐾 (See Los Angeles County map on pages 48–49)

Joe Dog and Bill Dog had a rollicking good time roaming and rolling in this very spacious park one sunny afternoon. Other dogs were having the same grand old time, and when they joined together, it was a major pooch party.

The park's 81 acres provide lots of leg room for dogs, but the creatures are supposed to be leashed. An Elysian green meadow stretches as far as you care to run with your dog. If tiptoeing through the grass isn't your idea of a good time, you can walk along the park's wide dirt hiking trail. It's a wise idea to stick to the trails anyway: Rattlesnakes seem to enjoy living at this address.

The craggy mountains towering north of the park make for an impressive backdrop. Enough trees grace the park that you can lounge in the shade while you admire the scenery and the friendly dogs who frequent the place.

Exit Highway 118 at Topanga Canyon Boulevard and drive south for almost 1.5 miles to Devonshire Street. Turn right and drive a few blocks into the park. 818/341-6595.

PLACES TO STAY

Summerfield Suites Hotel: The suites are big and their fireplaces are awfully inviting. Rates are $159–189. Better plan on staying for a few nights, because the dog fees aren't cheap. You'll pay between $150 and $200 for the length of their stay, depending on the room size. If your dog is staying only one night, it's the same price as dressing him in a human disguise and getting him his own room! 21902 Lassen Street 91311; 818/773-0707 or 800/238-8000; www.summerfieldsuites.com.

Granada Hills

PARKS, BEACHES, AND RECREATION AREAS

9 Moonshine Canyon Park

🐾🐾 (See Los Angeles County map on pages 48–49)

Our favorite part of this fairly narrow, twisty park is to the north of Highway 118. Within about two-thirds of a mile of the highway, you'll start to see the park and entries into it on your left.

Pull over and park on the road. (You'll see the parking possibilities on the southbound side of the street.) Enter the park at the trailheads that jut out of the edge of the canyon. Make a quick descent into the canyon bottom. Once there, it's best to go left on the trail. Going right will take you to a few dicey spots full of abandoned washing machines and cars, then to a busy road. The trail to the left, however, takes you alongside a creek, past brushy hills and the occasional songbird.

The hike is fairly secluded, with only an occasional glimpse of a house on a ridge. This is good and bad. It's good if you and your dog need to get away from civilization and see hardly a soul on the trail. It's not so good if you're worried about who might be lurking in the bushes. Remember: At all large urban parks, it's better to hike with a human companion than alone with your pooch. If you feel at all unsure about the safety of the park, go with someone else or don't go at all.

Exit Highway 118 at Tampa Avenue. If you drive south, the park will be immediately on your right. It stretches south along Tampa Avenue for another mile. If you drive north on Tampa Avenue, the road doesn't come very close to the park until after the golf course. The park will be on your left. 818/363-3556.

🔟 O'Melveny Park

🐾🐾🐾 (See Los Angeles County map on pages 48–49)

This 672-acre park offers so many great hiking opportunities that your dog won't know which trail to try first.

Jake would like to suggest a fairly flat two-mile hike that takes you along a tree-lined creek at the bottom of the canyon here. It's often pretty green, and the creek actually has water in it, so it's not like so many dry L.A. County canyon parks.

Jake likes this park because he knows he's going to get a picnic after his lei-

surely hike. The picnic tables are plentiful, and they're at the beginning/end of this particular hike, so he knows if we don't eat upon entering, we'll definitely have a bite before leaving.

Exit I-5 at Balboa Boulevard and drive south about a mile to Orozco Street. Turn right and drive to the parking lot for the picnic area. The trail starts at the north end of the picnic area. For info on tougher hikes in this park, call 818/363-3556.

Lakeview Terrace

PARKS, BEACHES, AND RECREATION AREAS

11 Hansen Dam Recreation Area

🐾🐾🐾 (See Los Angeles County map on pages 48–49)

This is 1,400 acres of hills, trees, shrubs, and grassy meadows. And the good news is that once again, it has a lake as its centerpiece. It disappeared for a few years during a long process of reclamation, but it's here to stay. Dogs enjoy sniffing around its perimeter and especially appreciate the horse trails here. They smell good to pooches, who may find an occasional munchy along the way (but try as your dog might, don't let him nibble these morsels).

From I-210, exit at Osborne Street and follow the signs for a couple of blocks. 626/899-4537.

Sunland

PARKS, BEACHES, AND RECREATION AREAS

12 La Tuna Canyon Park

🐾🐾🐾🐾 (See Los Angeles County map on pages 48–49)

Whether you're in the mood for an easy, cool, shady, wet hike, a more rigorous, steep, dry one, or something in between, you'll find what you're looking for at this 1,100-acre park on the north slope of the Verdugo Mountains.

If you and your leashed dog feel like taking it easy, head for The Grotto, a gorgeous, green cut in a canyon that seems to more verdant and cooler as you walk along the trail. The trees and steep surrounding slopes provide plenty of shade. Before you know it, you'll be at a beautiful waterfall, if there's still enough water to fall when you're there. (In early spring, it can really flow.) It's mossy, cool, and relaxing.

Other trails take you through canyons full of oaks and sycamores. If you go high enough, things get sagey, and the views become magnificent, if you happen to like views of one of the world's biggest metropolitan areas. (Most people come here trying to forget the city, but it looks pretty good from the ridgetop.)

Exit I-210 at La Tuna Canyon Road and drive west. If you want to hit The

Grotto, you'll find its parking and trailhead in a little under a mile, on the left. For the moderate La Tuna Canyon Trail, drive another half mile for parking, a picnic area, and the trailhead. This trail will lead you to other trails, which will take you out of the park and into other hiking areas—some steep and more demanding. 310/858-7272.

Burbank

PARKS, BEACHES, AND RECREATION AREAS

13 McCambridge Park

😺😺 (See Los Angeles County map on pages 48–49)

This nice little chunk of city park recently went through a million-dollar renovation, so it's an attractive place to walk your pooch. Lots of grass and trees. Unfortunately, the renovation didn't include any off-leash areas for dogs. (Thanks to Bill Thayer and his faithful black Lab for pointing us in the right direction.) The park is at North Glenoaks Boulevard between Andover and Amherst Drives. 818/238-5378.

14 Johnny Carson Park

😺😺 (See Los Angeles County map on pages 48–49)

Remember all of Johnny Carson's lines about "beautiful downtown Burbank"? Since the late *Tonight Show* host did his best to put Burbank on the map, the city decided to do the same for him. Just across from the NBC studios where he hosted his show year after year, there's a decent little park named after him.

The park, which used to be called Buena Vista Park, is a great place to visit with your dog if you're dropping off a friend at NBC or at the nearby Disney studios. It's well shaded and has many picnic tables and a footbridge that leads you to a fitness course. With Highway 134 roaring so close, it's not quiet, but who comes to this part of Burbank for tranquility?

A word of warning: Don't let your male dog lift his leg on the stone "sign" with Johnny Carson's mug engraved on it. We met a man who apparently sits on the grass all day watching for such indiscretions. He came running up to Joe after the dog did a quick leg lift. I thought perhaps he knew Joe or was running up to say Joe was a fine dog, but something about the way he was screaming "No, no pee on this! Bad dog!" led me to believe he had another mission.

Exit I-5 at Alameda Avenue and drive southwest for about 20 blocks. At Bob Hope Drive, turn left. The park will be on your left in about a block. 818/238-5378.

15 Wildwood Canyon Park

🐾🐾🐾 (See Los Angeles County map on pages 48–49)

The only way Jake would like this big park better than he already does would be if he could go leashless. It's beautifully manicured and surrounded by miles of forest. If he's in the mood to roll on the grass and enjoy a picnic near regal stone archways, we stay in the developed part of the park. If he's raring to explore nature and admire trees in his unique way, we take the myriad trails leading out from various points around the park.

His favorite kind of day involves a long hike through the hills, followed by a leisurely picnic at the serene, secluded, shaded picnic spots that dot the main area. You can't help but feel pampered in this lush park: It's run with such class that even the portable toilets are disguised to look distinguished.

Coming north on I-5, take the Olive Avenue exit and head northeast. Turn left at Sunset Canyon Drive. In six blocks, turn right on Harvard Drive, which will take you into the park. Make sure you bear right once you come to a fork in the road, or you'll end up on the adjacent golf course. 818/238-5378.

PLACES TO EAT

Chez Nous: Enjoy California Continental cuisine under the canopies with your pooch. 10550 Riverside Drive; 818/760-0288.

Priscilla's: If you and your pooch want to feel really welcome at a restaurant, come here. "We love dogs and would let them inside if we were allowed," says a manager. "We give them water, a little milk, whatever they want." You'll like the relaxed atmosphere on the patio with umbrella-shaded tables, as well as the gourmet coffees and tasty light fare. 4150 Riverside Drive; 818/843-5707.

Toluca Garden: This is a good Chinese restaurant where you and the dog can dine at umbrella-topped outdoor tables. 10000 Riverside Drive; 818/980-3492.

PLACES TO STAY

Coast Anabelle Hotel: Business travelers enjoy staying here. It's somewhat upscale but not very (cotton terry robes come with your room, but so do typical motel-style beds and bedding), and the pool and fitness center make even a long stay here a little more relaxing. Some rooms come with a full kitchen. Rates are $129–169. Dogs have to offer a $200 deposit (credit card is fine; you won't feel a thing if your dog doesn't do any damage) and sign a pet agreement. 2011 West Olive Avenue 91506; 818/845-7800 or 800/663-1144; www.coastanabelle.com.

Hilton Burbank: This large Hilton across from the Burbank airport recently underwent a huge renovation. The rooms, spa, pool, and fitness center are now to drool for, especially for dogs used to the typical business-style hotel.

Rates are $129–250. Dogs are $25 extra and need to weigh about 50 pounds or less. There's a grassy area on the grounds for little walkies. 2500 Hollywood Way 91505; 818/843-6000; www.hilton.com.

Holiday Inn: Rates are $110–135. Dogs are $10 and need to be under 50 pounds. 150 East Angeleno Avenue 91510; 818/841-4770; www.holidayinn.com.

Safari Inn: Dogs who dig colorful retro chic love staying at the Safari Inn. This is a fully restored and renovated classic from the 1950s, complete with an ultra-retro 1960s neon sign announcing the motel to the world. The rooms here are bright, cheery, and well appointed—a few steps up from a typical motel. (How many motels offer room service from their very own decent restaurant?) You can even get a "groovy martini" at the inn's restaurant/lounge, if you really want to stroll (stumble?) down memory lane. Relax in the pool under a few tall palms and the bright lights of the neon sign.

Rates are $92–129. Dogs require only a $200 deposit (a credit card deposit will do) and a signature on a pet policy. 1911 West Olive Avenue 91506; www.safariburbank.com.

Glendale

PARKS, BEACHES, AND RECREATION AREAS

16 Brand Park

🐾🐾🐾 (See Los Angeles County map on pages 48–49)

If you feel as if you're on the estate of William Randolph Hearst when visiting this green and verdant park, you're not far off. It's actually the former property of the late real estate tycoon Leslie C. Brand, a.k.a. "The Father of Glendale."

Upon entering the park, you'll be greeted by a great white Moorish/Indian-style mansion. The mansion is now a library, surrounded by lush, shaded land. You and your leashed dog can pass an afternoon in perfect serenity here. Go ahead, pretend it's your estate. Relax, read, sniff the flowers, and have a little picnic.

If you prefer a little exercise with your lounging, a fire road takes you through the park and up to a ridge with a great view. This hike is not for the fair of foot: It's almost a six-mile round-trip, and, to put it mildly, it's not flat. But it's one of the more enjoyable hikes we found in the Los Angeles area. And if you want to keep going, there are ways to access the thousands of acres of open space that lie outside the park's perimeter. Unfortunately, the leash law applies in this area, too.

Exit I-5 on Western Avenue and go northeast about 1.5 miles. The road will take you to the park's magnificent library entrance. 818/548-2000.

🐾🐾 Lower Scholl Canyon Park

🐾🐾 (See Los Angeles County map on pages 48–49)

Although this park is only six acres, it's easy on the eyes and on the paws. The grass here is almost golf-course-like, and the trees, while most are not tremendous, provide shade and a very pleasant atmosphere. (Some even turn colors in the fall.) Your leashed dog can go on an easy stroll along the walking paths or hang out while you watch your kids at the cute little play area. The park is at 2849 East Glenoaks Boulevard, at Glenoaks Canyon. For info, you can phone either 818/548-3795 or 310/858-7272. (It's managed by two different agencies.)

🐾🐾 Dunsmore Park

🐾🐾 (See Los Angeles County map on pages 48–49)

If, after a hike at the dusty, rugged George Deukmejian Wilderness Park (see below), you and your pooch are longing for mowed green grass, come here. It's only 10 blocks away and has many signs of civilization, including water fountains, shaded picnic areas, a large playground, and a fenced-in ball field.

Exit U.S. 101 on Pennsylvania Avenue. Go north a few blocks and turn left at Foothill Boulevard. Drive northwest about six blocks, then turn right on Dunsmore Avenue and drive four blocks north. 818/548-2000.

🐾🐾 George Deukmejian Wilderness Park

🐾🐾 (See Los Angeles County map on pages 48–49)

When we first heard the name of this park, we thought someone was making a joke. The words "George Deukmejian" and the word "wilderness" were often used in the same sentence when he was governor, but more like: "That George Deukmejian, he should have been more concerned about wilderness."

A couple of locals told us that back in the late 1980s, the Duke was actually against setting aside this large parcel of land for a park. But he was finally sold on it when a clever environmentalist came up with the idea to name the park after him. Whether this is true or just a semi-urban myth, dogs can be grateful to the governor for making room for this 700-acre square of land.

This isn't what you'd call a breathtaking park. It can be very dry and dusty, with only an occasional tree to provide relief from the sun in these chaparral-covered hills. But the dogs we've seen cavorting around the park really love it here. They seem to smile as they accompany their leashed people up and down the canyon.

Maybe they're smiling because of the lack of people or the abundance of singing birds. Maybe it's the scents of strange fauna on the couple of miles of dirt road here. Or perhaps they know that if they walk far enough, they'll be in Angeles National Forest, where they can run around in leashless ecstasy. (It will be 100 percent easier to get there once some trails connecting the two areas are completed.) Whatever the case, this is a park that you might not find aesthetically pleasing, but your dog will.

Exit U.S. 101 on Pennsylvania Avenue. Go north a few blocks and turn left at Foothill Boulevard. Drive northwest about six blocks, then turn right on Dunsmore Avenue. The road will lead you into the park in about a mile, where you'll bear right after the sign for the park and drive up a narrow paved road to a dirt parking lot next to a horse corral. Start your hike at the wide, gated road just above the lot. 818/548-2000.

PLACES TO EAT

Hot Wings Cafe: This little restaurant has a shaded outdoor area and a loyal following of dog-toting patrons. 314 North Brand Boulevard; 818/247-4445.

La Fontana Italian Kitchen: You and your dog will be surrounded by an impressive wrought-iron fence as you dine at one of the umbrella-topped tables. 933 North Brand Boulevard; 818/247-6256.

PLACES TO STAY

Days Inn: Rates are $83–104. Dogs require a $50 deposit and must stay in smoking rooms. 450 West Pioneer Street 91203; 818/956-0202; www.daysinn.com.

Vagabond Inn: Rates are $89–99. Dogs are $10 extra and are relegated to smoking rooms. 120 West Colorado Street 91204; 818/240-1700.

Pasadena

PARKS, BEACHES, AND RECREATION AREAS

Pasadena residents have been fighting to get a much-needed off-leash park or dog-run area for years. At press time, construction was about to start on what promises to be an incredible dog park located on Pasadena's east side, within Eaton Wash Park. The Alice Kennedy Frost Dog Park will be two acres, with tunnels, hills, and all kinds of fun dog doohickeys. It was scheduled to open during summer 2005. For an update, see www.pasadenapooch.org or phone the parks department at 626/744-4321.

20 Brookside Park

🐾🐾🐾🦴 (for restricted training purposes)

(See Los Angeles County map on pages 48–49)

Brookside Park, home of the Rose Bowl, is a beautiful place, with roses hither and thither. The park has a playground, ball fields, trees, and acres of green grass. When there are no major games going on, it's a quiet park. There's even a trail you and your leashed pooch can take to get farther away from the madding crowd, in case you happen to be accompanying someone who has only one Rose Bowl ticket.

Dogs are allowed off leash here only for training purposes, and only at a

designated area near the Rose Bowl. The hours for this training are 6 A.M.–
10 P.M. weekdays and 6–10 A.M. weekends. (A word about training: We're not
talking about training your dog to hike off leash or chase tennis balls. The
training clause is for specific feats that don't cover a lot of ground, such as
teaching your dog to come when called, to stay, and to heel. Be careful out
there; park rangers know the difference between truly training your dog and
walking around the park reading the newspaper with your dog.)

Exit I-210 at Seco Street and follow the signs to the Rose Bowl. As you
approach the Rose Bowl stadium, look for a big green meadow on your left.
It's part of this large park complex. 626/744-4321.

21 Central Park

🐾🐾 (See Los Angeles County map on pages 48–49)
Visiting Old Town Pasadena? Bring your leashed dog here for a little siesta
between your café-hopping adventures. The park has several tall old trees
that boy dogs are wild about, and plenty of other good dog amenities like big
grassy areas, a shaded paved path, and lawn bowling. (OK, they can't bowl,
but they enjoy watching for a few seconds.) The park is at Del Mar Boulevard
and Fair Oaks Avenue. 626/744-4321.

22 Eaton Canyon Park

🐾🐾🐾 (See Los Angeles County map on pages 48–49)
This wild and beautiful 184-acre park can be a little too enticing for dog
folks: Half of the users allow their dogs off leash, according to rangers. This
is something the rangers consider a big no-no, in part because of the wildlife
here (many a deer has been chased, they say), in part because of the horses
who share the trails (many a horse has been spooked, they say), and in part
because of the rattlesnakes and poison oak here (many a dog has encountered
both, the former with nasty results for the dog, the latter with nasty results
for the dog's human).

Rangers here say dogs may be banned if people continue to disobey the
leash law. "They're hanging on by the skin of their teeth," says one. If you
don't want to lose this park, use your leash. And use your poop bags. If you
don't have one, the park has Mutt Mitt dispensers.

Traveling east on I-210, exit at Altadena Drive and go north on Altadena.
Drive 1.6 miles. The main park entrance is on the right. Follow the winding
road to the park's nature center, where you can pick up a map and get your
bearings. 626/398-5420.

23 Lower Arroyo Park

🐾🐾🐾 (See Los Angeles County map on pages 48–49)
The dirt trails at this park go and go and go until you and your dog are so
pooped you can't go anymore. Wander through the bottom of the canyon, safe

from cars, free from the sounds of civilization. The canyon bottom is pretty wide, so you'll have your choice of paths. It's really important to keep your dog leashed here, because the park is home to wild animals, and some dogs have been harassing them out of their homes, according to park watchers.

If landlubbing activities like hiking fatigue you, try perfecting your casting skills at the casting pool next to the parking lot. Take advantage of this park, because the adjoining Arroyo Seco Park in South Pasadena doesn't even allow a dog to set paw inside it.

Take I-210 to its southernmost end. At its termination point, it becomes St. John Avenue. Go two blocks on St. John Avenue and turn right on California Boulevard. In about four blocks, the park will be directly in front of you. Turn right on Arroyo Boulevard and drive a couple of blocks. On your left is a driveway to the parking lot. 626/744-4321.

24 Victory Park

🐾 🐾 (See Los Angeles County map on pages 48–49)

Leashed dogs who enjoy watching people play softball like coming to this 25-acre park. It sports three softball diamonds and a baseball diamond, in addition to some open land and tree-studded picnic areas. Dogs who aren't sports fans can walk with you on the asphalt path that runs through the park.

The park is at Paloma Street and Altadena Drive. 626/744-4321.

PLACES TO EAT

All India Cafe: The food here is utterly delicious. It seems every time you sneeze, it gets lavished with yet another "best Indian cuisine" honor. Vegetarians and meat-eaters alike love the delectable cuisine. Dogs would be content to laze at the sidewalk tables in the shade of an awning, but as a bonus they get their own doggy delight: cool water and a treat! 39 South Fair Oaks Avenue; 626/440-0309.

Crocodile Cafe: You can't get crocodiles here, but you can get a terrific barbecue chicken pizza or a tiger shrimp salad. "Our food is swell," says a friendly waiter. Dine with your dog at the umbrella-topped tables out front. 88 West Colorado Boulevard; 626/568-9310.

Jake's: Jake Dog loves visiting this Old Town Pasadena eatery and smelling the big burgers, chicken strips, and chunky fries. Humans can wash it all down with one of many brands of brews, and dogs get a bowl of water if they're thirsty. Dogs and their people can sit at several well-shaded outdoor tables. 38 West Colorado Boulevard; 626/568-1602.

Mi Piace: In Italian, the name of this restaurant means "I like it." And I do. The Italian food has a light and healthy California bent. Try the Chicken Mi Piace, which is white-meat chicken sautéed with mushrooms in a garlicky-herby white wine concoction. (A menu writer I'm not.) The little pizzas are zippy. Eat with your dog under the sidewalk awning. Dogs get fresh water if thirsty. In Old Town Pasadena, at 25 East Colorado Boulevard; 626/795-3131.

Three Dog Bakery: Dogs take comfort in knowing that there's one place that always allows dogs inside in Old Town Pasadena. Pooches get to nose around and choose from dozens of fresh-baked treats and dog pastries while their people eye (and buy) fun dog gift items. Watch your dog dine at the one little table here. (Now you know how it feels when your dog watches you dine.) 24 Smith Alley; 626/440-0443.

Trattoria Farfalla: Dine on tasty pastas and pizzas at the sidewalk tables here. Dogs dig the mellow atmosphere and the water they'll get if thirsty. 43 East Colorado Boulevard; 626/564-8696.

PLACES TO STAY

Millard Campground: This tiny five-tent site is the perfect getaway just north of town. Since it's in Angeles National Forest, your dog is welcome. And outside the campground, he can go off leash on the many first-rate trails here. The beauties of this camping area are that you don't have to make a reservation and coming here is free. Exit I-210 at Lake Avenue and drive north to Loma Alta Drive. Go left on Loma Alta Drive. Follow the signs to the campground. 626/574-5200.

Quality Inn Pasadena: Rates are $59–79. Dogs are $10 extra and need to stay in a smoking room. 3221 East Colorado Boulevard 91107; 626/796-9291.

The Ritz-Carlton, Huntington Hotel & Spa: Remember all those times you've stayed at other hotels and shrugged off the postage-stamp-size towels or the paper-thin walls with a "Well, it ain't exactly The Ritz"? Well, this is

exactly The Ritz. Only lucky little dogs (under 30 pounds) get to experience this gorgeous, crème de la crème hotel. It's set on 23 acres of gardens with every luxury amenity imaginable. I won't go into more detail since most dogs are too big or too budget conscious to stay here and it would break their hearts. Rates are $200–320. (Suites can cost more than $3,000.) 1401 South Oak Knoll 91106; 626/568-3900; www.ritzcarlton.com/hotels/huntington.

Vagabond Inn: Rates are $89–99. Dogs are $10 extra. 1203 East Colorado Boulevard 91106; 626/449-3170.

The Westin Pasadena: If your dog is 40 pounds or under, he'll feel like a small human at this lovely hotel: Humans get the luxurious Heavenly Bed; dogs get the luxurious Heavenly Dog Bed. Humans get a fitness center; dogs get, well, free poop bags and some grass to peruse outside. Rates are $169–219. 191 North Los Robles 91101; 626/792-2727; www.starwood.com/westin.

Sierra Madre

25 Sierra Madre Dog Park

🐾🐾🐾🐕 (See Los Angeles County map on pages 48–49)

To visit this little dog park, you need to attend a tag sale of sorts. Dogs who come here need to wear a tag issued by the city. The tag is $25 for the calendar year, but the fee is prorated depending on the time of year you buy the tag. If you want to just check out the park for an afternoon, you're supposed to buy a daily pass for $5.

The park isn't even an acre, but it's got a separate fenced area for small or shy dogs, handicap access, lights, water, benches, and lots of dogs who are really fun to play with. It's within Sierra Vista Park, which has restrooms, should you need to heed nature's call after your dog does.

The park is at 611 East Sierra Madre Boulevard, south of the tennis courts in Sierra Vista Park. Call 626/836-8468 for park info. You can purchase tags at the city building at 232 West Sierra Madre Boulevard. The phone number there is 626/355-7135.

San Dimas

PARKS, BEACHES, AND RECREATION AREAS

26 Frank G. Bonelli Regional Park

🐾🐾🐾 (See Los Angeles County map on pages 48–49)

The good rating we're giving this park has nothing to do with friendliness. Park officials (the ones in the office, not out and about in the park) were so rude that we almost decided not to include this place in the book. If you can avoid it, don't go to the visitor center. At least don't go there and let them know you have a dog.

After they let us into the park ($6 at the time, $8 now), we drove past the entry kiosk and a tree immediately came crashing down. It would have landed right on the car, but I was able to swerve. The dogs ended up squished together in the corner, but at least they weren't squished to the floor by a lumberjack's mistake.

When we were done dealing with the humans here, it became obvious that this really is a great place to take a dog. Some 14 miles of trails can easily make you forget about any churlish people you may have encountered earlier. The trails are rugged and geared toward equestrians, so be sure to keep that leash on your dog. You can hike up grassy hills and scrubby, weedy areas to majestic views of the region. The best spot we found to start one of these hikes was right across from the entrance to the east picnic valley. It's perfect; after a rigorous hike, you can hang out at a shaded picnic table and enjoy a little wine/water and cheese with your dog.

Puddingstone Reservoir is the centerpiece of the park, and the bass and trout fishing here is rumored to be pretty hot. But dogs aren't allowed to swim in it. Too bad, because it covers a whopping 250 acres when full. When we visited, humans weren't even allowed to swim in the lake because of bacteria. But you can still pull a bunch of fish out and eat them for dinner.

The park is right next to the Raging Waters park, so it's a convenient place to take your dog if you don't feel like going home after you've dropped off the kids at that exhilarating attraction. From I-210, exit at Raging Waters Drive/ Via Verde and follow the signs east into the park. 909/599-8411.

Irwindale

PARKS, BEACHES, AND RECREATION AREAS

27 Santa Fe Dam Recreation Area

🐾🐾🐾 (See Los Angeles County map on pages 48–49)

When you're approaching this large county park, you'll find it hard to believe anything but industry could exist here. The area is utterly fraught with unsightly evidence of rampant "progress."

But in the middle of it all is a big patch of green doing its best to fend off the onslaught of civilization. It's not the most attractive park in the world, but it's a commendable attempt.

The park's Santa Fe Reservoir is a decent place to share a picnic with your dog. You can also fish for trout or launch a boat here for a relaxing morning on the water. You won't exactly feel like you're in the middle of Wisconsin, but it's better than some water holes we've seen down here.

The best time you can have with your dog at this park is if you take a hike on the nature trail. Signs and pamphlets point out the flora and fauna you'll come across in the 1,000-acre nature area. The trail provides a good hike, but it's not without its sad side: As if the surrounding scenery were not enough of a reminder, signs tell you how humans have destroyed the habitat. Do your part to protect it, and make sure your dog is leashed and doesn't disturb the birds and beasts here.

There's a $8 fee per vehicle, which you can avoid by parking on a nearby street. (If you have the $8, keep in mind that the county park system is financially devastated and can use every penny to keep parks running.) Exit I-210 at Irwindale Avenue and go south about 1.5 miles. Turn right at Arrow Highway, and within a few blocks turn right again at the signs for the park. To get to the nature trail, bear to the right after the entry kiosk and follow the signs. 626/334-1065.

Claremont

Claremont is a very dog-friendly place to be. Not only is there a fairly new leash-free dog park (Pooch Park), but now there's also a huge park where leashed dogs love to roam (the Claremont Hills Wilderness Park). All this, and Claremont is the home of famed rapper Snoop Doggy Dog. Just thought your own doggy dog would like to know.

PARKS, BEACHES, AND RECREATION AREAS

28 Claremont Hills Wilderness Park

🐾 🐾 🐾 🐾 (See Los Angeles County map on pages 48–49)

The city obtained a beautiful 1,200-acre chunk of land and turned it into a beautiful 1,200-acre chunk of park. Pooches can peruse this delightful acquisition, as long as they're on leash.

Claremont Hills is a hilly park (duh), with several miles of trails and fire roads leading through open land dotted with oaks and scrub. A creek runs through it during non-drought years. The park has cool, shaded canyons as well as terrific vistas of the surrounding valleys. All this makes it prime turf for mudslides. During rainy season, the entire park can close. Enter at the very south end of Mills Avenue. 909/399-5490.

29 Claremont Dog Park/Pooch Park

🐾 🐾 🐾 🐕 (See Los Angeles County map on pages 48–49)

Dogs are so happy to come here you can sometimes hear them baying from blocks away. It's the most popular park in Claremont, at least according to Ralph Dog and Zippity Dog, who are frequent visitors and can be trusted implicitly.

This 1.25-acre park is completely fenced, so dogs can run around to their heart's delight. It's a long park, which is great for dogs who want to work up a full head of steam before having to turn around and run in another direction.

Pooches love the green grass and the old trees that grace a couple of sides of the park. There are benches galore for people and a water fountain for pooches and their people. Two fire hydrants sit in the middle of the park and garner adulation from male dogs. Pooch Park is within College Park, on College Avenue, just south of First Street and the Metrolink station. 909/399-5490.

PLACES TO EAT

Winston, a zippy little Jack Russell terrier who has a penchant for human food, helped us sniff out the dog-friendly restaurants below. Good boy, Winston!

The Danson-Espiau's: This is Claremont's original sidewalk café, with oodles of outdoor tables for you and your happy dog. The Mexican and American food here is very tasty. If you're in the mood for a hearty salad, try the Mexican salad. Too virtuous? Chase it with a side of housemade chips. 109 Yale Avenue; 909/621-1818.

42nd Street Bagel: Dogs are frequent patrons of this terrific bagelry. Dine together at the two patio tables. Be sure to "accidentally" drop a bit of bagel for your patient pal below. 225 Yale Avenue; 909/624-7655.

Walter's Restaurant: Walter's has been a Claremont landmark restaurant since 1957, which is pretty much ancient history in these parts. You and your dog will lick your lips at the combination of California- and French-style cuisine using foods from around the world. "We have no boundaries," is how one manager describes the wonderful fusion foods. You'll find lots of terrific kabob dishes and menu items influenced by cultures from Afghanistan to India to Italy to Spain to Zaire. (Yes, that's A to Z.) Dogs are allowed at the sidewalk patio area but need to sit on the other side of the fence. (They can be pretty much at the feet of their humans; it's just that there's a little fence-y thing between you.) 308 Yale Avenue; 909/624-4914.

PLACES TO STAY

Ramada Inn and Tennis Club: This motel is so dog friendly that it even hosts dog shows. At times, all 121 rooms are taken up by dogs of the well-bred (literally) variety. The grounds have plenty of room for roaming with a leashed dog: The grassy courtyard alone is 31,000 square feet. Every room comes with a fridge and a continental breakfast. Work it off in the pool or at the motel's eight tennis courts. Rates are $69–99. 840 South Indian Hill Boulevard 91711; 909/621-4831.

Pomona

PARKS, BEACHES, AND RECREATION AREAS

30 Ganesha Park

🐾🐾🐾 (See Los Angeles County map on pages 48–49)

If you don't feel like paying $6 to get into the nearby Frank G. Bonelli Regional Park (see the San Dimas section), try this fee-free park. It's a popular place, but most visitors congregate around the swimming pool, tennis courts, and playground. Leashed dogs can zip around the rest of the park without much fear of crashing into hordes of people. The grassy, rolling hills and flat meadows are perfect for a good romp.

The park is at White Avenue, just north of I-10 and south of the Los Angeles County Fairplex. 909/620-2321.

PLACES TO STAY

Motel 6: There's a decent grassy area on the grounds. Rates are $48–60 for one adult, $6 for the second adult. 2470 South Garey Avenue 91766; 909/591-1871.

Sheraton Suites Fairplex: "The bigger the dog, the better," a staffer here told us. That's the attitude we like to see. If you and your dog are going to be spending some time at the adjacent Fairplex Exhibition Center, this might be the place to stay. It's pretty exotic for this area. Rates are $100–299. 600 West McKinley Avenue 91768; 909/622-2220.

Shilo Inn Hotel: Rates are $102–117. Dogs are $10 extra. 3200 Temple Avenue 91768; 909/598-0073 or 800/222-2244.

Westlake Village

PARKS, BEACHES, AND RECREATION AREAS

31 Triunfo Creek Park

🐾🐾🐾🐾 (See Los Angeles County map on pages 48–49)

Like wildflowers? Come here in the spring, when portions of this 600-acre park are blanketed with their beauty. Jake was really happy to learn that leashed dogs are allowed here, because the park is home to the *Pentachaeta lyonii*, an endangered yellow, daisy-ish flower you can find only in Southern California. Fortunately, I was able to successfully prevent him from making the flowers any more yellow than they are. (I don't know what happens when dogs do leg lifts on flowers that are listed as federally endangered, and I didn't want to find out.)

Some 90 species of wildflowers call the park home. Dogs who don't have a penchant for stopping and smelling the flowers can still enjoy a good romp on the trails, which take you through lush grasslands (in the spring) and oak woodlands. Jake liked the trees the best, partly because he's a boy dog, and partly because he's a shade-seeking missile of a dog, even in the more temperate months.

Exit U.S. 101 at Lindero Canyon Road and drive south to Triunfo Canyon Road. The road pretty much dead-ends at the main trailhead. 310/589-3200. You can get an update on the wildflower situation here and at 40 other sites in Southern California by phoning the Wildflower Hotline at 818/768-3533.

Agoura Hills

PARKS, BEACHES, AND RECREATION AREAS

32 The Paramount Ranch

🐾🐾🐾🐾 (See Los Angeles County map on pages 48–49)

Want to take your dog around the U.S. without leaving California? A visit to this 436-acre ranch could fool your dog into thinking he's in Tombstone, Dodge City, New Mexico, the Ozarks, Colorado's Royal Gorge, or colonial Salem. The Paramount Ranch has been a convincing backdrop for hundreds of films since the 1920s. Among the stars who made movies here are John Wayne, Gary Cooper, Cary Grant, Basil Rathbone, Roy Rogers, Lucille Ball, Kirk Douglas, Jane Russell, and Cornel Wilde. Your dog may not be able to sniff out their scents any more, but if he has a keen nose, he can probably still track down Jane Seymour, whose popular series *Dr. Quinn, Medicine Woman* was filmed here for several years in the 1990s. (The ranch is still a working set, and it works pretty hard, judging by a look at a recent filming schedule.)

But chances are that your dog be thrilled just to be allowed to join you at this fun park. The ranch is much smaller than it was in its heyday, but there's still plenty to see here, including an old Western town set complete with a saloon, a sheriff's office, and various stores. Several short trails, including the aptly named Backdrop Trail, take you past landscapes that will probably look very familiar thanks to their frequent use in films and TV shows.

Exit U.S. 101 at Kanan Road and follow it south for about three-quarters of a mile. Turn left on Cornell Road and drive about 2.5 miles to Paramount Ranch Road. Turn right and follow the road to the ranch. 818/597-9192.

33 Peter Strauss Ranch

🐾🐾🐾 (See Los Angeles County map on pages 48–49)

This beautiful 65-acre property was once the home of actor and producer Peter Strauss, most noted for his role in the TV miniseries *Rich Man, Poor Man.* He needed a place for his myriad collection of cacti and other succulent plants (he'd had hundreds of them on his apartment roof), and what better locale than this oak woodland? Although he moved on (and protected the property from development by selling it to the Santa Monica Mountains Conservancy), some of his plants can still be seen in the cactus garden here.

A few remnants of Strauss's predecessor, a resort and amusement park known as Lake Enchanto, also remain. In the 1930s and 1940s, the property had many amusement rides and the largest swimming pool in the West, with a capacity of up to 3,000 people. You can still see the circular pool from the lush lawn here. (The pool is empty, but try to imagine it in its heyday.) You and your leashed dog can also sniff out the lovely imported Italian terrazzo tile dance floor near the lawn.

The ranch is a fine place to bring a dog, especially if you have a child in tow. Although the rides are gone, there's a sweet playground (for human kids, not dog kids) overlooking the remains of Lake Enchanto's dam. The Peter Strauss Trail is less than a mile long, and it's an easy, pretty hike. It's shaded by coast live oaks, and ferns are everywhere. (There's a little poison oak here, which we mention only because it's not something you'd expect at such a well-groomed place.) A shallow creek runs through the property and along the trail at times, making the setting even more tranquil.

Exit U.S. 101 at Kanan Road and drive south for 2.8 miles. Turn left on Troutdale Road, and at the end of the road the park will be in front of you. To reach the entrance, go left on Mulholland Highway, cross the creek, and bear right, into the ranch's parking lot. 805/370-2301.

🐾 Cheeseboro and Palo Comado Canyons

🐾🐾🐾 (See Los Angeles County map on pages 48–49)

Some of the trails in these super-popular parks actually originated with the Chumash Indians, who lived here for several thousand years. Now it's hiker and mountain biker heaven, with leashed dogs getting a kick out of the place but always being on the lookout for the next passing bike.

Boy dogs thrill at the variety of trees, which include valley oaks, sycamores, coast live oaks, black walnut trees, and willows. The rolling grassy hills look so lush in the early spring, when they're actually green instead of the usual hue of dirty yellow Lab. (Jake blends right into the grass most times of year.)

Here's a bit of trivia that might be of interest to your dog if he's of the bird-watching bent. A ranger tells us that Cheeseboro Canyon has the largest concentrations of birds of prey nesting areas in the U.S. outside of Alaska. Jake was agog at the fascinating array of birds, although I think they all registered as "duck, duck, duck."

One of our favorite trails is the Cheeseboro Canyon Trail/Sulphur Springs Trail, an easy 4.6-mile hike with lots of shade from a valley oak savannah and a riparian coast live oak habitat. About 1.5 miles in, you'll come to a pretty picnic area next to a little stream. Have a bite and continue on—you may not want to eat when you get closer to stinky Sulphur Springs, although dogs go crazy for the scent. Jake couldn't get his nose off the ground as we approached. His schnoz flared and sniffed and snuffed as never before, and he looked positively devastated that he didn't find the dead animal that must have been causing that odor.

Take Highway 101 to the Chesebro Road exit and turn north, following Palo Comado Canyon Road (and the signs). Turn right onto Chesebro Road and continue to the end, where you'll find parking and picnic areas. 818/597-9192.

Calabasas

PARKS, BEACHES, AND RECREATION AREAS

35 Ahmanson Ranch/Upper Las Virgenes Canyon Open Space Preserve

😺😺😺😺 (See Los Angeles County map on pages 48–49)

Parts of *Gone with the Wind* were filmed on this stunning 2,983-acre wildland. But the land itself could have been gone with the wind starting as early as 2003 if Washington Mutual, Inc., had been able to proceed unimpeded: The corporation had planned a 3,050-home development here. Fortunately, the development was so contentious that the state ended up being able to buy the Ahmanson Ranch land from Washington Mutual and will keep it as an undeveloped wildlife refuge and park.

This is great news for the environment and excellent news for people and pooches who like to hike on oak-studded rolling hills, wide-open mesas, and cool canyon bottoms shaded by sycamores. A few trails are already up and running, with many more planned for the future. (A big bonus, if you aren't fond of itching: There's no poison oak here.) Some endangered species that helped save the land from development reside here, so leashes are the law.

Although the property is located entirely in Ventura County, we list it here because Los Angeles County provides the only access at this point. Access from the Simi Valley area is likely at some time, but for now, this is the way to get here: Exit U.S. 101 at Las Virgenes Road and follow it north all the way to the end. At press time, the Santa Monica Mountains Conservancy was trying to get the OK for a large parking lot at the end of Victory Boulevard. 310/589-3200.

36 Calabasas Bark Park

😺😺😺😺🐕 (See Los Angeles County map on pages 48–49)

This is the first dog park we've heard of that has a separate gated area not for small dogs, but for children! It's actually a good idea, because some children feel overwhelmed by big dogs running around. Apparently the area isn't used much. Most kids prefer to be with parents and canine siblings. But it's nice to know it's there. I know a few parents whose children would love to have their space separate from swirling dogs.

The park is two fenced acres of grass, with some shade trees, benches, poop bags, lights, and a dog drinking fountain. The park is at 4232 Las Virgenes Road, south of the Las Virgenes Municipal Water District. 818/878-4225 or 818/880-6461.

Topanga

PARKS, BEACHES, AND RECREATION AREAS

37 Red Rock Canyon Park

🐾🐾🐾 (See Los Angeles County map on pages 48–49)

There's a bone of contention about the old notion that dogs only see in black and white. Let's hope they don't, because if they see in color, they'll be wowed by the giant sandstone rock outcroppings here. They're red, as you may have guessed by the park's name. And because the rocks provide homes to various teeny forms of life, they can also be tan, white, and even purplish.

Contrasting the sandstone gorge is a fairly lush, cool riparian area with trees whose trunks boy dog noses love to explore. A fire road and trail takes you and your leashed dog through these different habitats. At some points, you come to incredible views of the surrounding mountains. Mountain bikes like it here, so keep your eyes peeled.

From Highway 1/Pacific Coast Highway, go north on Topanga Canyon Boulevard. At Old Topanga Canyon Road, turn left. Drive 1.7 miles to Red Rock Road. You can park at this intersection and walk nearly a mile to the park entrance, or you can drive all the way to the park entrance, but keep in mind that two-tenths of a mile of this road is an unimproved dirt road. You can also get to the park from U.S. 101, but you'll still end up dealing with the dirt road. 23601 West Red Rock Road; 310/589-3200.

Encino

PARKS, BEACHES, AND RECREATION AREAS

38 Westridge-Canyonback Wilderness Park

🐾🐾🐾🐾🐕 (See Los Angeles County map on pages 48–49)

Yes, that little running dog you see above really does belong there. It's not a typo—it's a miracle.

This is the only huge park (besides national forests and BLM lands) in the greater L.A. area where dogs under voice control are allowed off leash. Around these parts, dogs are usually relegated to fenced-in dog parks if they want to run around in the buff (sans leash). But thanks to the dog-friendly Santa Monica Mountains Conservancy, well-behaved dogs can be their doggy selves here and not be stopped by a fence in the face or a ranger with a citation book.

This 1,500-acre open space (and we're talking open—there's not much shade here, so bring lots of water for you and your dog) offers great views of the Pacific Ocean on clear days. The fire road along the north-south ridgeline is a popular hiking area, but it's also big with mountain bikers, so be careful with your off-leash pal.

At one point, the property had been slated for a 500-home development. It was also approved as a landfill (dump). Now that it's in the hands of the conservancy, it won't have to face those terrible fates again.

From I-405, take Mulholland Drive west 2.7 miles to the 17000 block. You can park in a 20-car roadside parking area and walk 10 minutes to the park entrance and the trail. 310/589-3200.

39 Sepulveda Basin Off-Leash Dog Park

🐾🐾🐾🐾 🐕 (See Los Angeles County map on pages 48–49)

It's big, it's fairly grassy, and it has four boy dog toilets (OK, fire hydrants). What more could a dog want? Water? It's here at four mud-free drinking stations. Shade? There are enough small shade trees for comfort during the summer months. If those won't do, there are plenty of picnic tables. Dog friends? Yup. A section for small dogs? Yap! Sirloin strip? OK, the park doesn't have everything.

This is a heavenly place to visit if you're a dog who longs to be off leash, or if you're a dog person who longs to see your dog off leash. "It's been successful beyond our wildest dreams," says Ken Novak, a manager with the city of Los Angeles Recreation and Parks Department. Even the fencing is terrific here: It's green, so it matches the park. Ivy has been planted at its base, and it's starting to creep up toward its goal of becoming a wall of ivy. Outside the fence, there's a little more acreage for leashed dogs who want to lounge around on the grass and/or have a picnic with their people pals.

The park is at the corner of White Oak Avenue and Victory Boulevard; 818/756-8616 or 818/756-8191. For info on dog events at the park, phone 818/343-0013.

40 Balboa Park and Lake Balboa

🐾🐾🐾 (See Los Angeles County map on pages 48–49)

Balboa Park is completely recreation-oriented, which is good news for leashed dogs, for once. Pooches are allowed on the many playing fields that make up this large city park. And they're welcome on the big empty fields where no sports are played. If your dog likes to hike on forested trails, this place won't be his idea of heaven, since there are none. But if he enjoys a good roll in the grass, take him here at once. If no one is playing soccer or softball, he's in for a real treat.

Lake Balboa, across Balboa Boulevard from the park, is another story. It's officially considered part of the park, although people here seem to think of it as its own entity. Leashed dogs and the people they're attached to find it a more pleasant place, with a wide 1.3-mile walking path around the lake's edge. "It's more fun than a regular leash park," writes reader Sheryl Smith, mother of Gracie Dog. "There's an occasional fish flopping around to bark at, that some fisherman has just landed, and there are ducks and white and blue herons.... There must be lots of good smells there, because Gracie's nose is always to the ground there." If you ever run into Sheryl and Gracie, ask them about their collection of dog license tags from around the world. Their incredible collection numbers about 1,000, and some of the designs should be museum pieces.

Exit U.S. 101 at Balboa Boulevard, drive a couple of blocks north, and you'll be at Balboa Park's entrance. 818/756-9642.

Sherman Oaks

PARKS, BEACHES, AND RECREATION AREAS

41 Dixie Canyon Park

🐾🐾 (See Los Angeles County map on pages 48–49)

If you like your urban walks on the wild side, take a hike at Dixie Canyon. This 20-acre park, donated to the Santa Monica Mountains Conservancy by Warren Beatty, is a pretty decent place to take a leashed dog. There's lots of shade from the California black walnut trees and coast live oaks, and the park's trail takes you by a year-round stream in the middle of the canyon. Watch out for poison oak: It's very thick on the canyon's east side. You should be OK if you stay on the trail.

From the intersection of Ventura Boulevard and Dixie Canyon Avenue, go south on Dixie Canyon Avenue for eight-tenths of a mile and then turn left on Dixie Canyon Place. You'll quickly come to the end of the road (actually, a cul-de-sac). Park and take the stairs to the park's entrance. 310/589-3200.

42 Van Nuys–Sherman Oaks Park and Recreation Center

🐾 (See Los Angeles County map on pages 48–49)

The backdrop is ugly, scattered as it is with little apartment buildings. But the park itself is one huge, green, grassy field, with a great fitness course. You'll have no excuse not to exercise here, but dogs have to be leashed.

Take the Van Nuys Boulevard exit from U.S. 101 and drive north to Hartsook Street. The park will be on your right. 818/783-5121.

PLACES TO STAY

Best Western Carriage Inn: Rates are $99–189. 5525 Sepulveda Boulevard 91411; 818/717-2300.

Van Nuys

PARKS, BEACHES, AND RECREATION AREAS

43 Woodley Park

🐾🐾🐾 (See Los Angeles County map on pages 48–49)

If you like your parks big and grassy, check out this one. Dogs really enjoy it here. There's ample shade, plenty of picnic areas, and a fitness course to keep you and the pooch in good condition. Unfortunately, there's also an unattractive water reclamation plant on the north side of the park, but they have to put them somewhere.

The park is between I-405 and U.S. 101. Take the Burbank Boulevard exit from I-405 and drive west into the park. Turn right on Woodley Avenue and drive past signs for the Japanese garden. The meadow area will be on your right. 818/756-8891.

Studio City

PARKS, BEACHES, AND RECREATION AREAS

44 Laurel Canyon Park

🐾🐾🐾🐾🐾🐕 (See Los Angeles County map on pages 48–49)

Yee haw! Dogs, throw off your leashes and come here to be all the dog you can be! This is the biggest of the off-leash dog runs in Los Angeles County, and many consider it the best. It's nearly 20 acres, and there are sufficient trees and picnic tables to make everyone comfortable.

If you and your dog like to socialize, you couldn't ask for a better place. Canine rush hour (around 5 P.M., depending on the time of year) is a real scene. On a typical dog day afternoon, you'll find more than 100 dogs running like mad, sniffing each other in unmentionable places and pushing their noses to the ground in search of unusual odors. Their owners, meanwhile, chitchat about this and that (often, "this" being their dog and "that" being your dog).

People flock here from all over Los Angeles and the San Fernando Valley. There's plenty of water, plenty of poop bags, plenty of fence, and, most importantly, plenty of good dog fun. And for people who like to watch the stars, we hear that celebrities sometimes frequent the place on weekends.

(Note: We've heard about some aggressive dogs who have attacked other dogs here, and about their people who have given false contact information to avoid taking responsibility for their dogs' behavior. These are rare problems, but since I heard from more than one person about this, I'd be negligent not to mention it. Fortunately, most dogs here never even hear a cross word from another dog, much less feel their teeth.)

Get here early so you can nab a parking space. The park is on Mulholland Drive, about a quarter mile west of Laurel Canyon Boulevard. From Laurel Canyon Boulevard, go west on Mulholland and take the first left. The road winds down a hill and into the parking lot. 818/756-8189.

45 Wilacre Park

🐾🐾🐾 (See Los Angeles County map on pages 48–49)

This scrubby, shrubby 128-acre park is the former estate of silent-movie star Will Acres. It's in the middle of one of Studio City's more posh neighborhoods, but once you're hiking, you'll feel like you're in the middle of nowhere. Dogs are welcome here, but so are horses and bikes, so be sure to leash. For a really fun hike, take the 2.7-mile loop trail to the very dog-friendly Coldwater Canyon Park (see Beverly Hills), headquarters of a forest-friendly organization, TreePeople. If you hike up toward TreePeople's main building, you'll find a doggy drinking fountain along the way.

If it's toasty out, sniff out a narrow road at Wilacre that takes you to a shady canyon thick with big oak and eucalyptus trees. It's a popular spot for filming, so if you see a crew, you'll have to head back. The park is at the intersection of Laurel Canyon Boulevard and Fryman Canyon Road. The address is 3431 Fryman Canyon Road; 310/589-3200.

PLACES TO EAT

Jumpin' Java: Don't let the name fool you. There's more than just coffee for your canine here. You can get breakfast, lunch, and dinner, too. The Mediterranean-style cuisine makes for tasty, light eating. Dine with your dog at the covered patio with six tables. 11919 Ventura Boulevard; 818/980-4249.

Studio Yogurt: If the cool, creamy, refreshing frozen yogurt they serve here is beyond your caloric capacity, order one of the fat-free or sugar-free treats. They taste every bit as good. Your dog won't complain either. Dip your spoon with your dog at the covered patio. 12050 Ventura Boulevard; 818/508-7811.

North Hollywood

PARKS, BEACHES, AND RECREATION AREAS

46 Whitnall Off-Leash Dog Park

🐾🐾🐾🐕 (See Los Angeles County map on pages 48–49)

Before this park became a dog park, it had really gone to the dogs: It was a haven for drug dealing, gang activity, and illegal dumping. Then along came the dog park in 2002, and now it's clean as a whistle (a stray dog poop or two notwithstanding). Three cheers for the dogs and their people! (And for "Three-Dog Dave" Hepperly and Tamar Love Grande for giving us the heads-up about this place.)

The park is a couple of grassy acres. It's got all the usual dog park amenities, including drinking fountains, shade umbrellas, benches, poop bags, double gates, and trees. Small dogs have a 100-by-200-foot section to call their own. Not bad for bitsy beagles. At the corner of Cahuenga Boulevard and Whitnall Highway; 818/756-8060.

Universal City

If you go to the exciting Universal Studios tour/theme park here, your pooch will be pleased to know that she can accompany you at least part of the way.

Universal Studios has a kennel, which dogs of visitors get to use for free. Bring a blanket and her favorite toy so she'll rest in comfort while you get jostled around a bit by King Kong or get the wits scared out of you at the Revenge of the Mummy ride. (Your dog should actually be glad she's not allowed on the rides.) The climate-controlled kennel is unattended but locked. Water is supplied. You can visit your dog any time by getting a key-bearing information booth employee to accompany you. A nearby bushy and grassy area serves as the squat spot.

To use the kennel, bring your leashed dog to the information booth just before the main entrance. 818/622-3801 or 800/UNIVERSAL (800/864-8377); www.universalstudios.com.

PARKS, BEACHES, AND RECREATION AREAS

47 South Weddington Park

🐾🐾 (See Los Angeles County map on pages 48–49)

Golf, anyone? This park is so green and trim that you can't help but think of Arnold Palmer. Joe Dog liked it because of its proximity to Universal Studios—it's right across the street. He enjoyed the kennels there (see above for details), because he knew a cat could end up spending the day just down the row from him.

The park is bordered by a couple of small side roads, so it's fairly safe from traffic. But since dogs are supposed to be leashed, that's not something you have to worry about.

Heading south on Lankershim Boulevard, go right on Bluffside Drive (directly across from the north gate of Universal Studios). 818/756-8188 or 323/923-7390.

PLACES TO STAY

Sheraton Universal Hotel: How often do you get to sleep on the back lot of a major motion picture studio with your dog? Stay here, and you will actually be on a back lot of Universal Studios together. (It's as close as your dog will come to Universal, except for being in the kennel there.) And what a fun, imaginatively designed, attractive hotel this is. It's big, with cushy, well-appointed rooms. Some of the rooms and suites are theme rooms, embellished with Universal characters and movie decor. Our favorite is the Shrek Suite, with its pine log furniture and large pictures of Shrek and his cohorts. You'll feel as if you're in his living room. Dogs feel right at home here.

Dogs love staying at any room here: As part of their stay, they get to use a comfy dog bed (the Sheraton Sweet Sleeper Dog Bed, the smaller cousin of the Sheraton Sweet Sleeper Bed for humans) and get bowls for their food and water. Dogs need to weigh less than 80 pounds (Jake could get in by sucking in his belly) and you can have only one per room. Rates are $149–199. Suites start at $269. 333 Universal Hollywood Drive 91608; 818/980-1212; www .starwood.com/sheraton.

Hollywood

Tinseltown just isn't what it used to be. The wealth of Art Deco architecture and grandiose theaters has faded. The half-mile Hollywood Walk of Fame is home to the homeless (although there are plans in the works to improve the area). But it's still worth visiting, for the myth and lure of Hollywood will never completely fade. (If you visit toward dusk, you may be glad you brought your dog.) Meanwhile, if you can foot the bill, a stay in the fabulous Chateau Marmont (see Places to Stay) might restore a little of the old glow of Hollywood for you and your dog.

PARKS, BEACHES, AND RECREATION AREAS

48 Trebek Open Space

🐾🐾🐾 (See Los Angeles County map on pages 48–49)
The category: Generous Gentlemen.

The answer: A 62-acre parcel of wilderness with fire roads for leashed dogs, mountain bikers, equestrians, and hikers was donated by this game show host who's always looking for life's questions, not answers. (Be sure to phrase your response in the form of a question.)

If you answered "Who is Alex Trebek?" you're right! (If you said only "Alex Trebek," your dog wins.) The popular, longtime *Jeopardy!* host donated this rugged, hilly area to the Santa Monica Mountains Conservancy, and even dogs who don't know a thing about his show are game for a vigorous romp here. It's adjacent to the leash-free Runyon Canyon Park (see below), should your dog hanker to throw his leash to the wind and trot around naked. (Runyon is easier to find and easier to park at, so if you like convenience—and a leash-free romp—you're better off there.)

Exit U.S. 101 at Hollywood Boulevard and drive west for about two miles. Go right (north) onto Nichols Canyon Road. Roadside parking will be on your right in a little less than a mile. It's signed, but poorly signed, so keep your eyes peeled. 310/589-3200.

49 Runyon Canyon Park

🐾🐾🐾🐾🐾 (See Los Angeles County map on pages 48–49)
Dogs are actually allowed to be their leash-free selves at this 125-acre undeveloped park. It's full of overgrown weeds and brush, but dogs don't care. In fact, they like it this way. Besides, there are plenty of trees to keep their interest while they walk up and down the hilly paths here.

And while it happened a long time ago, Jake thought you might want to know a little Hollywood lore a park ranger told us: This is the very same park where Errol Flynn was caught with a minor, causing a major public scandal. (Was this at the same time he was making the film *Assault of the Rebel Girls*?)

The park is on Fuller Avenue, north of Franklin Place. 323/666-5046.

PLACES TO STAY

Best Western Hollywood Hills Hotel: Rates are $100–190. Dogs are $25 for the length of their stay. 6141 Franklin Avenue 90028; 323/464-5181 or 800/287-1700.

Chateau Marmont Hotel: This is that grand, white, castle-like building that makes you do a double take as you're driving on Sunset. Yes, dogs really are allowed to stay in this legendary Hollywood hideaway. Joe Dog was on his best behavior when we checked it out, walking rather regally and not even stopping to scratch his ears.

The chateau, which opened in 1929, is modeled after an elegant Loire Valley castle. You'll hear a lot of French around here. Actually, the staffers speak several languages, including "discreet." That last language has helped make the Marmont very popular with Hollywood's icons over the decades.

Huge suites and romantic bungalows offer privacy, and many are set among lush, peaceful gardens. There's something for nearly every robust budget, from a 400-square-foot room to a two-bedroom penthouse suite with two bathrooms, a dressing area, a large living room with hardwood floor and working fireplace, a full kitchen, a formal dining room, and a 1,250-square-foot private terrace with great views of Hollywood. I think that's the room Joe Dog once wanted, but we ended up elsewhere. (The Motel 6 in Long Beach, to be exact. Hey, you can't tell one place from the other when the lights are out. Well, not when there's no moon and you're sleeping. Deeply.)

If you and a human friend want to go out for a night on the town sans pooch, the concierge can help hook you up with a pet sitter. Room and suite rates are $295–2,000. Dogs pay $100 extra per visit. 8221 Sunset Boulevard 90046; 323/656-1010 or 800/242-8328; www.chateaumarmont.com.

DIVERSION

Compare Paw Prints: On a visit to the forecourt of **Mann's Chinese Theatre** in Hollywood, Joe Dog found out his paws were as big as the heels of Gene Autry's boots. Since he was an old Western movie buff (we'd caught him watching Westerns on TV), it was doubtless a thrill for him to see that he could, if necessary, walk a mile in Autry's boots. You and your dog can spend part of a fun-filled Hollywood afternoon measuring your feet and paws against the footprints of the stars. Be sure to bring a camera. Everyone else will have one, and your dog is likely to have his mug snapped more than once. The theater itself is at 6925 Hollywood Boulevard, Hollywood; 323/461-3331 or 323/464-6266.

When you're done comparing shoe sizes with the stars, take your feet for a stroll down the **Hollywood Walk of Fame.** It's on Hollywood Boulevard, between Gower Street and La Brea Avenue, and along Vine Street, from Sunset Boulevard to Yucca Street. More than 2,500 celebs are immortalized with stars planted into the sidewalk featuring their names. Your dog might be especially interested in seeing the stars for Rin Tin Tin and Lassie. The walk is free, but be prepared for a barrage of homeless people and scam artists with their paws out. For a list of the stars and their locations, go to www .hollywoodchamber.net.

West Hollywood

Dogs love hanging around West Hollywood. It's an eclectic place with what seems like a higher-than-normal percentage of dog lovers. Jake simply loves all the attention lavished on him and others of his ilk here.

PARKS, BEACHES, AND RECREATION AREAS

50 William S. Hart Park

🐾🐾🐾 ➤ (See Los Angeles County map on pages 48–49)

A Parisian pooch named Boo had his Parisian person Birgit write to tell me about this dear little park. "It isn't much bigger than an oversized handkerchief, but the dogs love it anyway," they wrote. And indeed they do. Lots of off-leash pooches trot around here with big smiles on their snoots. It's a very pretty little fenced park with trees and a doggy water fountain. Maintenance crews try to keep the park green, but with up to 100 thundering paws at a time, it's an onerous task.

It's easy to confuse this park with the big William S. Hart Regional Park in Newhall. (See Newhall.) They're both named for the same Old West movie

DIVERSION

Doggy Day Care, L.A. Style: I don't normally write about dog boarding in my books. After all, the *Dog Lover's Companion* series is about where to go with your dog, not where to leave your dog behind.

But I just can't help mentioning the chichi extras available at doggy day care centers around L.A. These centers go many steps beyond the basic doggy day care model of a cage-free setting with lots of dogs running around. These are day cares for the seriously pampered pooch. Here's what's offered at some of the higher-end establishments:

- Exclusive boutiques offering the latest in canine couture
- Party rooms for birthdays, "barkmitvahs," and other special occasions
- Aromatherapy grooming
- Swimming time
- Customized massage
- Lounge beds
- TVs and VCRs

This sounds better than my last vacation, and by the looks of the price lists I've seen, it's far more expensive.

Some of the more popular day care centers around L.A. include **Chateau Marmutt** (not to be confused with the lovely dog-friendly hotel, the Chateau Marmont), 8128 West 3rd Street, Hollywood, 323/653-2062, www.chateaumarmutt.com; **Hollywood Hounds** (ironically, this one's across the street from the Chateau Marmont Hotel), 8218 Sunset Boulevard, Hollywood, 323/653-2062, www.hollywoodhounds.com; and the **Kennel Club,** 5325 West 102nd Street (near LAX; this one offers full boarding, too), 310/338-9166, www.kennelclublax.com. Others exist and thrive, but this is all we have room for here. Your local yellow pages can help you find more.

star, but that's where the similarities end. While the Hart Park in Newhall is his 200-plus-acre former ranch, this Hart Park is essentially the yard of his former West Hollywood home. It's fitting that dogs are allowed to romp on both his country and his city property. He was a cowboy through and through, and he'd have liked this.

Dogs can visit on leash any time, but they can only run around naked 7–9 A.M. and 5–7 P.M. daily. (This is an ongoing test program, so please check hours before letting your dog loose.) The park is at 8341 De Longpre Avenue, just off North Sweetzer Avenue, one block south of West Sunset Boulevard. 323/848-6400.

PLACES TO EAT

Basix: Every meal here is a joy. For breakfast, try the "Croissant Very French Toast." It's served with real-deal maple syrup. The blackened chicken pasta is a hit with the lunch crowd. (And the dog crowd.) Your dog may join you at the covered patio area. 8333 Santa Monica Boulevard; 213/848-2460.

Comedy Store: Have a drink and an appetizer on a Friday or Saturday night with your best bud at the comedy palace of Los Angeles. As you sip your screwdriver and eat your little pizzas at the outdoor patio bar, you and your pooch can watch for your favorite comic. Sometimes comics do a little warm-up act on the patio. Your dog will be howling. 8433 West Sunset Boulevard; 323/656-6225.

Irv's Burgers: You and your dog can dine on great, meaty burgers and some healthier cuisine at this beloved eatery across from city hall. You sit on a stool at the counter while your dog looks on from below. 8289 Santa Monica Boulevard; 323/650-2456.

Joey's Cafe: Dine with your doggy at one of six shaded sidewalk tables here. The omelets are droolworthy. Jake and I suggest the oven-roasted sun-dried tomato omelet with basil, spinach, and goat cheese. 8301 Santa Monica Boulevard; 323/822-0671.

Mel's Drive-In: This isn't a real drive-in, but you and your dog can park yourselves at the many umbrella-topped tables out front. Enjoy classically good burgers, fries, and shakes here. With all this decadent food floating around, the doggy drool can flow. Sneak yours a little bite of something and watch your dog smile. 8585 Sunset Boulevard; 310/854-7200.

Rage: It's all the rage to eat the Continental cuisine with your dog at the shaded tables out front. 8911 Santa Monica Boulevard; 310/652-7055.

Tail O' the Pup: This is one of the last examples of architectural kitsch in L.A. The counter where you order food is encased in a giant hot dog, complete with mustard and bun. Jake the Dog looked utterly bewildered when he first laid his hungry eyes on it. I could just see his thought process: "It smells like a hot dog, but there's something weird about it."

More than one million hot dogs have been served here since it opened in 1945. (It may be tacky, but it's beloved.) Burgers and the like are also popular here. Dine with your dog (furry, not hot, although that works too) at the large outdoor seating area. Thirsty dogs get water. 329 North San Vicente Boulevard; 310/652-4517.

Tango Grill: Chicken and steak are the specialties here, and they're pretty tasty, too. Dine outside with the dog of your choice. Your dog will get water if she asks for it. 8807 Santa Monica Boulevard; 310/659-3663.

PLACES TO STAY

The Grafton Balboa: The rooms at this gracious, first-rate hotel have a "Feng Shui reverential decor," according to the friendly manager. I think this means you and your dog will find it a peaceful place, but that could have more to do with the comfy beds and lovely furnishings than the fact that mirrors aren't facing the door. You'll adore the large, beautiful courtyard pool and Mediterranean gardens, but dogs need to keep their paws dry at the pool and down at the gardens (if ya know what I mean).

Rates are $119–300. Dogs pay a $100 fee for the length of their visit. The hotel is on the Sunset Strip, at 8462 West Hollywood Boulevard 90069; 323/654-4600; www.graftononsunset.com.

Le Montrose Suite Hotel/Hotel Gran Luxe: This attractive French-influenced hotel is homey, cozy, and nestled in a lovely neighborhood. You'll get fresh fruit and mineral water upon check-in, and homemade cookies when you leave. (Dogs will want to leave again and again.) Pooches get a bowl of water upon request. All rooms have fireplaces and some have kitchenettes. Rates are $145–950. Dogs pay a $100 fee for their stay. 900 Hammond Street 90069; 310/855-1115 or 800/776-0666; www.lemontrose.com.

Le Parc Suite Hotel: Stay at this all-suite hotel and you'll get twice-daily maid service, a robe, and even slippers, which some dogs find quite fetching. All rooms at this quiet, out-of-the-way hotel have kitchenettes and separate living/dining areas. Some even come with a fireplace. While the hotel boasts that it has beautiful balconies, it doesn't matter to dogs, who need to stay in the first floor (smoking) rooms during their visit. Rates are $155–300. There's a $75 fee for the length of your dog's stay. 733 North West Knoll Drive 90069; 310/855-8888 or 800/578-4837; www.leparcsuites.com.

Beverly Hills

This golden city offers dogs first-class treatment. "I never felt so at home as when I visited Beverly Hills," reports Shelby, a large chocolate Lab mix, via his translator Heidi. "I got to go shopping and eating and everyone was giving me pats on the head." Shelby writes that his best time was at Loews Beverly Hills Hotel. (See Places to Stay.) It's a four-paw experience you shouldn't miss, and the price is startlingly affordable. (Relatively speaking.)

PARKS, BEACHES, AND RECREATION AREAS

Dogs aren't allowed in the stunningly beautiful Greystone Park. But then again, neither are cameras or picnics, so canines shouldn't feel too offended.

As for the rest of the parks, a woman at the parks department here had to double-check the dog rules with a supervisor when we called to update the book. When she came back to the phone, she had this answer: "I'm told we prefer the wind-up type, but we'll take the live ones." We give four paws for self-effacing humor in the land of 90210. If you want to sniff out a little wilderness in the land of opulence, Franklin Canyon Park and Coldwater Canyon Park offer big, wild chunks of dog heaven.

51 Beverly Gardens Park

🐾🐾 (See Los Angeles County map on pages 48–49)

Stretching from Wilshire Boulevard to Doheny Drive, this narrow, 20-block-long park is great for dogs on the go. It runs along the north side of Santa Monica Boulevard, so if you and your dog are trying to sprint from one end of town to the other, you couldn't ask for a greener way to go.

The strip of park has a path, so you're not relegated to the sidewalk. But since it does parallel the busy boulevard, it's not without its share of exhaust fumes and honking Mercedes. Dogs must be leashed. 310/285-2537.

52 Coldwater Canyon Park

🐾🐾🐾🐾 (See Los Angeles County map on pages 48–49)

Los Angeles Magazine touted this 45-acre park as "one of the 300 best reasons to stay in Los Angeles," and dogs couldn't agree more. Although it's not one of the bigger Santa Monica Mountains Conservancy lands, it's one of the better ones for dogs who like a little socializing on their jaunts: It's rare to come here and not see several other people out hiking with their happy leashed dogs.

Boy dogs are especially tickled when they visit, because the park is headquarters for TreePeople, a grassroots group helping to keep trees in L.A., educating non-tree-people about the importance of urban forests, and planting oodles of arbors around L.A. There are plenty of trees along some of the trails here, and there's a trail for every hiking ability. The park is part of a 1,000-acre cross-mountain park, so you're not relegated to Coldwater property. Good trail maps can help you and your dog figure out where you want to hike. Before you head for the hills, top off your dog's tank with a swig from the doggy water fountain, near the TreePeople headquarters. (And as always when hiking in this region, don't forget to pack along plenty of water for you and your dog.) If you want to treat your dog to an extra special treat, take him on a full-moon hike here. They're out of this world. (See the Diversion Give Your Dog the Moon.)

The park is at Mulholland Drive and Coldwater Canyon Avenue. 12601 Mulholland Drive. 818/753-4600.

53 Franklin Canyon Park

🐾🐾🐾🐾 (See Los Angeles County map on pages 48–49)

Dogs dig this 605-acre park. It has everything dogs love, from lakes to woodlands to hilly grasslands. Most of all, it has space—a hot commodity in these parts. Dogs need to be leashed, but they still love sniffing around the park and trotting down the various trails. Jake's favorite is the Hastain Trail, a

DIVERSION

Shop with a Canine Customer: If your dog enjoys shopping and is well behaved, many **Beverly Hills stores** will welcome your business (but not your dog's business, if you know what I mean—walk your dog first).

Dogs don't even have to be itsy-bitsy, or well-heeled, at many of these stores. "We've had cow-sized dogs shop here," says a sales clerk at the **Gap** store at 371 North Beverly Drive (310/274-0461). "As long as they're good dogs, they're welcome."

Sometimes this Gap even supplies canine customers with treats. Carol Martinez, media maven for the Los Angeles Convention & Visitors Bureau, says she once shopped here with her granddog, a seven-pound teacup terrier named Killer. "They had treats up on the counter, and he just stood there and ate them all up right out of the bowl," she says. "Of course, no one dared say anything when they found out his name."

Several small boutiques also allow the occasional pooch, but they asked not to be mentioned for fear of being besieged with giant dogs and dogs with bad bathroom habits.

One place you'll have to avoid with your dog is Neiman Marcus. A dog in another Neiman store bit a customer a few years back, and the Beverly Hills store has had to go along with a company policy banning all dogs. Instead, try **Saks Fifth Avenue** at 9600 Wilshire Boulevard (310/275-4211). (Should you feel like taking a little drive, the Saks in Pasadena allows well-behaved dogs of "just about any size"; 35 North DeLacey Avenue; 626/396-7100.) Saks management prefers small dogs—the kind you can comfortably tuck under your arm—but I've seen some well-coifed medium-sized dogs here.

fairly arduous 2.3-mile round-trip that leads to an overlook with great views of the area. On a clear day, you can't see forever, but you can allegedly see the Pacific. (We couldn't; the smog was rather thick when we checked it out.)

The park is home to dozens of species of birds in the Pacific flyway, so bring your field glasses if you and your dog like bird-watching. It's also home to a nature center, amphitheater, and auditorium, but dogs need to steer clear of all these.

The best way to get there from U.S. 101 is to take the Coldwater Canyon Boulevard exit and drive south to the intersection of Coldwater Canyon and Mulholland Drive. Make a 90-degree turn onto Franklin Canyon Drive. (Note: There's no signage for the street.) At press time, there was also no signage for the park, but when you see a sign that says "Road Closed 800 Feet" and "Sunrise to Sunset," you're at the park entrance. You can park in the north end of the park near the nature center or keep driving south to get to other areas to park and explore. 2600 Franklin Canyon Drive; 310/858-7272.

54 La Cienega Park

🔥 (See Los Angeles County map on pages 48–49)

If your pooch wants to fraternize with the cream of the Beverly Hills canine corps, there are fancier places to take her. But this is a passable neighborhood park with fenced-in ball fields and a playground. If the ball fields are in use, there's not much room for you and your leashed dog to roam, but you can always find a strip of grass.

The bulk of the park is on the east side of La Cienega Boulevard, between Gregory Way and Schumacher Drive. A smaller segment of the park is on the west side of La Cienega Boulevard. 310/285-2537.

55 Will Rogers Memorial Park

🐾 🐾 (See Los Angeles County map on pages 48–49)

Dogs and their elegantly clad people come to this lush park to lounge the afternoon away. Dogs have to be leashed here, and it's not a large park, but it is verdant and rich with the colorful sights and sounds of Beverly Hills. When Joe, Bill, and I visited, we witnessed a tiny bit of a dog being led out of a Rolls by a chauffeur who had the same air of noble servitude as if he were escorting the queen of England. He walked the little thing around once and said "Now, Emily." The dog did her little business on command. The chauffeur scooped and they sped off, no doubt to more pressing engagements.

The Will Rogers Memorial Park is a triangular chunk of fine real estate at the corner of Canon and Beverly Drives and Sunset Boulevard, right across from the Beverly Hills Hotel. 310/285-2537.

PLACES TO EAT

The eateries listed on Beverly Drive are all near a free two-hour parking lot.

California Pizza Kitchen: Your dog can dine outside with you here, but she has to be tied up on the other side of the wrought-iron fence. 207 South Beverly Drive; 310/275-1101.

Champagne French Bakery: If your dog doesn't mind being tied up on the other side of the railing (right next to you, though), this is a fine place to come for some tasty food and some sun. Thirsty dogs get water upon request. 200 South Beverly Drive; 310/271-4556.

Frida Mexican Cuisine: This is some of our favorite Mexican food. Try the Pollo Pipian (chicken simmered in a ground pumpkin seed sauce) or the Torta Vegetariana (grilled cactus with tomato, avocado, beans, and other yummies). Dine with your doggy at the neat little row of four white-tablecloth-festooned sidewalk tables. If your dog is thirsty, she can get a bowl of water. 236 South Beverly Drive; 310/278-7666.

DIVERSION

Give Your Dog the Moon: You and your dog will have a howl of a good time at the popular **full-moon walks** at Coldwater Canyon Park in Beverly Hills. **TreePeople** (see Coldwater Canyon description for more on this great group) welcomes your good dog to accompany you on fun, one-hour hikes. You can choose from two or three hiking levels and topics of discussion. (The guides here aren't silent: You're going to learn something about insects or trees or the moon on their walks. Even your dog may come back more knowledgeable.)

The walks are given on the night of the full moon April through October. They start at sundown or, more precisely, moon-up. They're free to members of TreePeople and $5 for plain old people. Dogs are free. For details and schedules, check out www.treepeople.org or phone 818/753-4600.

Il Tramezzino: The eggplant parmesan here is *delizioso*. Eat it at one of the umbrella-topped tables. 460 North Canon Drive; 310/273-0501.

Jacopo's Pizzeria: Besides pizza, you can get chicken, seafood, and pasta at the outdoor tables here. Got a thirsty dog? Just ask for a bowl of water. 490 North Beverly Drive; 310/858-6446.

Sansai Japanese Grill: Enjoy good, fast Japanese with your dog at this local chain's two sidewalk tables. 281 South Beverly Drive; 310/274-2070.

Subway: Yes, Virginia, there is a Subway in Beverly Hills. Dine with doggy at the outside tables. 279 South Beverly Drive; 310/278-7827.

PLACES TO STAY

Beverly Hilton: This elegant hotel has gone from allowing even the biggest moose of a dog to permitting pooches only if they're under 25 pounds. Even these wee dogs must sign a damage waiver. Rates are $199–399. Dogs are $25 extra. 9876 Wilshire Boulevard 90210; 310/274-7777; www.hilton.com.

L'Ermitage: If you can afford the first-class European elegance of this exclusive and very private hotel, you won't regret a night or two here. You and your medium-to-small dog (40 pounds or less) will be pampered beyond belief. A chauffeur comes with your stay, so you and the pooch, who will be treated like anything but a pooch, can hitch a ride to nearby locales. A wonderful array of goodies awaits you daily and nightly in your suite. The marble bathrooms alone come complete with a steam room, phones, a TV, and a plush robe.

Dogs get a doggy bowl, a pooch bed, and a menu upon check-in. It's the most fascinatingly expensive and fancy pet room-service menu I've ever seen. Some of the items: grilled filet of beef with organic rice and brown gravy ($28), poached salmon belly in frothed milk (for kitties, I imagine; $23), and the pièce de résistance, beluga caviar with a hard-poached egg ($155; again, it must be a rich cat thing—I've never spent that much on a dinner for four, much less on an appetizer for a pet).

Room rates are $295–895 ($3,000 for a suite that's to drool for). Dogs are charged a $150 fee for the length of their stay. 9291 Burton Way 90210; 310/278-3344; www.lermitagehotel.com.

Loews Beverly Hills Hotel: If you want vintage-style glamour with super dog-friendly service, you'll find it at the delectable Loews Beverly Hills Hotel. From the palm-tree-lined entrance to the stylish lobby to your sumptuous

DIVERSION

Shop for Canine Couture: As any diva dog knows, being naked just doesn't cut it in certain circles. Why should a pampered pooch wear her birthday coat when there are so many other stylish options out there these days?

Fido fashion is big in L.A., and the hot canine clothier du jour is **Fifi & Romeo** (7282 Beverly Boulevard; 323/857-7214; www.fifiand-romeo.com). This gorgeous, chandeliered French-style boutique reportedly appeals to the likes of Bette Midler, Barbara Streisand, Meg Ryan, Drew Barrymore, Robert Downey Jr., Cameron Diaz, Madonna, Ray Romano, Christina Aguilera, Kid Rock, and Lucy Liu (to drop a few names from the star-studded list of F&R fans).

Besides little cashmere sweaters, you can find leather coats, fancy raincoats, hand-embroidered clothes, and stunning beaded numbers. If your dog can't find the clothes of her dreams here, fear not: There are plenty of other places around town to shop for upscale goodies. The sizzlingly popular doggy fashion designer Corey Gelman offers his line, **Chic Doggie by Corey,** at various stores, including the Saks Fifth Avenue in Beverly Hills. (Or you can see his latest designs at www.chicdog.com.)

A word to the wise: After you spend $200 on an itsy-bitsy pink and white hand-stitched cashmere coat, be sure to take it off before heading for the dog park. A local real estate agent, who would prefer to remain anonymous, said she left her little dog's new coat on at a park "and as soon as we walked in, she went right over to the one puddle and looked straight at me, and rolled in it," she says. "I like to think she was telling me, 'Mommy, you don't have to give me expensive things like this for me to love you.' I haven't bought her anything that nice since."

room (complete with an amazingly comfortable TempurPedic bed), this place is all about seemingly effortless class and luxury.

Unlike many other hotels of this genre, Loews welcomes dogs of any size. Thanks to the popular "Loews Loves Pets" program, dogs get the VIP treatment here. Upon their arrival, they receive a note from the hotel's manager welcoming them and giving them tips about nearby dog-friendly places. They also get some treats, a toy, and food and water bowls and can have use of a dog bed if they need one. In addition, gourmet room service awaits them. "The chefs prepare meals for dogs just like they do for our other guests," says the friendly concierge. Well, the menu may be different, but the prices and quality are right up there with those of the human meals.

The concierge can arrange for in-room pet sitting or for dog walking, should you be otherwise occupied in the heated outdoor pool or on Rodeo Drive. In fact, the hotel will loan you a "puppy pager" in the event of a pooch emergency while you're elsewhere.

The rates are fairly reasonable here, considering the locale and amenities. They start at $149, and the normal room rates go up to about $200. Large suites can run up into the four-figure arena. It costs nothing to bring a dog. You'll only pay for the extras, like room service and pet sitting. What a deal! 1224 South Beverwil Drive 90035; 310/277-2800; www.loewshotels.com.

Regent Beverly Wilshire: This hotel puts the "E" in elegance and the "L" in luxury. Unfortunately, it also puts the kibosh on dogs who are barely larger than most cats. There's a 20-pound weight limit. Don't read any further if you don't want your larger dog to get tears all over your shoulder. Normally I wouldn't write much about a place that has such restrictive weight limit, but the Beverly Wilshire deserves the full treatment, despite its rather archaic pooch size limit.

Upon arrival, your tiny pooch will be presented with a silver tray containing two ceramic bowls. One has Milk-Bones and is accented by a sprig of fresh mint, the other bowl is for the bottle of Evian water your dog gets. Also on the tray are two white linen napkins, a rubber squeeze toy, and a vase with a long-stemmed rose. Your dog will also get a special pillow for napping. And all this is free! In addition, for a fee, the hotel provides dog sitting and dog walking. They'll even arrange for a vet or a groomer to come to your room, should you need one. Special gourmet meat selections are also at your dog's pawtips.

Oh, yeah, the hotel. Well, it's in the heart of Beverly Hills, at Wilshire Boulevard and Rodeo Drive, and it's exquisite. It's a historic hotel, built in 1928, and has 275 luxurious guest rooms, including 69 suites. All the rooms have a marble bathroom with deep-soaking bathtub, fully stocked private bars with fridges, fresh flowers, terry robes, a private safe, foam and down pillows, 100 percent cotton linens, an in-room fax, twice-daily maid service, and so on. You get the picture. There's even a heated outdoor pool—but no dog-paddling pooches, please.

The hotel is probably best known in recent years as the setting for the hit movie *Pretty Woman.* The more intimate scenes between Richard Gere and Julia Roberts took place in the hotel's Presidential Suite. For a mere $5,000 per night, you and your dog (and your human guests) can stay here, too. For the price, you get 4,000 square feet of space with gobs of rooms, two fireplaces, and lots of special touches (not the kind of touches in *Pretty Woman,* though). Some notables who really stayed in the Presidential Suite are Elvis Presley, the Dalai Lama, King Hussein and Queen Noor, Prince Andrew, Andrew Lloyd Webber, Elton John, and Mick Jagger.

If you want something a little simpler (cheaper), you can stay in a gorgeous room for as little as $365. The average room rate runs about $450. There's a $125 deposit for dogs. 9500 Wilshire Boulevard 90212; 310/275-5200 or 800/241-4354; www.regenthotels.com.

Los Angeles

Many communities and districts within the city have their own headings. Check individual headings if you don't find the area you need here.

PARKS, BEACHES, AND RECREATION AREAS

The dogs of Los Angeles are keeping their paws crossed for more off-leash spaces. Several different dog groups are working hard to find leash-free park areas. At press time, a group of Northeast Los Angelenos were within a bone's throw of getting approval for a nice chunk of leash-free land at Hermon Park in the Montecito Heights area. For more info, or to support their efforts, check out www.montecitohts.org/dogpark.

5 6 Elysian Park

🐾 🐾 🐾 (See Los Angeles County map on pages 48–49)

The views of Dodger Stadium and downtown Los Angeles don't get much better than from this 585-acre park. The hills here often rise above the smog, and the Los Angeles skyline actually looks attractive from a couple of high-altitude picnic spots.

Angel's Point is a must-see for leashed dogs and baseball fans. Dogs like the breezes that blow in from the different sections of the city. Ball fans enjoy being able to peer into a little segment of Dodger Stadium. The park is conveniently nestled between I-5, U.S. 101, and I-110. To get to Angel's Point and the many roads and trails beyond, exit I-5 at Stadium Way and follow the signs to the park. Once you're in the park, take your first left, Elysian Park Drive. If you're on your way to drop off friends at a Dodgers game and your dog needs a quick walk, take your first right after you enter the park. It's a very green, tree-laden area that won't take you far off track from your destination. 213/485-5054.

57 Ernest E. Debs Park

🐾🐾🐾 (See Los Angeles County map on pages 48–49)

There's something for almost every dog at this large park. Adventurous leashed dogs can accompany you along the fire roads here, while pooches who prefer to lounge around can stretch out on the manicured grass. And those who prefer to eat with you can do so with gusto at the dozens of picnic tables in the civilized part of the park.

The park is between the communities of Lincoln Heights and Highland Park. The best way to enjoy any of this difficult-to-access park is to take the entrance just south of Terrill Avenue, off Monterey Road. Be forewarned: The speed bumps will drive you crazy. The phone number for information is that of Griffith Park: 323/913-4688.

58 Griffith Park/Griffith Park Dog Park

🐾🐾🐾🐾🐕 (See Los Angeles County map on pages 48–49)

This 4,017-acre park has something for dogs of every stripe (and spot), from dogs who need to run off leash to dogs who want to check out the famous "Hollywood" sign.

Since most dogs enjoy the leash-free life, we'll start with the dog park. It's a fenced-in park, with double-gated entries and a separate section for little or shy dogs. It's half grass, half dirt; not one of the prettier dog parks in the area, but it does the trick. To get to the Griffith Park Dog Park, exit Highway 134 at Zoo Drive and follow Zoo Drive into the park. The dog park is next to the John Ferrar soccer field, on the right side of the road. (The freeway is on the left side.)

Anywhere else in this giant park, dogs must be leashed. Much of the acreage is taken up by such non-dog attractions as the city zoo, an observatory and planetarium, a bird sanctuary, an outdoor theater, an equestrian center, golf courses, tennis courts, a swimming pool, a transportation museum, and a Western heritage museum. But fortunately, two-thirds of the park is wild and wonderful, straddling the eastern end of the Santa Monica Mountains. You can explore the undeveloped sections of the park via more than 57 miles of trails! This is the U.S.A.'s largest municipal park, and it can be a quite an attractive place considering it's in the middle of three major freeways in the city that puts the "M" in metropolis. About 100 tree species thrive here, including oaks, pines, and even redwoods. Birds are abundant, which makes sense when you consider their alternatives in the urban realities beyond the park's perimeter.

With all the trails here (few are very developed), you have myriad choices about what kind of hiking you and your dog can do. Here are two suggestions to get you started:

1. Get a map before you arrive, so you'll have time to plan out your trek. Call the number below and the rangers will send you a free map showing all the trails.

2. Be careful. Because of the remoteness of some of the trail areas, they've become dumping grounds for bodies. And we're not talking bodies of literature, bodies of evidence, or even pigeon and squirrel bodies. Even with your dog at your side, you may not want to venture too far by yourself.

One fun hike you can take is the one that winds you as close as is legally possible to the infamous "Hollywood" sign. From central Hollywood (Franklin Avenue and Beachwood Drive), go north on Beachwood Drive about 1.5 miles. At the street's northernmost end, it will come together with Hollyridge Drive. Park around here, and after walking about a block, you'll come to a wide trail on your left. It's not marked, but it will take you about 1.5 miles up Mt. Lee, where you'll be stopped by an ungracious fence. The fence is there at least in part because of the radio tower at the hilltop. (Maybe they also don't want dogs doing leg lifts on this oft-molested sign.)

One of the most entertaining activities you and your dog can share at Griffith Park is a train ride. U.S. 101, I-5, and Highway 134 surround the park. A popular entry is off I-5 at Los Feliz Boulevard. 323/913-4688.

59 Hancock Park

😾 😾 (See Los Angeles County map on pages 48–49)

Take your dog to a tar pit that once trapped scads of Ice Age animals! What fun! The tar still bubbles up from its pond-like setting, but fear not: It's well fenced, so even the most ardent water dogs will be safe from the alluring mire. You can see how animals were drawn here thinking it was a place to splash around and guzzle some liquid refreshments. A few replicas of mammoths charging into the tar pit add a prehistoric air to the park.

The park itself has enough green grass for a pleasant stroll, but it's not big enough for a major exercise experience. There's a snack bar near the tar pit, but hanging around here probably won't give you an appetite, since on a hot day it can smell like roofing tar.

Hancock Park is alongside the George C. Page Museum, which houses skeletons and re-creations of formidable prehistoric animals trapped in the Rancho La Brea Tar Pits during the Ice Age. The Los Angeles County Museum of Art flanks the park's other side, so the park is convenient if you have to drop off a culturally minded friend.

The park is between Sixth Street and Wilshire Boulevard and Curson Avenue and Ogden Drive. Your best bet for free parking is along Sixth Street. The park is "owned" by one government entity and operated by another, and no one seems to want to take phone calls for it. In fact, last time we talked to them, no one even knew the park existed. Scary! Well, here's the number for the museum. Whoever answers the phone will have information on the park. 323/857-6311.

60 Kenneth Hahn State Recreation Area

🐾 🐾 🐾 (See Los Angeles County map on pages 48–49)

Here's a Los Angeles–area park where the birds singing in the trees are actually louder than the drone of the freeways! The hilly section of this large park is a fascinating place to visit. Not only can you and your leashed dog do some intense hiking, you can also experience the world-uniting feel of the Olympics.

In 1932, the area was the site of the 10th Olympics. Then in 1984, Los Angeles again hosted the Olympics, drawing athletes from 140 nations. To serve as a continual (and growing) reminder of the events, 140 trees have been planted together on the hills where the 1932 events occurred. Each tree represents a nation that took part in the 23rd Olympics.

Watching their young leaves blowing in the breeze is enough to send patriotic shivers up your spine. It's also enough to make most male dogs stretch their leashes to pay their kind of homage to these saplings. But they can't. The trees are fenced in until they are big enough to withstand such assaults.

But there are many other trees to sniff in this large park. Several trails branch out from the parking lot at the Olympic Forest. Most take you up the hill, but you can also hike down by the lake and stream in the adjoining section of park.

Fees are $4 per vehicle on weekends and holidays. Driving north on La Cienega Boulevard in the Ladera Heights neighborhood north of Inglewood, you'll pass an oil drilling site, then come to signs for the park. Although it's a state park, it's operated by Los Angeles County. 323/298-3660.

61 Lincoln Park and Recreation Center

🐾 🐾 🐾 (See Los Angeles County map on pages 48–49)

There's plenty of shade here, so it's great for leashed dogs in the summer. And there's a really funky Egyptian-themed playground for kids, so the young

DIVERSION

Choo on This: From your seat aboard one of **Griffith Park's miniature trains,** you and your dog will see goats, horses, llamas, pigs, and a little Native American town. Your dog's ears will flap with wonder as the open-air train chugs gently along. The ride lasts only about eight minutes, but the price is right: Dogs go for free. ("Dogs can't hold down a job, so they shouldn't have to pay," a funny train lady told us.) Humans are $2, be they of the adult or child variety. The train departs from the section of Griffith Park around Los Feliz Boulevard and Riverside Drive, Los Angeles. Call 323/664-6788 for more information.

DIVERSION

You Can't Be Sirius: But you can check out this bright "dog star" and millions of other heavenly bodies when you attend a **Los Angeles Astronomical Society star party.** Well-behaved, non-klutzy canines are welcome to join you when you observe the universe with other astronomy buffs a few times a year at the Griffith Observatory hill in Los Angeles.

These nice folks who share their expensive equipment with the public deserve the utmost in consideration. If they ask you to take your pooch home and come back because of crowds, or for whatever reason, please respect their wishes. For a schedule of upcoming star parties, or to get in touch to ask about your dog attending, go to www.laas.com; 213/673-7355.

---

ones like it year-round. The 46-acre park is centered around a small lake, where neighborhood folks come with their fishing rods and a lunch and spend the day.

Exit I-10 at Soto Street and drive north to Valley Boulevard. Turn left and then go right at the next intersection. There's usually plenty of street parking. 213/847-1726.

62 Pan Pacific Park

😸 😸 (See Los Angeles County map on pages 48–49)

Set next to CBS Television City and the farmers' market, this park is in a fun, central location. It's a long, narrow park that stretches between Beverly Boulevard and Third Street at Curson Avenue, on the former site of the exquisite 1930s Pan Pacific building (which an arsonist burned down in 1989). It's primarily made up of playing fields, but a paved path winds through the other sections of the park. There's not much shade, so it can be relentlessly hot on summer days.

At the Beverly Boulevard end of the park is a memorial to victims of the Holocaust. If you approach it from the opposite side, it's a very moving, powerful monument. 323/939-8874.

63 Silver Lake Park Dog Park

😸 😸 😸 🐕 (See Los Angeles County map on pages 48–49)

It's hard to believe, but right in the middle of what has traditionally been the Land o' Leashes (that is, in the metro region of the city rec and parks department) lies this small, fenced, leash-free mecca.

The trees here are relatively wee, but dogs still are relatively happy weeing on them. Someday when the trees get big and strong, they won't mind so much. The park also has water for pooches and people. The benches here make for more comfy human visits, and also make a great place to sit down and talk to a new human acquaintance. (The park draws lots of singles from the surrounding community. We've heard there have been some matches made in heaven here.)

The park is on Silver Lake Boulevard, just south of Silver Lake and a bit north of Sunset Boulevard. 323/644-3946.

PLACES TO EAT

This is just a sampling of the eateries in Los Angeles proper. Some of the best dog-friendly restaurants are in surrounding areas. See listings for other cities/areas for doggy dining details.

King's Road Cafe: The breakfasts here are to drool for, especially the omelets. And if you like your coffee big, this is the place for you: The coffees here come in giant bowls. Boo the Parisian Dog originally raved so much about the atmosphere at the dog-friendly patio that we had to sniff it out for ourselves. Indeed, the wait staff here is super friendly, and the patrons are generally laid-back. There's a terrific newsstand just around the corner so you can have a good read while you eat good eats. It can get crowded here, especially on Sundays, so if you and your dog can make this a weekday destination, you'll probably enjoy it more. 8361 Beverly Boulevard; 323/655-9044.

Melrose Baking Company: If you want great baked goods at a fun outdoor setting, don't skip this place. 7356 Melrose Avenue; 323/651-3165.

Sante LaBrea: This is among our favorite California restaurants. The outdoor area is lovely, they like dogs, and the food is healthful and very delicious. 345 North La Brea Avenue; 323/857-0412.

Stir Crazy: They love dogs at this coffee shop. "We don't discriminate against anyone," one of the managers told us. 6917 Melrose Avenue; 323/934-4656.

Trattoria Farfalla: The people-watching at this Los Feliz eatery is fun, and the food here is tasty. Jake Dog apparently loves the lamb chops, but the closest he came to them was when he decided to visit a neighboring table—ostensibly at the invitation of the couple sitting there—and ended up with his snout resting firmly on their table, dangerously, pleadingly, close to the meaty dish. (I was eating one of their signature ultra-thin-crust pizzas.) Dine with doggy at the sidewalk tables. Thirsty dogs get water here. 1978 Hillhurst Avenue; 323/661-7365.

PLACES TO STAY

Please see other cities and communities (like Beverly Hills, Westwood, or West Hollywood) for nearby hotels.

Beverly Laurel Motor Hotel: You'll get a decent room for a decent price here. And it's in a great location, three blocks from CBS and near the farmers' market. Cool off with a dip in the pool after a long day of exploring. The motel was built in 1964, and it looks it. Rates are $94–110. Dogs are $25 extra. 8018 Beverly Boulevard 90048; 323/651-2441.

Four Points Hotel Sheraton L.A. Airport: This one's near the airport, which is convenient for traveling pooches. Rates are $119–175. There's a $50 deposit for dogs, who also have to pay $10 extra nightly. 9750 Airport Boulevard 90045; 310/645-4600 or 800/529-4683.

Holiday Inn Brentwood-Bel Air: This is that funky old cylindrical tower you see right off the 405 when stuck in traffic. Dogs under 40 pounds can stay here. Rates are $99–129. 170 North Church Lane 90049; 310/476-6411.

Hotel Sofitel Los Angeles: "We love dogs here," more than one dog-happy manager has told us. This big, attractive, upscale hotel is near the best of Beverly Hills. Rates are $189–329. 8555 Beverly Boulevard 90048; 310/278-5444; www.sofitel.com.

Le Meridien at Beverly Hills: You'll get contemporary European-style digs at this beautiful hotel. The rooms aren't chichi, but delightfully comfortable in a clean, spacious, overstuffed kind of way. Amenities include a robe and slippers, a deep-soak tub, and a free nightly shoeshine. (Don't wear tennis shoes here if you want to get your money's worth.)

Rates are $179–235. Your dog can stay for up to four nights for $100 extra. (So one night will be $100, as will four nights.) After four nights, it's $25 nightly. 465 South La Cienega Boulevard 90048; 310/247-0400; www .lemeridien.com.

The St. Regis Los Angeles: It's elegant. It's sophisticated. It's expensive. But if you have some extra change jingling around your pockets, and you like sleek, modern luxury accommodations, it's worth a visit. They're super dog friendly here: Dogs get St. Regis's own brand of dog biscuits, a "silver" (read stainless steel) bowl, and use of a doggy bed. And the hotel isn't just for fluffy-wuffy dogs. "As long as your dog isn't the size of a wildebeest, it's OK," says a manager. (I'm not sure exactly what the average wildebeest weighs, but I think most dogs could safely make a reservation here. If not, it's gnus to me.)

Rates are $369–469. (Well, at least your dog doesn't cost extra.) 2055 Avenue of the Stars 90067; 310/277-6111.

Travelodge Hotel at LAX: Rates are $64–109. Dogs are $10 extra. 5447 West Century Boulevard 90045; 310/649-4000 or 800/421-3939.

Vagabond Inn Figueroa: Rates are $89–109. Dogs are $10 extra. 3101 South Figueroa Street 90007; 213/746-1531.

Westin Hotels and Resorts: There are three Westins within city limits, but we'd run out of space if we went into the detail each deserves. Suffice it to say they're all luxurious (the Westin Century Plaza has hosted presidents), stylish, and very welcoming for medium-size or smaller dogs: Each offers the doggy version of their ultra-comfy beds for people. "Dogs love the

Heavenly Dog Beds," says one concierge. "I would too if I were a dog." One offers bowls, another treats.

The **Westin Century Plaza Hotel and Spa** (2025 Avenue of the Stars 90067; 310/277-2000) is the most pricey, with standard rooms $259–325. Dogs must be 35 pounds or under. The **Westin Bonaventure Hotel and Suites** (404 South Figueroa Street 90071; 213/624-1000) will run you $109–259 and allows dogs under 40 pounds. The **Westin Los Angeles Airport** (5400 West Century Boulevard 90045; 310/216-5858) is the least expensive, with rooms $104–180, and allows the biggest dogs, up to 50 pounds. You can get more details on all the hotels by checking out www.starwood.com/westin.

City of Commerce

What a quaint, cozy name for a city. *Not.* Well, at least if you need to do business here, and you're lucky enough to have your dog with you, you'll have one great place to stay.

PLACES TO STAY

Ramada Inn: "We're very pet-friendly," boasted one of the managers of this hotel. At a typical Ramada, that usually means dogs are allowed. Period. But at this Ramada, it means dogs are as welcome as their humans. Dogs get their very own doggy bed and enough rawhide chews to make their jaws look like Arnold Schwarzenegger's biceps. (This was originally written years before he became the Governator, but it still hold true.) This is wonderful news for dogs on the go. Speaking of dogs on the go, there's even a dog exercise area for leashed pooches in the back of the hotel.

The hotel asks that only small- to medium-sized dogs stay here, but we're told the rule can be bent for some big dogs. Rates are $59–85. 7272 Gage Avenue 90040; 562/806-4777 or 800/272-6232; www.ramadainn.com.

East Los Angeles

PARKS, BEACHES, AND RECREATION AREAS

64 Belvedere County Park

🐾🐾 (See Los Angeles County map on pages 48–49)

Although Highway 60 bisects this county park, it's still a decent place to take a leashed dog for a romp. In fact, the freeway's proximity makes it attractive to dogs on the go who find they have to go.

Just exit Highway 60 at Atlantic, go north a block, and turn west on First Street. Proceed on First Street about 10 blocks. The north half of the park will be on your right. Park in the lot and enjoy acres of green grass and a few trees. 323/260-2360.

Pico Rivera

PARKS, BEACHES, AND RECREATION AREAS

65 Pico Park

☘☘ (See Los Angeles County map on pages 48–49)

This is your typical, respectable-sized neighborhood park. It's grassy, with picnic tables, a playground, ball fields, and quite a few trees. It's not dog heaven, but it's large enough for leashed dogs to at least stretch their hairy legs. Dogs need to be licensed (and wearing their license) to set paw in the park.

From I-605, take the Beverly Boulevard exit west across the San Gabriel River. The park will be on your left within a few blocks. 562/942-2000.

South El Monte

PARKS, BEACHES, AND RECREATION AREAS

66 Whittier Narrows Regional Park

☘☘☘ (See Los Angeles County map on pages 48–49)

Is your pooch picky about parks? This one is bound to please: There's something for almost every dog in this very large chunk of county land. For dogs who like to hang out near lakes, the park is home to the Legg Lakes. These are actually three ponds connected together. The fishing for trout is about as good as it gets in the middle of a major metropolitan area. The section of the park with the lake also has a long path around it for dogs who prefer not to get grass on their paws.

For dogs who like to explore nature, try the self-guiding nature trail at the Whittier Narrows Nature Center. Starting at the visitor center, get a pamphlet explaining the various phenomena you might encounter on the half-mile nature trail. Make sure your leashed dog doesn't disturb this precious little piece of nature. There's a chicken who sometimes runs around the parking lot, so beware in case your dog plans to be self-sufficient for dinner.

And for chow hounds, a very big area east of Santa Anita Boulevard is devoted almost entirely to picnic tables. When it's not crowded, it's a great place to run around with your dog. Although dogs are supposed to be leashed, it's nice to know that two sides of this large section are fenced.

There's actually a small segment of the park where dogs are allowed off leash for sport training. Call the park to find out the details.

From Highway 60, exit at Rosemead Boulevard, go south to Durfee Boulevard, and turn left. The Legg Lakes part of the park is in about three-quarters of a mile, and the parking lot is on the left. On summer weekends there can be a $4 fee per car, but there's plenty of free street parking if you drive a little farther and go left on Santa Anita Avenue. This is also the place to park if you want to take your dog to the very large picnic section of the park. For the nature trail, continue on Durfee past Santa Anita Avenue and follow the signs to the visitor center. The park also extends north of Highway 60, both to the east and west of Rosemead Boulevard. 626/575-5526.

Whittier

PARKS, BEACHES, AND RECREATION AREAS

67 Arroyo Pescadero

🐾🐾🐾🐾 (See Los Angeles County map on pages 48–49)

Jake Dog and I were excited when we planned our first trip to this Puente Hills wildlife corridor (former Chevron land): It encompasses 1,700 acres—a really big chunk of wildland for these parts. But when we arrived, we found that there's just one trail here, a two-mile loop trail, which barely makes a dent into the vast acreage.

To our delight, however, our hike proved to be an excellent one, even with the mandatory leash. The trail starts out as an ADA-accessible interpretive path with some interesting displays and educational info about the park's flora, fauna, and importance as a wildlife corridor. Once Jake read the signs and got educated, we proceeded toward the hiking trail, which took us through a variety of environments, including coastal sage, chaparral, and a riparian community near a streambed. That was our favorite part, with plenty of greenery and relatively cool shade. He didn't want to leave, but we had more parks to sniff out, other Pescaderos to try. (Jake made me write that ghastly pun.)

We hear that Arroyo Pescadero may get more trails in the future, but for now, this one really is all you'll need. The address is 7531 South Colima Road. Exit Highway 72 at Colima Road and drive north to the park entrance. Access is on the west side of Colima, across from the Murphy Ranch ballparks. 562/945-9003.

Hacienda Heights

PARKS, BEACHES, AND RECREATION AREAS

68 Hacienda Hills Open Space

🐾🐾🐾 (See Los Angeles County map on pages 48–49)

If your dog enjoys a hike on land dotted with trees (and more than dotted; at points, it's canopied), and you want to choose from different levels of trail difficulty, this 300-acre open space fills the bill nicely. It encompasses three canyons, which affords some strenuous hiking if you take the perimeter trail. Most dogs prefer the interior loop trail, which is shorter, flatter, and doesn't get quite so many mountain bikes.

Depending on where you hike, you and your leashed dog will see towering sycamores, oak woodlands, coastal sage scrub, sumac and toyon chaparral (in fact, one of the canyons here is the Toyon Canyon), and some riparian habitat. And if you go high enough, you'll have some fine views of downtown L.A. (not that this is what you came here for).

You can enter Hacienda Hills in two places in Hacienda Heights. Your best bet is to exit Highway 60 at South 7th Avenue and drive south to the end of the street, where you'll find the entrance. The address is 1600 South 7th Avenue. (The other entrance is at 14100 Skyline Drive, and that entails getting off the freeway at the same exit but taking a more circuitous route.) 562/945-9003.

Rowland Heights

PARKS, BEACHES, AND RECREATION AREAS

69 Schabarum Regional Park

🐾🐾🐾 (See Los Angeles County map on pages 48–49)

Your dog will enjoy rolling on the many acres of well-manicured grass here almost as much as he enjoys sniffing the hundreds of trees for the history of dogs who have visited before him. You can explore this park via a fitness trail or a winding paved path, or just traipse through the meadows. Dogs need to be leashed. It's a good idea here, because there's a horseback riding school on the premises. While dogs can be awestruck by what they think are the gods of dogs, they can also decide these dog gods look like fun things to chase.

We like driving to the end of the park, near Picnic Area No. 8. When it's a fairly crowded day, this is where you're bound to find the fewest people.

If you find street parking or arrive early enough, you won't have to pay the $4 fee that's charged on weekends and holidays. But don't grumble if you pay—the county needs every penny it can get to maintain these parks. Exit Highway 60 at Azusa Avenue and head south. Turn left on Colima. The park will be immediately on your right. 626/854-5560.

Malibu

This mountainous oceanfront community is L.A.'s final frontier. Too remote for some, too expensive for others, it's one of the more natural and untouched areas in the county. Malibu's combined incorporated and unincorporated areas cover about 45,000 acres and are 27 miles long and up to eight miles wide. Only 28,000 people live here. Compared with the typical Los Angeles ratio of people to acres, this seems like the countryside. Below you'll find a few magnificent parks where you and your happy pooch won't believe you could be within a bone's throw of one of the world's largest cities.

PARKS, BEACHES, AND RECREATION AREAS

Many of the Santa Monica Mountains National Recreation Area parks are found here. Malibu is also home to the only beach in L.A. County where pooches are permitted. (See the Long Beach section for info on a leash-free beach pilot program, Dog Beach Zone.)

70 Leo Carrillo State Beach

🐾🐾🐾 (See Los Angeles County map on pages 48–49)

Leashed dogs are allowed to trot around a portion of this 6,600-foot-long beach that straddles Los Angeles and Ventura Counties. Dogs can sniff around the beach north of Lifeguard Tower 1 and south of Lifeguard Tower 3. Ask a ranger about this area's location when you park.

Dogs may also camp at one of the 136 sites here. Dogs prefer the campsites by the beach, but they go fast, so reserve ahead. Sites are $20. Call 800/444-7275 for reservations; 805/488-1827 for beach info. The beach entrance is on the 36000 block of Pacific Coast Highway, just south of the county border.

71 Zuma/Trancas Canyons

🐾🐾🐾🐾 (See Los Angeles County map on pages 48–49)

You and your leashed dog can take a short, easy hike or a rather arduous hike, but whatever you do, you're going to love this enormous patch of Santa Monica Mountains National Recreation Area land. At 6,229 acres, it's a biggie, with myriad choices for both the tenderpaw and the experienced canine climber.

Jake, being a dog who seeks shade above all else in life (except for left-overs), likes to stick to the more verdant expanses here. The streams that flow through the lands give rise to the "Zuma" part of the parkland's name. It's from a Chumash word meaning abundance, and the streams do indeed provide abundant plant and animal life. Jake's favorite hike is the Zuma Loop Trail, along the base of Zuma Canyon. The two-mile loop features a hard-wood riparian habitat, which is apparently a rare phenomenon. The shade provided by sycamores, willows, black walnuts, and oaks makes Jake a happy hiker. (More accurately, a happy reposer by the time he gets to this spot.) He especially likes this trail because it's easy and bans bikes.

We also enjoy a good jaunt on the Ocean View Trail and Canyon View Trail (which extend from the Zuma Canyon Trail). They wend through a chaparral environment with less shade, but the ocean views are worth the effort. It's a moderate three-mile loop, which also doesn't permit bikes.

Duty-bound to sniff out a more challenging hike, we once made it to the Zuma Edison Road trail, which was a beauty, but as soon as we got to the most scenic part Jake started pulling on the leash to go back. Being rather pooped myself, I acceded to his request.

There are a couple of entrance options for the more popular trails. The simplest is to take the Pacific Coast Highway/Highway 1 to Busch Drive (near Zuma Beach, where dogs aren't allowed) and drive north on Busch until it ends. 805/370-2301.

72 Escondido Canyon Natural Area

🐾🐾🐾 (See Los Angeles County map on pages 48–49)

You don't have to drive all the way to Yosemite National Park to see one of California's most stunning waterfalls. Just drive to Malibu and take an easy 4.2-mile hike (round-trip) with your leashed dog. The Escondido Canyon Natural Area is home to a one-mile trail that takes you through grasslands, wildflowers (seasonally), and riparian woodlands, to the base of Escondido Falls—a 150-foot multitiered limestone waterfall that cascades over ferns and moss and is so beautiful it looks almost otherworldly. (Jake was frightened when he saw and heard the waterfall—his very first. He fluffed up, barked once, and decided it was time to pull me back to the car. With the aid of a couple of dog biscuits, he realized it was not, indeed, a car wash running amok and regained his rumpled composure.)

Late winter through spring is the best time to visit for the biggest flow. Come in August and you'll still have a decent hike, but you'll be looking at the Escondido Trickle.

Getting to this verdant nirvana on the one-mile trail is a joy. Getting to

DIVERSION

Pack Off to Canine Camp: If images of overnight camps from your childhood still haunt you (oh the food, oh the homesickness, oh the mandatory weaving of multicolor potholders), it's time to get over it. And what better way to do this than to go to camp with your dog? **Iron Dogs Training Camp** in Malibu is a three-day, two-night weekend for people to learn about dogs and dogs to have a ball and learn a few things themselves. You can choose from all kinds of activities, including flyball, agility, and the ever-ridiculous "musical mats" party game. You can also learn about things like clicker training, canine first aid, and doggy massage.

Cabins in the scenic Malibu canyons house 2–20 people on bunks and an even greater number of dogs on the ground. (Bring earplugs if the sound of many dogs licking themselves or scratching or gnawing or snoring in unison would keep you awake.)

The fee is $299 and includes training, food, and lodging for one person with up to two dogs. See the camp's website, www.iron-dogs.com, for more information, or phone 818/335-9889.

the trail itself is a unique experience. From the parking area you have to walk a mile or so through a very upscale Malibu neighborhood brimming with gorgeous homes. You may feel a little out of place with your hiking duds, but at least you'll have your dog at your side. From the main part of Malibu on Highway 1/Pacific Coast Highway, drive about five miles west to Winding Way (there will be a large sign for the Winding Way Trail). Turn right, and you'll almost immediately come to the parking lot. 310/589-3200.

🐾🐾🐾 Circle X Ranch

🐾🐾🐾 (See Los Angeles County map on pages 48–49)

On a clear day, the 360-degree views from Circle X's magnificent Sandstone Peak are to drool for. You'll see the Channel Islands, Santa Catalina Island, Mount Baldy, and sometimes even San Gorgonio Peak. At 3,111 feet, Sandstone Peak is the highest point in the Santa Monica Mountains. It's a moderate-to-difficult hike to the top, though. In fact, most of the trails at this 1,665-acre park are not for tenderpaws. But one, the Canyon View Trail, offers good views and hiking that even a couch potato pooch can handle. "It was my first hike ever and I loved it," brags Lacey, a Welsh Corgi, via his interpreter Sue. "Since then, my stubby legs have taken me to lots and lots of cool hikes around here, but my friends are still impressed I hiked the Circle X."

Take Highway 1/Pacific Coast Highway to Yerba Buena Road. Turn inland and drive 5.4 miles to the park entrance. 805/370-2301.

🐾🐾 Malibu Bluffs

🐾🐾 (See Los Angeles County map on pages 48–49)

Want to watch some whales? Come to this six-acre park's whale-watching station with your leashed dog during the right time of year, and you may well see some. The park is of the community variety, and although dogs need to stay off the ball fields, they're welcome on the jogging path and the par course. 24250 Pacific Coast Highway; 310/317-1364.

🐾🐾🐾🐾 Charmlee Wilderness Park

🐾🐾🐾🐾 (See Los Angeles County map on pages 48–49)

If you and your dog don't like to sweat when you hike, but do like being rewarded with great ocean views on the trail, leash up and head to this 560-acre park. The Meadow Trail starts at a point high enough to see the Pacific from your very first steps. It's easy, often breezy terrain, and since the trail is actually a fire road, it's wide enough to accommodate you and your furry friend and any passing mountain bikes or horses. It's great for beginners or anyone not needing a big challenge. (It's a good choice for dogs getting on in years but still up for tackling something more than the corner hydrant.) You can loop around and come back for a bite to eat at the park's picnic tables.

The park has a nature center (sorry, no dogs inside) and an informative native plant display. Come from February through April and you'll be agog with all the wildflowers here.

There's a $3 fee per car. The park is at 2577 South Encinal Canyon Road. From Highway 1/Pacific Coast Highway in the Zuma Beach area, take Encinal Canyon Road north for four miles to the park. Turn left at the entrance and drive about a half mile to the parking area. 310/457-7247.

76 Corral Canyon Park

🐾🐾🐾🐾 (See Los Angeles County map on pages 48–49)

We love this 340-acre park because it has such a variety of habitat, plus terrific views. You and your leashed dog can take a 2.5-mile loop trail that takes you through pristine wilderness, ancient marine terrace, sage scrub, coastal salt marsh, and a lush creek area with alders, oaks, sycamores, willows, and other trees that make boy dogs happy. At the top, you'll have terrific views of the Pacific and surrounding mountains.

The trailhead is conveniently located at 25623 Pacific Coast Highway, between Malibu Canyon Road and Kanan Dume Road. It's a civilized place to start a hike, with water, restrooms, picnic benches, and yes, even parking. (Note: Although a trail from here leads to Dan Blocker State Beach, dogs aren't allowed there, so don't even try it.) 310/589-3200.

PLACES TO EAT

Coogie's Beach Cafe: Enjoy gussied-up diner-style food with a few twists, including dishes like Italian-style egg rolls and charbroiled garlic turkey salad. Dine with doggy at several outdoor tables. Palm plants try to shield you from the traffic at this fairly new shopping area. Coogie's is at Malibu Colony Plaza, 23750 Pacific Coast Highway; 310/317-1444.

Johnnie's New York Pizza: Small dogs are preferred here, but if you've got an angelic larger pooch, you can bring him to eat with you at the outdoor tables if it's not too crowded and it's OK with your neighbors. 22333 West Pacific Coast Highway; 310/456-1717.

Malibu Kitchen & Gourmet Country Market: The extra-good sandwiches and salads make this place a hit with dogs and their people. Sandwiches range from the sublimely vegetarian (warm seasonal roasted veggies with balsamic vinaigrette, goat cheese, and mixed greens) to the sublimely meaty. The "Better than Mom's Meat Loaf" sandwich, with ketchup, on homemade rustic bread, is a huge hit with dogs whose people tend to drop bits of food while eating. Dine at the seven outdoor tables. It's in the heart of Malibu, at 3900 Cross Creek Road; 310/456-7845.

PLACES TO STAY

Leo Carrillo State Beach: See Leo Carrillo State Beach, above, for camping information.

Topanga Ranch Motel: Stay at these cute, simple motel-style cottages from the 1920s if you want to be close to the only beach for many, many miles that officially allows dogs. (See Leo Carillo State Beach, above.) They're white with red trim and little white fencing around the rosebushes. (This makes them sound more charming than they really are. They're fine, but nothing storybook-like.) All 30 units have fridges, and about half have private patios. The canyon is your backyard.

Rates are $75–105—very affordable for this pricey area. 18711 West Pacific Coast Highway 90265; 310/456-5486; www.topangaranchmotel.com.

Pacific Palisades

PARKS, BEACHES, AND RECREATION AREAS

🐾🐾 Temescal Canyon Park

🐾🐾 (See Los Angeles County map on pages 48–49)

This park is nearly a mile long, running from Bowdoin Street to the Pacific Coast Highway. It's narrow in places, and at times it seems to disappear, but the bulk of the park is wide enough so that if you want to pull off the path and picnic in the shade, there's plenty of room.

It's a fun walk. We see people running their dogs from the top of the hill down to the ocean. It's green and tranquil, despite the fact that it's bisected by Temescal Canyon Road. 310/454-1412.

🐾🐾 Will Rogers State Historic Park

🐾🐾🐾 (See Los Angeles County map on pages 48–49)

"It's great to be great, but it's greater to be human," said humorist and actor Will Rogers, who made his home here during the 1920s and 1930s. Dogs may not exactly agree with this sentiment, but they do appreciate being able to peruse this 186-acre park.

Leashed dogs may explore along the trails that wind past a polo field, a roping ring, and Rogers's ranch house. Dogs can't go into the ranch house and should stay away from the stables and from the polo fields on weekends, when polo matches are held.

A major warning: Heed the leash law. Rattlesnakes abound in the far reaches of the park, and nosy dogs who are allowed to romp off leash find them fairly frequently. Rangers here say about one dog a month gets bitten in the summer. Half survive it. Half don't. The trail here is wide, and if you stay toward the middle, you'll have no problems.

There's a $5 parking fee. The park is at 1501 Will Rogers State Park Road, off Sunset Boulevard. 310/454-8212.

PLACES TO EAT

A La Tarte Bistrot: Want a ménage a trois? You can order one right off the menu. After all, this is a French place! (The ménage is actually just a three-part salad. Sorry.) This chic French bistro has some delectable food. Dine at several shaded outdoor tables with your dear doggy at your side. (After all, this is a French place!) 1037 Swarthmore Avenue; 310/459-6635.

Jacopo's: My favorite pizza here is Max's Big Apple. It's about as close to real New York pizza as you and your dog will get in these parts, and you won't have to deal with airline hassles. But if Jake could choose, he'd probably pick the barbecue pork pizza. It has smoky pork, barbecue sauce, corn, and cilantro. (It's enough to make the stomach turn, isn't it?) 15414 Sunset Boulevard; 310/454-8494.

Palisades Bakery: Choose from a variety of foods here, from burgers to Chinese food to Indian specialties. Eat at umbrella-covered tables with your pooch. 15231 1/2 La Cruz Drive; 310/459-6160.

Brentwood

PARKS, BEACHES, AND RECREATION AREAS

79 Barrington Dog Park

🐾🐾🐾 🐕 (See Los Angeles County map on pages 48–49)

This oddly shaped park (it looks kind of like a bow tie) features a separate area for small dogs and is a couple of acres of grass and wood chips, with poop bags, water, tennis balls galore, and trees that offer pleasant shade for humans and pleasant leg-lift spots for boy dogs. People can rest their laurels on aluminum benches. (The folks here, the Friends of Barrington Dog Park, don't rest on their laurels long—they're always striving to make some kind of improvement in this fairly new park.)

The park is closed for maintenance Tuesday 6–10 A.M. It's at 333 South Barrington Avenue. Since it's close to I-405, here are directions from the freeway: Take the Sunset Boulevard exit and head west to Barrington Place. Go left on Barrington Place and drive past the entrance to Brentwood School. Go left immediately after the post office. The park is behind the post office. 310/840-2187. The Friends of Barrington Dog Park have a fun website: www.fobdp.org.

PLACES TO EAT

Belwood Bakery: You and your pooch can dine on tasty baked goods and sandwiches at the three outdoor tables here. 11625 Barrington Court; 310/471-6855.

Westwood

This lively University of California community is a fun place to have a dog. People around here genuinely like them.

PARKS, BEACHES, AND RECREATION AREAS

80 Westwood Park

 (See Los Angeles County map on pages 48–49)

For a flat, squarish park, this isn't a bad place for a leashed dog. Long dirt paths wind their way through very green grass, past modern sculptures and many shaded picnic tables.

From I-405 take the Wilshire exit heading toward Westwood. Take your first right (on Veteran Avenue). The park will be on your right shortly after the federal building. Another section of the park is on Sepulveda Boulevard, just north of Ohio Avenue. 310/473-3610.

PLACES TO EAT

Stan's Corner Donut Shop: Lots of local cops hang out here, so it's got to be good. If you're in the mood for Indian food or a hot dog, Stan's serves this, too. Stan says, "I love dogs. I have a little French blood in me!" And dogs love the outdoor tables on this sunny corner and the water they'll get if thirsty. 10948 Weyburn Avenue; 310/208-8660.

Tanino Ristorante Bar: The Italian food here is *delizioso,* and the menu is full of wonderful choices. If you like mushrooms, you're really in for a treat. Tanino features a small menu *"per l'amante dei funghi"*—for mushroom lovers. You can start with a mushroom soup with fontina cheese and fungus your way through a mushroom soufflé, quail stuffed with yummy things in a mushroom sauce, and a couple of other tasty 'shroom dishes. Most dogs prefer the grilled T-bone steak, should you have any doubts. Dogs can join you at the covered patio. 1043 Westwood Boulevard; 310/208-0444.

PLACES TO STAY

The official mailing address of these two hotels is Los Angeles, but they're true Westwood glories.

Beverly Hills Plaza Hotel: This is a gorgeous hotel, upscale from the ground floor up (it's only four stories tall, but still...). There used to be a

30-pound size limit, but management is smart and now permits any size well-behaved pooch. There's a $200 cleaning fee for dogs and a $500 deposit, so bring the bankroll or the credit card if you decide to stay here. Rates are $185–525. 10300 Wilshire Boulevard, Los Angeles 90024; 310/275-5575 or 800/800-1234; www.beverlyhillsplaza.com.

W Los Angeles: Dogs really dig this luxurious, peaceful, ultra comfortable and super-dog-friendly hotel. The beds have featherbed toppers and goose-down comforters and pillows. (Not that your dog should go on the bed or anything.) It's an all-suites hotel, so you can relax in your lush terry robe (hotel-supplied) on your cushy sofa in your roomy suite with your faithful, happy, furry friend at your side.

The doggy details are just as splendid: Visiting pooches will get a cozy pillow bed, bowl, food, treats, and a leash. The W gives new meaning to the phrase, "It's a dog's life." The suites are $300. 930 Hilgard Avenue, Los Angeles 90024; 310/208-8765; www.starwood.com/whotels.

Santa Monica

Even though tourist dogs don't have many places to run around off leash (dogs must be licensed Santa Monicans to use the two off-leash areas here), Santa Monica is a great place to be a dog. It's laid-back, upscale, and down to earth. Dog-friendly eateries abound, and the city is home to some of the most dog-friendly hotels on earth. Soon, there may even be a leash-free beach, if the dogs of Santa Monica win over the hearts of decision makers (see below).

PARKS, BEACHES, AND RECREATION AREAS

A note to dogs who like to run leash-free at beaches (in other words, 99.999 percent of dogs): At press time a movement was apaw to open a portion of Santa Monica Beach to naked (leashless) dogs. This would be a major boon to the Santa Monica area's 5,000 dog people and their praying pooches. See www.unleashthebeach.org for updates or info on how you can help.

Leashed dogs are permitted in all city parks. (You must have a poop bag–type implement showing, or you could get a ticket. It's best to carry an extra, in case a cop comes after your dog goes.) The two dog parks allow only licensed Santa Monica dogs. It's not great if you're just in town for the day, but it's good for local dogs anyway.

🐾 Joslyn Park Dog Park

🐾🐾🐾🐕 (See Los Angeles County map on pages 48–49)

The park may be small, but it's beautiful. It's set on a grassy hill with a few trees and has great views of the city. It's completely enclosed, so those lucky pooches who get to go leashless are safe from traffic. It has poop bags, lighting, and a separate area for small dogs.

Licensed Santa Monica dogs may run leashless 7:30 A.M.–8:30 P.M. on weekdays and 8:30 A.M.–8:30 P.M. on weekends. They must stay away from the playground and recreation area. All other dogs must be leashed, so it's best to keep them out of the dog run and explore other parts of the park. The park is at 7th Street and Kensington Road. 310/458-8974.

82 Pacific Park Dog Park

🐾🐾🐕 (See Los Angeles County map on pages 48–49)

This small, fenced dog park, right next to a kennel, won't provide your pooch with endless miles of leash-free exercise, but it will provide her with endless leash-free socializing. If your dog is a social pooch, she'll probably get all the exercise she needs here while engaging in faux wrestling matches and chase games. The park has everything a dog needs, including water, a little shade, occasional grass, and benches to chase each other under.

Licensed Santa Monica dogs may run leashless in the enclosed section west of the tennis courts 7:30 A.M.–8:30 P.M. on weekdays and 8:30 A.M.–8:30 P.M. on weekends and holidays. All other pooches have to be leashed, so it's best to stay outside the doggy area. The park is at Pacific and Main Streets. 310/458-8974.

PLACES TO EAT

If we listed all, or even most, of the restaurants in the popular eating parts of Santa Monica, we'd run out of pages in the book. So here are just a few.

Some of Santa Monica's most unusual and trendy restaurants reside on the **Third Street Promenade** between Wilshire and Broadway, and most have outdoor areas. That doesn't necessarily mean your dog is welcome at all of them, but your chances are better than when walking down a row of restaurants in Tahoe in January. You may want to watch your food, though, because a few of the homeless have been known to sneak up and grab it out from under you.

Restaurants along Santa Monica's **Main Street** are in a quieter setting than the restaurants in the Third Street Promenade. Unfortunately, we've found that most of the more upscale eateries won't allow dogs to dine with you outside.

Acadie Hand Crafted French Crepes: The crepes here are out of this world, with down-to-earth prices. My favorite is the Cevenol, with chestnut puree and crème Chantilly. Jake's favorite is anything that drops on the ground. The outside eating area houses several functional steel tables with plenty of room for pooches. 213 Arizona Avenue (at the Third Street Promenade); 310/395-1120.

Café Dana: We've been welcomed at this café's wonderful brick courtyard before, and even offered a bowl of water (Jake has, I haven't), but we're now told dogs may have to be relegated to the sidewalk tables. Be sure to ask before you bring your dog to the enchanting courtyard. The house specials lean toward Greek food, but there's a wide variety of dishes here. If you like things English, try the afternoon tea, which comes with all the fixin's you'd get at a tea house. 1211 Montana Avenue; 310/394-0815.

Joe's Diner: Joe Dog liked this one. He thought the name was in good taste, but thought the good old-fashioned American cuisine was even tastier. Eat at one of two outdoor tables. 2917 Main Street; 310/392-5804.

Newsroom Espresso Cafe: Dine with your dog at the many umbrella-topped outdoor tables here. A must-try dish, even if you're not a vegetarian, is the Ultimate Maui Veggie Burger. 530 Wilshire Boulevard; 310/319-9100.

Peets Coffee: There's a big water bowl right by the front door here. Dogs can lap while you latte. 800 14th Street (at Montana); 310/394-8555.

Starbucks Coffee Company: Sip a cup of java at the tables out front while your dog gets that Maxwell House expression on his face. You'll recognize it. It's that "Ahh-I'm-so-content-with-the-world-because-I'm-smelling-good-coffee" look. 2671 Main Street; 310/392-3559.

Sunset Bar & Grill: Eat continental cuisine on the happening patio with your happy pooch. Actually, your happy pooch has to be tied to the other side of the rail, but she'll still be well within petting (and mooching) distance. 1240 Third Street; 310/395-7012.

PLACES TO STAY

Some of the most posh, dog-friendly hotels in California call Santa Monica home. The more affordable lodgings, like the local Best Westerns and Comfort Inns, don't allow dogs. If you want to stay in this beautiful coastal city, be prepared to dig deep in your wallet.

The Fairmont Miramar Hotel Santa Monica: You and your smallish dog (under 30 pounds) can live in California-style casual elegance when you stay at this sprawling, lovely hotel. You can sleep in a 10-story tower, a bungalow surrounded by beautiful gardens with little waterfalls, or a gorgeous six-story wing of the hotel. Rates are $300–1,200. 101 Wilshire Boulevard 90401; 310/576-7777; www.fairmont.com/santamonica.

Le Merigot: This opulent oceanfront gem has been described as "reminiscent of the fine hotels on France's Côte d'Azur," and also of "blending European elegance with the vibrant lifestyle of Southern California" *Brides* magazine describes the hotel as "Zen meets the millennium." You get the idea. It's cool, it's sleek, it's to drool for. Even the luxury spa here has won coveted awards. The rooms' ultra-cushy "Cloud Nine" beds—festooned with Frette linens, down duvets, and feather pillows—should win an award for comfort.

"Yada, yada, yada," your dog might be saying right about now. "But what's in it for me?" Well, doggy, Le Merigot has a marvelous program called "Club Meg," which allows dogs up to 100 pounds to be pampered guests at the hotel. (The brochure for the program features a dog who's the spitting image of Jake. Jake as the mascot for a luxury hotel pooch program is a funny thought, indeed.)

Dogs get pooch cookies, a dog magazine, and some other doggy amenities. They can also order dog-food room service. The kibble isn't as appealing as Loews's dog cuisine, but it's nothing to quibble about. There's also a grassy dog walk area next to the hotel.

Rates are $250–460. Dogs require a $150 deposit and are $35 extra for the length of your stay. 1740 Ocean Avenue 90401; 310/395-9700; www.lemerigothotel.com.

Loews Santa Monica Beach Hotel: Everything about this elegant beachside resort is first-rate, from the gorgeous rooms to the sumptuous spa and health club. The lobby is to die for, too. It's also a great place to have a cocktail with your dog. Karen Dawn, founder of Dawn Watch, an animal rights media-watch organization, stayed at the hotel with her two dogs and significant other when they first moved to L.A. "We'd come into the lobby's lounge area and order cocktails, and they'd put a little mat down for Paula and Buster and give them a bowl of water," she says. "They're incredibly dog friendly." Paula, a pit bull rescued from the Bronx, is still dumbfounded by the whole experience. (So is Buster, her big mutt, who trotted to the edge of the pool one day, leaned a little too far in to sniff at a ball, and tipped right in, much to his consternation.)

Loews is, indeed, dog friendly. The "Loews Love Pets" program considers all pet visitors VIPs (Very Important Pets) and starts their visit with a personal welcoming note from the hotel's general manager. Attached to the letter is a listing of pet-friendly places in the area. Dogs get a complimentary bag of biscuits, a toy, special placemats, and food and water bowls. If you want to borrow a doggy bed, that's no problem—they've got them for every size of pooch. Loews offers dogs gourmet room service with items like grilled lamb with rice, and even a vegetarian alternative should your dog be so inclined. Dog walking or pet sitting is available, too.

Rates are $275–625. Dogs cost nothing extra but do have to pay for room service, pet sitting, other bonus services. 1700 Ocean Avenue 90401; 310/458-6700 or 800/235-6397; www.loewshotels.com.

Venice

Looking around Venice these days, you can see barely a hint of the dream of Abbot Kinney, the city's founder. In 1900, he began creating a city that was a near duplicate of Italy's Venice, complete with canals, Italian architecture, and imported singing gondoliers. He had hoped to create a cultural renaissance in America.

If he could see the scantily clad roller skaters, the punkers with metal in every conceivable body part, the homeless, and the body builders and religious zealots in action, old Mr. Kinney would shudder. But despite the wayward ways of those inhabiting his dream, the place has a wild charm, a playland quality. And what really counts is that dogs think Venice is cool.

DIVERSION

Do It All at the Dogromat: All the Milk-Bones your dog can eat and a bath to boot. That's the way life is at the **Dogromat,** one of the most engaging self-service "dog laundromats" in the West.

Even dogs who hate baths don't mind coming here. There's something in the air that says, "It's OK. Thousands of dogs before you have been bathed here and survived, and you're next, and you won't die." Plus, as one of the owners freely admits, "We're notorious for feeding treats." Humans like it even better than dogs. It's much easier to bathe a dog here than at home because the tubs are waist high and everything you need is at your fingertips. Other benefits include ready advice from the staff (which is made up of grooming professionals), socializing in a dog-friendly atmosphere, and letting flea carcasses wash down someone else's drain.

The *Los Angeles Times* wrote that "What Chuck E. Cheese is to children, this place is to dogs." And your dog won't have greasy pizza drippings all over his clothes when he leaves. Dogromat rates are based on the size and hair type of your pooch. The average is $12. Dogromat is at 12926 Venice Boulevard, Venice; 310/306-8885.

There are plenty of dogs here. As of this writing, they're not allowed on the beach, but there's a big battle being waged about that. A terrific group, Freeplay, is working hard to get beach access and more off-leash parks. Freeplay started as an acronym standing for Friendly, Responsible, Environmentally Evolved Pet Lover's Alliance—Yes (not short, but the resulting acronym was worth it); www.freeplay.org.

PARKS, BEACHES, AND RECREATION AREAS

83 Westminster Dog Park

🐾🐾🐾🐾🐕 (See Los Angeles County map on pages 48–49)

Since Freeplay helped open this fenced-in park a few years back, beach-area dogs have joyously awaited their daily or weekly jaunts here. The park is more than an acre within very tiny Westminster Park, with plenty of shade and a few benches.

Small dogs have a choice of running with the big boys or playing in their very own smaller fenced-in dog run area. Most tiny canines we know would opt for the chance to be as big as they feel and not be set apart as a little dog. But it's a great feature for dogs in need of some protection from giant paws.

The park is at Pacific and Westminster Avenues. The regional park office phone is 310/837-8116.

DIVERSION

Stroll to a Different Drummer: Since Venice's parks are so tiny, most people like to take their dogs for a jaunt along **Ocean Front Walk,** between Rose Avenue and Venice Boulevard. It's about as close to the beach as dogs are allowed, and for many, it's close enough. This is where you can consult a psychic; have your cards read by a tarot dealer; listen to street musicians; buy incense, T-shirts, or sunglasses; and watch skaters skate and lovers love.

If you like to check out bikini-clad babes—apparently one of Jake Dog's favorite pastimes—this is a hot spot. Jake smiles pantingly as cuties skate or jog or saunter by. Sometimes he even steps out into their path, urging them to stop with his big brown eyes. They often do, and they lavish him with pats and coddles. On a recent visit, a human dood saw the lovin' Jake was getting and asked if he could borrow him "just for 15 minutes." "Your dog gets more attention in five minutes than I got all week here," he said. Jake wanted to tell him that losing the nose ring and the nipple rings and covering his very hairy chest might help, but he remained politely silent.

You never know what you'll run into here. One day Joe Dog, Jake's predecessor, was trotting merrily along sniffing the air for all the great, cheap places to eat along the walk, when suddenly a hand appeared on the path before him. It wouldn't have been a big deal, except the hand wasn't attached to a body. It was writhing and doing sickening somersaults. Joe trembled and ran backwards right into a juggler. He stood there wrapped around the juggler's leg until the hand crawled away, back to the pile of motionless rubber hands from which it had strayed. He gave a shudder, unwrapped himself, and marched onward, never glancing back.

PLACES TO EAT

In addition to these restaurants, little eateries abound along Ocean Front Walk. Just grab a chair and table from the communal sidewalk restaurant furniture and enjoy one of the most scenic and unusual lunches you've ever experienced. See the restaurant listings for Marina del Rey for more super-close eateries.

Abbot's Habit: Your dog will want to make a habit of visiting this laid-back hangout, especially after he's offered a bowl of fresh water and you've bought him some of the crunchy dog treats they sell here. Everyone from surfers to artists (often one and the same) comes here for their delectable baked goods and rich coffees. The sidewalk tables, where dogs are allowed, offer great people-watching opportunities. 1401 Abbot Kinney Boulevard; 310/399-1171.

Figtree's Cafe: The food here is fantastic and eclectic. You may eat at the patio as long as you tie your dog to the other side of the rail. She'll still be at your side, but there will be a couple of bars between you. A water bowl is available. 429 Ocean Front Walk; 310/392-4937.

Massimo's: Dogs are welcome to join you at the cozy covered patio in back here. The shade is essential, because you don't want your delectable gelato to melt all over the place. The salads, sandwiches, and baked goods are also a delight. Dogs get water if thirsty. (A big thanks to Skye Dog and his person, Barbara, for giving us the heads-up about Massimo's.) 1029 Abbot Kinney Boulevard; 310/581-2485.

Pasta Factory: The pasta and breads are made fresh right here every day. You'll give your crunchy boxed pastas at home the evil eye after you taste the difference. The pizzas and seafood are tasty, too. Dine with your dog at the outdoor tables. 425 Washington Boulevard; 310/823-9838.

Marina del Rey

PARKS, BEACHES, AND RECREATION AREAS

84 Burton Chace Park

🐾 🐾 (See Los Angeles County map on pages 48–49)

Water dogs love this 10-acre park, because it's on a spit surrounded by water on three sides. But unless you visit via a boat (guest docks are available for a reasonable fee), dogs don't really get access to the water here. It's Dock City here.

Leashed dogs of all ilks enjoy sniffing the salty breeze from this lovely, well-groomed park. The lawn can be golf-course-green, and the pathways are immaculate. This is a popular spot for weddings and group picnics, which you'll need to steer clear of, even if your dog loves parties. 13650 Mindanao Way; 310/305-9595.

PLACES TO EAT

The Cow's End: This is a fun coffeehouse where you can sip your stuff under a canopy. They're so doggone friendly here that your dog may even be offered a tasty dog biscuit if he plays his cards right. 34 Washington Boulevard; 310/574-1080.

Mercedes' Cuban Grill: The Cuban-Caribbean creations here are spicy and exotic. The ambience inside is cozy and creative, and outside, where dogs are allowed, it's pure fun in the sun. (Or in the moon, if you choose to have dinner here.) If you're thirsty for a unique drink, try the banana mojitos. Dogs get only a bowl of water if they're thirsty, but that's OK, because who wants a dog with banana breath? 14 Washington Boulevard; 310/827-6209.

Inglewood

PARKS, BEACHES, AND RECREATION AREAS

85 Edward Vincent Jr. Park

🐾🐾🐾 (See Los Angeles County map on pages 48–49)

With 55 acres of hills, meadows, and trees, this park is large enough for a good walk with your good leashed dog, but not so big that you're going to get lost. The path through the park is wide, so you, your dog, and a passerby all won't be squished together as you mosey along.

The best place to park is along Warren Lane, near Centinela Avenue. 310/412-5370.

El Segundo

Are you near the airport and looking for a place to run your dog off leash? Be sure to sniff out El Segundo's little off-leash gem. And if the dogs of L.A. County get their way, there could be an off-leash beach at Dockweiler Beach by the next edition of this book. A terrific group, Freeplay, is trying hard to make this happen. See www.freeplay.org for updates and info. For now, dogs have to be content to only camp there in an RV, on leash, and away from the water (see Places to Stay).

PARKS, BEACHES, AND RECREATION AREAS

86 El Segundo Dog Park

🐾🐾🐾🐕 (See Los Angeles County map on pages 48–49)

Like plane spotting? Bring your furry pal to this dog park. It's on a grassy bluff that has views of nearby LAX, and you can watch the planes take off and land all day if you like. But chances are that your off-leash dog will have more important things to do at this long, 1.5-acre park, like sniff trees, sniff other dogs, run around a lot, and sniff more dogs. The park has water, benches, poop bags, double gates, and a separate section for small dogs.

It's on East Imperial Avenue between McCarthy Court and Sheldon Street, across from Imperial Avenue School. 310/524-2700.

PLACES TO STAY

Dockweiler Beach RV Park: Got an RV and an urge to cozy up to the ocean? Stay at one of the 118 sites here for a couple of nights. Pets must be leashed, and they can't officially go to the nearby beach. Rates are $25–32.

From I-405 about 12 miles south of Santa Monica, exit at Imperial West Highway and drive four miles west to Vista del Mar. That's where you'll find the park. Call for reservations. 310/322-7036.

Summerfield Suites by Windham: You and your dog never have to leave your suite (except for the occasional potty break at the hotel's little dog walk area…uh, for your dog) when you stay at this clean, comfortable lodging that's a favorite among people doing business near the airport. The suites all have a full kitchen, cozy living room, nice bedroom, and business-oriented services features like high-speed Internet and a large, attractive working area. If you want your groceries delivered, that can be arranged for no extra fee (except for the groceries).

Of course, you'll want to leave your suite so your dog can get some well-deserved off-leash exercise. And what better place than El Segundo Dog Park, which is a quick car ride away.

Dogs need to be under 60 pounds to stay here. Rates for suites are $129–189. There's a $150 fee per visit for dogs in the one-bedroom suites and a $200 fee per visit for dogs in the two-bedroom suites. 810 South Douglas Street 90245; 310/725-0100; www.wyndham.com.

Manhattan Beach

Dogs and people usually take an automatic liking to this seaside town. It's a friendly place, with people who stop you in the street to talk about how much they like your dog. This is not that common in these parts, so enjoy it. Unfortunately, the friendly attitude doesn't extend to the city's beaches or parks. Only one allows pooches.

PARKS, BEACHES, AND RECREATION AREAS

87 Manhattan Beach Parkway Park

🐾 🐾 (See Los Angeles County map on pages 48–49)
This is a jolly green continuation of Hermosa Beach's Hermosa Valley Greenbelt. It's skinny, dozens of blocks long, and it's the only public green in town that allows dogs. Leashes are a must, and don't even think about going on the beach with your pooch. Sorry, water dogs.

The park runs along Ardmore Valley Avenue for much of its length. 310/545-5621.

PLACES TO EAT

El Sombrero: They make a mean burrito here. Try one at the sidewalk benches. 1005 Manhattan Avenue; 310/374-1366.

Hennessey's: Dogs can dine with you at the sidewalk tables here, but not the patio tables. Try the granola French toast. Yum! 313 Manhattan Beach Boulevard; 310/546-4813.

Local Yolk: If you want a great breakfast, this place is just killer. (And this is not a reference to the cholesterol-raising dishes here.) A photo inside shows a man with a dog outside the restaurant. It says, "A safe place for dogs" (or something like that). And it is. Dogs are welcome to dine with you at the outdoor tables here. 3414 Highland Avenue; 310/546-1407.

Sloopy's Beach Cafe: Inside, this is a very funky place. It looks like a jungle or forest with tons of plants and tree-trunk tables. Outside there are just a few little tree-trunk tables with plastic chairs. Dogs can dine with you on tasty breakfast food and California lunch fare.

Uncle Bill's Pancake House: This is one of the more dog-friendly eateries around. "We love dogs!" says a manager. Uncle Bill's has been hailed as "the king of the South Bay breakfast eateries." Try the cheddar and bacon waffle. You'll be drooling as much as your dog. (Thirsty dogs get a bowl of water.) Dine with your furry friend at tables out front. 1305 Highland Avenue; 310/545-5177.

PLACES TO STAY

Residence Inn by Marriott: You and your dog can get a roomy apartment-style suite here. Some come with fireplaces, and all come with a kitchen, which is a mighty convenient feature when traveling with a pooch. Rates are $139–199. There's a $75 deposit and a $100 cleaning fee for the length of your stay when you visit with a dog. 1700 North Sepulveda Boulevard 90266; 310/546-7627 or 800/321-2211.

Hermosa Beach

PARKS, BEACHES, AND RECREATION AREAS

Dogs aren't allowed at any of Hermosa Beach's beaches.

88 Hermosa Valley Greenbelt

🐾🐾 (See Los Angeles County map on pages 48–49)

This long, narrow strip of green runs 30 blocks—the entire length of the city. It's got a pleasant soft dirt/chipped bark path down the middle, which leashed dogs really enjoy treading on. It's shaded in parts and can be fairly quiet, considering that it's sandwiched by two roads. But it's quite narrow, not ideal for a dog who likes to do heavy-duty exploring.

You can enter the park almost anywhere along Ardmore Avenue or Valley Street. The park continues north into Manhattan Beach (see Manhattan Beach Parkway Park). 310/318-0280.

PLACES TO EAT

As if to make up for the lack of poochy beach access, dog-friendly eateries abound here.

Good Stuff: This delightful eatery is right by the strand and the beach. Dine on everything from traditional (really yummy) breakfast dishes to burgers,

122 THE DOG LOVER'S COMPANION TO LOS ANGELES

from wraps to pretty darn good Mexican food. Dogs can join their people at the many outdoor tables. If it's busy, you have to sit at the side tables with your dog. 1286 The Strand; 310/374-2334.

Hennessey's: Hennessey's outdoor area is a hit with the dog set: Water bowls are always out and almost always filled with fresh water. People like the big heaping plates of food that's not necessarily the healthiest in the world (burgers, corned beef hash, beer-battered onion rings, and the like), and dogs like to sit around and wait for food to fall to the ground. If it's busy, dogs are relegated to the other side of the patio fence, but they can still be right beside you. 8 Pier Avenue; 310/372-5759.

Java Man: Dogs enjoy this old, funky sandwich/coffee/soup place. It's on a busy part of the street, but dogs don't seem to mind: The folks here give dogs treats and water, and the dogs don't notice the traffic passing by. 157 Pier Avenue; 310/379-7209.

Le Petite Cafe: "We are very happy to tell you we are very dog friendly," announced the manager when last we spoke. Dogs can join you at the outdoor eating bar, where you can get a great omelet or a beefy burger. 190 Hermosa Avenue; 310/379-1400.

Martha's 22nd Street Grill: They'll often let your dog sit beside you at the outside tables here, but if it's crowded, you'll be asked to tie your dog up to one of the poles on the side. The food is really good—and good for you, too. The menu includes apple pancakes, Monte Cristo sandwiches, and veggie burgers. Your dog can get a bowl of water if his whistle needs wetting. 25 22nd Street; 310/376-7786.

Redondo Beach

PARKS, BEACHES, AND RECREATION AREAS

Dogs are banned from all city parks, beaches, and open-space lands, with one very special exception. When you're done getting down and dirty at the dog park, take a trip to the Ushampooch, a fun, clean self-serve dog wash just one block from the park, at 1218A Beryl Street; 310/798-7300; www.ushampooch.com.

🐾 Redondo Beach Dog Park

🐾🐾🐾🐾🐾 🐕 (See Los Angeles County map on pages 48–49)
A few years ago, dogs were thrilled to have a 2.5-acre leash-free, fenced park to call their very own, even though there was no shade and much of the park ran under big power lines. After all, before that, dogs couldn't even set paw in any local parks. But now that the park has been expanded and gussied up a bit, dogs are positively ecstatic.

The park is now six big acres. It's divided into three parts—two big parks that switch off being open to give the grass a chance to grow, and one smaller park for small dogs. The park also has about 30 fairly new trees. The trees are still too small to give shade, but at least they give hope for shade in the near future.

The power lines over a swatch of the park don't do much for the place aesthetically, but dogs don't care. There's doggy drinking water, cool green grass, good sniffs, and lots of other dogs to pal around with. In fact, a survey shows that the dog park is the busiest park in the city, with about 1,500 visitors on some of the busy weekends.

The park is at Flagler Lane and 190th Street. Driving north on Highway 1/ Pacific Coast Highway, go right on Beryl Street. In about 10 blocks you'll come to Flagler Lane. Go left on Flagler. Parking is on the right, before the stop sign on the top of the hill. 310/318-0610; www.rbdogpark.com.

PLACES TO EAT

Catalina Coffee Company: They roast their own beans here, and it smells divine. Have a sandwich and a café drink with your dog at your side at the spacious, shaded outdoor area. Thirsty dogs can get a bowl of water. 126 North Catalina Avenue; 310/318-2499.

Coffee Cartel: Buy books and a cuppa joe at this older, fun place with a literary bent. Coffee Cartel sponsors everything from poetry readings to bluegrass bands. Dogs can join you at the outdoor tables. 1820 South Catalina Avenue; 310/316-6554.

Petit Casino: Who says food at a mini mall has been chain-restauranted to death? The food's not fancy, but it's not cookie-cutter, either. Dine at the outdoor tables with your dog. 1767 South Elena Avenue; 310/543-5585.

Redondo Beach Brewing Company: The grilled food is great, and the ales are all that. For something different, try the Greek tacos or the scrumptious chicken adobo sandwich. Drink and dine with your dog at the shaded tables out front. 1814 South Catalina Avenue; 310/316-8477.

Zazou: This terrific restaurant offers a fun mix of California-Provençal cuisine. The dishes are flavorful and, for the most part, healthful. (Dogs long for the braised rabbit, but the butternut squash and ginger raviolini are truly droolworthy.) You can eat at the tables out front with your dog, but you can't drink alcohol out here. (Neither you nor your dog, if that makes you feel better.) 4810 South Catalina Avenue; 310/540-4884.

PLACES TO STAY

Best Western Redondo Beach Inn: Rates at this attractive Best Western, which features a pool and spa, are $89–109. Dogs are $50 extra for the length of their stay. 1850 South Pacific Coast Highway 90277; 310/540-3700.

Torrance

PARKS, BEACHES, AND RECREATION AREAS

90 Columbia Park

🐾🐾 (See Los Angeles County map on pages 48–49)

The park may be under many power lines, but it has the most amusing dog-rule signs we've seen. Joe didn't even try to lift his leg on them when he visited. If other cities would approach the poop-scooping issue like this, it would make the task much more pleasant. Stop by and check them out. When you do, you may as well trot around the huge swaths of grass with your leashed dog.

Exit I-405 at Crenshaw Boulevard and drive south about 15 blocks. Go right at 190th Street and right again into the park. 310/618-2930.

91 Miramar Park

🐾 (See Los Angeles County map on pages 48–49)

Is your dog thirsty? This tiny, grassy park overlooking the ocean provides the best dog-watering hole in the county. Fido Fountain was built in 1990 because dogs were drinking from the human water fountain and many humans were complaining. "The large dogs jump up as their masters turn on the water for them," wrote one resident. "Very upsetting to me, and others, if they knew they were drinking after dogs. I myself love my dog, but I do not eat or drink after my own dog."

Fortunately, City Hall didn't allow such letters to result in more regulations against dogs. The city just went ahead and built a dog-sized fountain right beside the other drinking fountain. Then the tables were turned: Sand-covered humans started rinsing off their feet in the Fido Fountain. So the city built a miniature headstone reading "Fido Fountain—Dogs only, please." It did the trick. Now human feet and dog lips rarely come together at Miramar Park.

The park is at the northern border of the city, just south of Redondo Beach on Paseo de La Playa. 310/618-2930.

Palos Verdes Estates

PARKS, BEACHES, AND RECREATION AREAS

92 Malaga Park

🐾 (See Los Angeles County map on pages 48–49)

We mention this tiny park only because it's so close to a really lovely European-style part of this luxurious city. You and your leashed dog can catch a refreshing ocean breeze at Malaga Park, since it's high on a hill. Dogs like to relax on the small plot of lush grass and contemplate what it would be like if their backyard looked like this. People enjoy sitting on the stone benches and contemplating the same thing. In the spring, a little garden comes alive with color. Make sure your leashed dog doesn't think the park is larger than it is and accidentally wander into the flower beds.

From Palos Verdes Drive going west, go right on Via Corta. Park on the street. The park is immediately on your left. Don't blink or you'll miss it. 310/378-0383.

PLACES TO EAT

Rive Gauche: Elegance is the operative word at this four-star French restaurant. Yet the managers gladly permit pooches to dine with you at the patio tables. "We're very dog friendly here," they say. Some patrons have been bringing their dogs here for years, much as they would if this restaurant were in France. One regular told us that sometimes her dog manages to mooch a little something from her waiter. But I don't think that's the norm here. Still, maybe your dog will get lucky.

There's a canopy over the patio, so you and your *chien* can dine without the sun smacking you in the eyeballs. 320 Tejon Place; 310/378-0267.

Rancho Palos Verdes

PARKS, BEACHES, AND RECREATION AREAS

93 Ladera Linda Community Center

🐾🐾 (See Los Angeles County map on pages 48–49)
This isn't the biggest park in Rancho Palos Verdes, but since it doesn't get nearly as much use as many others, it's one of the better places to take a dog. It covers about 33 acres, much of it devoted to playing fields and open space.

From Palos Verdes Drive in the Portuguese Bend area, go north on Forrestal Drive. The park will be on your left in a few blocks. 310/541-7073.

Harbor City

PARKS, BEACHES, AND RECREATION AREAS

94 Harbor Regional Park

🐾🐾 (See Los Angeles County map on pages 48–49)
This 210-acre park between Harbor City and Wilmington is right beside a huge oil refinery. Yum, yum. The air is often an otherworldly hue. It's not the most appetizing place, but you can manage to stomach a picnic here. To the park's credit, there's a good-sized lake along the east end. It may not be a prime fishing spot, but at least it's good old H_2O.

The best thing about this park is its proximity to I-110. If you have a dog who's in dire need during a Sunday drive, a jaunt to this park won't take you far off course. Exit I-110 at Highway 1/Pacific Coast Highway and drive west a short half mile. The entrance is on your left. 310/548-7515.

San Pedro

Stick close to the waterfront here and you'll have a great time. Los Angeles Harbor is a working harbor where you can see tankers, container vessels, cruise ships, and pleasure craft going about their business.

San Pedro is a point of embarkation for one of the ferry lines to Catalina. It's a fun excursion to take with a sea-loving pooch. (See the Santa Catalina Island section for more on the ferry services.) For more on fun things to do in this town, check out www.sanpedro.com. The folks who run this site are very helpful and have a couple of dogs themselves.

PARKS, BEACHES, AND RECREATION AREAS

Angel's Gate Park looks huge and green on the map, but don't let cartographers fool you. Except for an area around the Korean Friendship Bell, the place is almost entirely off-limits to hikers, since it's got roads and barracks-like buildings almost everywhere. A good bet is to try Fermin Park, on the ocean just below Angel's Gate Park. But the paws-down favorite of dogs is the new Knoll Hill Dog Park. If you're in the area, it's a must-visit kind of place.

95 Point Fermin Park

🐾 🐾 (See Los Angeles County map on pages 48–49)

Lined with palm trees, this long, green park would be attractive enough inland, but since it's on the ocean, it's especially appealing. Dogs have to be leashed, which is only appropriate since the park is narrow and close to the road. But they still have a fun time sniffing the sea breezes and rolling on the lush lawns here.

The park is on Paseo del Mar, just west of Gaffey Street. It's a convenient place to visit if you're taking your dog to Ports O' Call or any of the other Port of Los Angeles attractions. 310/548-7671 or 310/548-7705.

96 Knoll Hill Dog Park

🐾 🐾 🐾 🐾 🐕 (See Los Angeles County map on pages 48–49)

This three-acre dog park has everything a dog could ask for, and something a dog would never think of asking for: great views of the Port of Los Angeles. Set on a hilltop above the hustle and bustle of the city, the park is a wonderful place to visit if your dog needs to burn off steam while you take a breather on one of the park's chairs or benches.

The park is divided into two sections: a two-acre section for all dogs and a one-acre section for small dogs. The parks have water stations, poop-bag dispensers, multiple fire hydrants, and some trees. There's ample parking, which is reason alone to visit in these parts.

This pooch paradise is on top of Knoll Hill—which announces itself in big white letters against the hillside—just north of the Vincent Thomas Bridge. Exit I-110 at Highway 47 and drive east. In less than a mile you'll come to the Harbor Boulevard exit, just before the bridge. Follow it north (it will actually be signed as Front Street once you exit) and make a left at the second Knoll Drive (the first Knoll Drive is a one-way street away from the hill) and head up the hill. The park is being managed and maintained by its users. They're hopeful that the city will take over one of these days. Meanwhile, if you have questions or want to contribute or help with upkeep, contact Peninsula Dog Parks, Inc., 310/514-0338; www.dogparks.org.

PLACES TO EAT

Sacred Grounds: In case you end up downtown, here's one dog-friendly downtown eatery. Desserts, pastries, and robust coffees are the specialties.

Eat, drink, and be merry with your good dog at the sidewalk tables. 399 West 6th Street; 310/514-0800.

PLACES TO STAY

Holiday Inn San Pedro—L.A. Harbor: Rates are $95–125. Dogs pay a $25 fee for the length of their stay. 111 South Gaffey Street 90731; 310/514-1414.

Vagabond Inn: Rates are $70–80. Dogs are $8 extra. 215 South Gaffey Street 90731; 310/831-8911.

Long Beach

After 36 years of a strict no-dog policy on the beach, dogs are being given their day in the sun. Depending on how things turn out, it could end up being a long, sunny day or a short chilly one. Please see Dog Beach Zone, below, for more on this long-term pilot program.

No matter how it turns out, you and your pooch can at least have your day on a ferry. Long Beach is where you can board a fast (about 75 minutes) ferry to beautiful Catalina. (See the Santa Catalina Island section for details about the ferry service.)

PARKS, BEACHES, AND RECREATION AREAS

97 Dog Beach Zone

🐾🐾🐾🐾🐕 (See Los Angeles County map on pages 48–49)

This three-acre chunk of sand and surf is the only beach in Los Angeles County that allows off-leash dogs. By the time you read this, we're hoping it has permanent off-leash status. But a parks department coordinator tells me that unless more people start following the rules during the beach's extended pilot program, doggy days here could be numbered. So here's a message to dogs: Tell your people to heed the rules. They need to scoop your poop, keep you in the off-leash section, come during the appointed hours, and not bother non-dog people.

Before heading to this 235-yard-long stretch of beach, head to your computer or phone and contact the park district (562/570-3100; www.lbparks.org) to see if dogs are even allowed on the beach anymore. You can also check the website of Haute Dogs (www.hautedogs.org), the high-energy organization that started the off-leash movement here. (While you're at the Haute Dogs site, be sure to check out the schedule for some of its fun events.)

Originally, Dog Beach Zone hours were limited to the early morning and the evening. At press time, the beach was open to dogs 6 A.M.–6 P.M. Be sure to check the hours before you set paw on the beach.

Even if the pilot program doesn't end up peachy for pooches, all may not be totally lost: "No matter what, we're hoping we can continue, at least in some manner," says Geoff Hall, of the city parks department. One scenario entails dramatically limited doggy days here—more than Haute Dogs had started with on its once-a-month permit basis, but nothing like the pilot program. "We want this to work for everyone, and we'll keep working together on this," says Geoff.

The pilot off-leash section is approximately between Roycroft and Argonne Avenues. You'll see the signs (or you won't, if dogs aren't allowed anymore). Parking at the metered beachfront lot (enter off Bennett Avenue) is a quarter per 25 minutes. You don't pay a cent after 6 P.M., though, but that's kind of a moot point with the current off-leash hours. There's also free parking along Ocean Boulevard.

A final note: If your pooch works up a powerful thirst during her escapades at the beach, be sure to visit the nearby Fountain of Woof, next to the restrooms at the end of Granada Avenue. Even if dogs no longer have their day at the beach, they'll always have their fountain by the restrooms.

🐾🐾 El Dorado Regional Park

🐾🐾🐾 (See Los Angeles County map on pages 48–49)

You and your dog can fish in the lakes here, watch dozens of ducks waddle around, stroll down shaded winding paths, or frolic together on the park's numerous huge fields of green.

Pooches have to be leashed, so it's not quite as dog heavenly as it could be. But you don't find too many 450-acre parks in these parts, so your pooch will be pleased as punch to visit here.

Fees are $3 per vehicle on weekdays, $5 on weekends and holidays, but free street parking is available on some of the side streets. Exit I-605 at Spring Street and drive west about a quarter mile to the park's entrance, on your right. The nature study area of the park, where dogs aren't allowed, is on your left. 562/570-3100.

🐾🐾 Recreation Park Dog Park

🐾🐾🐾🐾🐾 (See Los Angeles County map on pages 48–49)

Pooches passing through or living in Long Beach are extremely lucky dogs. This is an incredibly fun, attractive park for leashless dogs and their people.

The fenced park is about two acres with a few big old shade trees, 20 benches, several picnic tables, poop bags, doggy water fountains, and a small fenced area for small or shy dogs. Dogs tremble with excitement as they approach. It's wonderful to watch their joy as they bound from one end of the park to the other, somersaulting and crashing into each other with gleeful abandon.

The park is also very human friendly, with bathrooms and a water fountain for people. It's not cheap to keep up a park like this, so if you feel like donating to the cause, please put some spare change in the parking meter at the park's gate to help keep the park in good working order.

Exit I-405 at Bellflower Boulevard and drive south about two miles to 7th Street. Turn right and drive about another mile to the sign for the park's maintenance yard and dog park. Turn right again and park in the lot next to the dog run. Dogs are allowed in other parts of Recreation Park, but they must be leashed. 562/570-3100.

100 Shoreline Park

🐾🐾🐾 (See Los Angeles County map on pages 48–49)

If your dog appreciates a good view, this park's for her. More likely, she'll appreciate the potent smells to be found here.

Eyes and noses have a feast at this 40-acre shoreline park. Among the sights you can see clearly, if the smog isn't like pea soup, are Shoreline Village, the marina, and the *Queen Mary*. Among the smells dogs can snort are tracks from other dogs who frequent the park, fish being caught in the lagoon, and enticing food from nearby restaurants.

The only trees here are palms, so there's little shade on hot days. If you're going to have a picnic at the many tables, make sure you pick a cool day.

From downtown Long Beach, take Pine Street to its southernmost end and turn right. 562/570-1581.

PLACES TO EAT

Dogs are banned from the charming Shoreline Village shops and restaurants. Too bad, because it's the perfect atmosphere for well-behaved pooches and their people. But here are a few places that will make you forget about Shoreline's lack of doggy dining.

Fleur de Lis: Your dog will think he's in pooch paradise when dining at

DOG-EAR YOUR CALENDAR

If you like Easter, and your dog has a sense of humor, put the **Haute Dog Easter Parade** in Long Beach on your must-do list. Leashed pooch participants trot down the street in their Sunday best. Prize categories include best Easter hat/bonnet, best Easter attire, most whimsical outfit, best kissin' canine, longest ears, shortest tail, dog-person lookalike, and best dog legs. The parade takes place in a very dog-friendly section of town and benefits local charities. For details and this year's dates, log on to www.hautedog.org. You'll also find info there on other terrific dog events, including the Haute Dog Howl'oween Parade and an interfaith blessing of the animals. In addition, the lively and beautifully designed site features info on the Dog Beach Zone, a leash-free (at least for now) section of beach that Haute Dog has been behind all the way.

this lovely café's shaded outdoor tables on its lower terrace. From here, you get wonderful bay views. Dogs love this, because there's just something about big bodies of water that sets a dog's nose aquiver. But that's not the half of it. The Fleur de Lis staff makes sure dogs feel welcome by giving them tasty dog biscuits and big bowls of water. That puts the "wow" in bow-wow.

The food here is scrumptious. Among the mouthwatering menu items: warm brie with tomato and basil, portobello and grilled eggplant sandwich (complete with all kinds of roasted veggies), and a salad consisting of tangy grilled chicken breast, apples, caramelized walnuts, and bleu cheese, on a bed of spring lettuce tossed in a raspberry vinaigrette dressing. (Forgive me, I'm drooling.) The café is near Recreation Park and a couple of popular dog-walking areas. Open for breakfast and lunch. 335 Nieto Avenue; 562/494-4668.

Johnny Rockets: If you and your dog are fans of the '50s, you'll feel right at home at the outside tables here. Try the chocolate malted. It's really decadent. 245 Pine Avenue; 562/983-1332.

Polly's Gourmet Coffee: Sip fresh coffee and chow down on house-baked muffins and pastries at this café's patio with umbrella-topped tables. Polly's actually shares the patio with a couple of other restaurants (including Z Pizza), so your dog can smell everything from pizza to fried chicken while accompanying you for your meal. 4606 East 2nd Street; 562/433-2996.

Rubio's Baja Grill: The fresh Mexican food here is delicious and reasonably priced. If you're a seafood hound, try the lobster tacos. Dine with your dog at the restaurant's brick patio. Got a thirsty dog? The friendly servers will provide him with a bowl of water. 4702 East 2nd Street. 562/439-8317.

Z Pizza: This pizzeria may be the last one in the phone book, but it's tops with dogs. You can get every kind of pizza imaginable here. Dine at the patio Z Pizza shares with a couple of other restaurants, including Polly's Gourmet Coffee. (Or if you're staying in a nearby hotel, Z will deliver, by bicycle.) 4612 East 2nd Street; 562/987-4500.

PLACES TO STAY

It's not easy being a medium-to-large dog who needs to stay in Long Beach. Only a couple of accommodations are accommodating. The rest are for the small-dog set.

Days Inn: Ooh, your dog has to be itsy-bitsy to stay here. Fifteen pounds is the limit. At that rate, Jake Dog couldn't even get a beefy leg in the door. Rates are $70–90. Your tiny canine will cost you $10 for your entire visit. 1500 East Pacific Coast Highway 90802; 562/591-0088; www.daysinn.com.

GuestHouse Hotel: This one's close to California State University, Long Beach. Humans enjoy the outdoor "tropical" pool and attractive decor. Your stay includes a continental breakfast and passes to a health club nearby. Got kids? Try the bunk-bed rooms. Rates are $89–129. Dogs are $10 for the length of their stay. 5325 East Pacific Coast Highway 90804; 562/597-1341 or 800/990-9991; www.guesthouselb.com.

Hilton Long Beach Hotel: This used to be called the Long Beach Hilton at the World Trade Center, but 9/11 put an end to that. This is a beautiful hotel in a jazzy location. There's a big fitness center, too, in case walking your dog isn't enough exercise. (Then you can use the steam room or the pool for that spa feel.) Unfortunately, only small dogs (under 25 pounds) can stay here. Those little guys need a $100 deposit. Rates are $90–245. 701 West Ocean Boulevard 90831; 562/983-3400 or 800/445-8667; www.hilton.com.

Holiday Inn—Long Beach Airport: Rates at this retro round tower are $79–139. Dogs are $25 extra and require a $150 deposit. The only size limit: "No St. Bernard-size dogs," says management. 2640 Lakewood Boulevard 90815; 562/597-4401.

Residence Inn by Marriott: You and your small to semi-medium-size dog (pooches must be under 35 pounds) can have a very comfortable stay at this all-suite lodging. Condos and townhouses are also available. The hotel welcomes many dogs every week. It's a good place to stay if you're in town for a while, because your suite comes with many of the comforts of home, including a little kitchen area and a living room. Most rooms come with VCRs, and a few even have fireplaces.

Guests get a complimentary hot breakfast every day. Once a week the hotel hosts a fun barbecue by the pool. It's a great way to mix and mingle with other guests. The property even has two outdoor areas designated for leashed dogs to walk and do their thing. (Don't forget to scoop.)

Rates are $113–189. Dogs are $6 ($5 after 10 days) and require a $40–60 fee for the length of their stay. (The fee depends on the size of your suite.) The manager can work out a simple and fair doggy fee if you stay awhile. 4111 East Willow Street 90815; 562/595-0909; www.residenceinn.com.

The Turret House: If your dog is looking for a delectably dog-friendly getaway, The Turret House should be very high on your list of places to stay. It's a painstakingly restored 1906 Victorian that's as dog friendly as it is beautiful.

Owners Brian and Jeff, career flight attendants who cut their bed-and-breakfast teeth on an inn in coastal Maine, are some of the most welcoming hosts you and your dog will ever come across. So are their two friendly English bulldogs, Waldo and Winston, and their sweet 14-year-old chow, Alli. "They love it when we have dog guests," says Brian. "They're very good hosts." The apple doesn't fall far from the tree.

The inn itself is gorgeous, with claw-foot tubs in every bathroom and fireplaces in each of the five bedrooms. But since your dog is probably reading over your shoulder right now, let's talk about the doggy extras: Dogs are given all-natural pooch treats upon arrival. The backyard is completely fenced, and dog doors lead from the house to the yard. Well-behaved dogs get to wander around and trot outside when they need to water the grass.

What a treat! Some dogs have been known to wander out of the main house through a doggy door, across the backyard, and into Brian and Jeff's adjacent cottage through their doggy door. "We've had some fun surprise visits," says Brian.

Pet sitting and dog walking are available for an extra fee, should you decide to strike out sans dog for a while. Room rates are $99–125. The price includes an expanded continental breakfast buffet and snacks, sodas, beer, and wine. 556 Chestnut Avenue 90802; 562/624-1991 or 888/4-TURRET (888/488-7738); www.turrethouse.com.

Santa Catalina Island

Catalina is slowly becoming an easier place to vacation with your dog. Getting here with a dog has never been a problem, thanks to the ferries being so dog friendly (see the Diversion Nautical Dog!). It used to be that once you arrived on the island, there was no place to spend the night with your dog. But now two hotels permit pooches! And to add to a dog's vacation pleasure, by the time you read this, there will even be a very small dog park in the charming seaport village of Avalon—the only city on the island.

Neva Jennings, the personable former longtime president of the Avalon Humane Society, is the force behind the little leash-free area. "I've been yapping and carrying on for two years to try to get this little space," she says. The park, which was an unused patch of grass behind a skate park, will be in the middle of town—an easy walk from the ferries. Don't be expecting your typical two-acre dog park: This one will be no bigger than a very modest backyard and will have only the most basic amenities. But compared to the off-leash opportunities that existed before, it's heavenly. For info on its status, phone the city at 310/510-0220. (Neva hopes the park will be named Bark Park. Jake and I think it should be named the Neva Jennings Bark Park—not just because she helped win this little patch of land for dogs, but also because of her 21 years as president of the humane society here.)

As far as stretching your dog's legs elsewhere, it's pretty restrictive. With the exception of the magnificent and wild Catalina Island Conservancy lands and a 10-by-10-foot patch of dog-dedicated dirt on the way from the ferry to town, dogs are not allowed at any parks, beaches, or along most of Avalon's main oceanfront drag, Crescent Avenue. Be sure to carry a poop bag and some spares with you any time you're with your dog: If you're walking with your dog and you get caught without a cleanup bag in your possession (regardless of whether you've already used it and won't be needing another one), you can be fined.

If there's no room at the two dog-friendly hotels, or if you just want a little time to explore Avalon with the human you came with, Neva Jennings can help you here, too. In addition to all her other work on behalf of dogs, she

runs the Avalon Boarding Service. This is no kennel: This is Neva's own home. Happy dogs who stay with her get to make her home their home. Neva knows dogs, loves dogs, and will treat your pooch kindly and warmly. Even the most skittish dogs tend to feel content at her side.

Neva says she's "very elastic" about pick-up and drop-off times, and she'll meet you somewhere other than her home if it's easier for you. She'll even just board your pooch for the day, if that's all you need. Dog boarding starts at $15 for 24 hours, which includes high-quality pooch food and some exercise. You can phone her at 310/510-0852 or write her at P.O. Box 701, Avalon, CA 90704.

PARKS, BEACHES, AND RECREATION AREAS

If you don't know where to go, this place can be hell for a dog. It seems like every time you find a decent spot of green or beach, you also spot a "No Dogs Allowed" sign or a ranger with his hands on his hips and a frown on his lips.

But by the time you read this there will be a small off-leash area in the middle of Avalon. And lucky local water dogs know of couple of spots where pooches can do the dog paddle: Casino Point and Pebbly Beach. These are not public beaches but decent little swimming holes. We've been implored not to include directions to these unofficial dog patches in our book, because last time we did there was a backlash against dogs using them. But any local can tell you where to find them.

The bulk of the island is undeveloped. Dogs are permitted on these natural lands if they have a permit and wear a leash. See below for details.

101 Catalina Island Conservancy land

🐾🐾🐾 (See Los Angeles County map on pages 48–49)

Catalina Island is 76 square miles. A whopping 85 percent of this land is maintained by the county and by the Catalina Island Conservancy, whose mission is to keep this beautiful terrain in its natural state.

Dogs are allowed to join you on the trails here. Leashes are the law, and for good reason: Conservancy lands truly are where the buffalo roam and the deer and the antelope play. (To be more precise, it's where the American bison roam and the mule deer and black buck antelope play. But let's not get carried away with details.) It's also home to the endangered island fox and some shrews, bats, and snakes that are considered California Species of Concern—a few steps below threatened or endangered, but nothing you want your dog trying to chase down anyway. Rattlesnakes also slither about, although you'll be unlikely to see any if you stay on the trails. And poison oak is among the 600 or so plant species here, quite common in the canyons and creek beds. Keep your eyes peeled and your dog leashed and you'll enjoy a terrific hike on any of several trails that loop around the island's wild lands. There's a trail for just about every level of hiker.

Dogs aren't allowed to stay at developed campgrounds, but if you have your own boat, you'll be happy to know that your dog can join you in the primitive boat-in campsites. (Primitive as in there's no water, no bathroom, and hooray!, no tourists thronging about. You must bring your own water and your boat's portable toilet if you plan to go to the bathroom during your stay.) Rates are $12 per adult, $6 per child. Dogs are free but must be leashed or on a lead at all times. (This is a service not only to the delicate wildlife but to your dog. You might get a visit from some wild boars, and not of the crashingly-so variety.) See www.campingcatalina.com for more important boat-in camping information. Phone 310/510-3577 for reservations.

You'll need a permit to hike anywhere but Avalon. The permits are free, and they can be obtained at the conservancy office in Avalon, 125 Clarissa Avenue; 310/510-2595. Two other locales on the island also offer permits. See www.catalinaconservancy.org for details. Or phone 310/510-1421. You can get a free hiking map by sending a self-addressed stamped envelope to the Catalina Island Conservancy, Attention Visitor's Services—Hiking Map, P.O. Box 2379, Avalon, CA 90704.

PLACES TO EAT

Casino Dock Cafe: This is the only restaurant on the island that openly welcomes dogs! Dine outside, overlooking Avalon Bay, at the base of the casino. The cuisine is of the burger-seafood-chicken variety. Thirsty dogs get a bowl of water. 2 Casino Way; 310/510-2755.

DIVERSION

Nautical Dog!: Unless you have your own boat, you're going to have to rely on passenger ships to take you to Santa Catalina Island. Although dogs must be leashed and muzzled, most seem to enjoy the scenes, smells, and sounds they experience aboard these big boats. (Muzzles can be of the lightweight nylon and Velcro variety. Many dogs barely notice them.)

The *Catalina Express* is the fastest passenger boat to the island's only real town, Avalon. The excursion takes a little more than an hour. If it's foggy, however, the trip can last a long time, so the short cruise time is not a guarantee. Our last excursion to Catalina on this line took well over two hours because of the drippy September morning fog. Trips leaving from San Pedro and Long Beach cost $47.50 round-trip per adult, a little less for seniors and children. Trips leaving from Dana Point take a little longer and cost a bit more. Although you'll pay $6 to bring a bike, surfboard, or stroller on either excursion, dogs still go for free! Reservations are highly recommended. 310/519-1212; www.catalinaexpress.com.

PLACES TO STAY

Best Western Catalina Canyon Resort: This 72-room hotel permits pooches under 40 pounds. It has a pool, a day spa, and a hot tub. Nice for humans, but dogs don't care that they can't get massaged or soak their paws. They're just happy to be here. It's more than a half mile to the water, and there's no ocean view, but dogs don't care about that either. There's a restaurant on the premises, but no pooches there, please. We think dogs do care about this, but you can always get a doggy bag. Rates are $195–300. Dogs are $50 for the length of their stay. 888 Country Club Road, Avalon, CA 90704; 310/510-0325; www.bestwestern.com.

Catalina Island Conservancy Boat-In Camping: Please see Catalina Island Conservancy land, above, for camping information.

Edgewater Beachfront Hotel: Any size dog is welcome to stay at this fun and funky harborside hotel. Carlton, a very cute cocker spaniel mix, is the official hotel greeter, and can be found hanging out in the lobby most afternoons. Nothing makes you feel more at ease about bringing your dog to a hotel than having a friendly resident dog on hand. "It was like he was saying 'It's OK, come on in, we love dogs here!' when we visited," writes Jeannie, whose terrier, Smurfboy, felt utterly at home during his stay.

The rooms are all different. Our favorite has a brick wall and a nautical theme, but there are big suites with Jacuzzi tubs and several other rooms to choose from. All rooms include dual-headed shower tubs, mini fridges, microwaves, and "electric" fireplaces (this just means there's no wood, but there is a flame). The ocean-view rooms are worth the extra price, if you don't get to view much ocean where you're from. Rates are $79–300. Dogs are $50 for the length of their stay. 415 Crescent Avenue, Avalon, CA 90704; 310/510-0347; www.edgewaterbeachfronthotel.com.

138

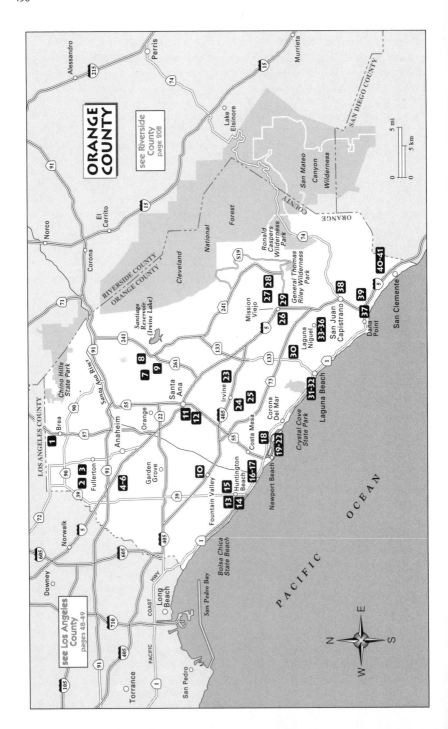

CHAPTER 3

Orange County

This is the amusement capital of America, and that's not an amusing thought to dogs. They're banned from such first-rate attractions as Disneyland and Knott's Berry Farm. But the county is also home to some dog-friendly places that just might put a grin on your pooch's rubbery lips and make a stay well worth his time.

The scent of money is unmistakable here—the land is some of the most expensive in the country. That ends up being a boon for dogs, since the communities can afford to support hundreds of parks.

Dogs are allowed at all county-run parks except wilderness parks. The only beaches that permit pooches are those of Huntington Beach, Newport Beach, and Laguna Beach, and dogs are very restricted as far as times they can visit the parks or sections they can use.

If you and your dog are salty sea dogs, make a beeline to Newport Beach's Balboa Pavilion. You can sail away with a few companies here. You won't go far—the shorter trip lasts three minutes, while the longer trip goes around the harbor for a couple of hours. But you will have a splashingly smashing good time.

PICK OF THE LITTER—ORANGE COUNTY

BEST DOG PARKS
Best Friend Dog Park, Huntington Beach (page 149)
Bark Park, Costa Mesa (page 152)
Central Bark, Irvine (page 160)

BEST LEASH-FREE BEACH
Dog Beach, Huntington Beach (page 148)

MOST SNOUT-LICKING-GOOD DOG MENU
Park Bench Cafe, Huntington Beach (page 151)

BEST FREE DOG BAGELS
Bruegger's Bagel Bakery, Newport Beach (page 158)

MOST WELCOMING RESTAURANT
Britta's, Irvine (page 161)

MOST DOG-FRIENDLY PLACES TO STAY
Westin South Coast Plaza Hotel, Costa Mesa (page 154)
Four Seasons Hotel Newport Beach, Newport Beach
(page 159)
Casa Laguna Inn, Laguna Beach (page 165)
St. Regis Monarch Beach Resort & Spa, Dana Point
(page 168)

BEST WATER ADVENTURES
Ferries and cruises, Newport Beach (page 156)

SWINGIN'EST POOCH POOL PARTY
Three Dog Bakery, Newport Beach (page 157)

NATIONAL FORESTS

The National Forests and Wilderness Areas resource at the back of this book
has important information and safety tips on visiting national forests with
your dog and has more information on the Cleveland National Forest.

Cleveland National Forest

Brea

PARKS, BEACHES, AND RECREATION AREAS

1 Carbon Canyon Regional Park

🐾🐾🐾 (See Orange County map on page 138)

This 124-acre park is nestled among the rolling foothills of the Chino Hill Range. It has the usual recreational facilities, including tennis courts, ball fields, and tot lots. But by far the favorite attraction for dogs and their people is a 10-acre grove of coastal redwoods near the Carbon Canyon Dam. Jake thinks I should mention that dogs can also check out the pepper trees, sycamores, eucalypti, and Canary Island pines. But be careful not to let the trails lead you into the adjacent Chino Hills State Park. Pooches are not permitted in most places there.

The entry fee here is $3 per car on weekdays, $5 on weekends, $7–10 on major holidays. Exit Highway 57 at Lambert Road and drive four miles east (Lambert becomes Carbon Canyon Road). The park entrance is one mile east of Valencia Avenue. 714/973-3160.

PLACES TO STAY

Hyland Motel: Small, well-trained dogs are welcome here. Rates are $55–75. 727 South Brea Boulevard 92621; 714/990-6867.

Fullerton

PARKS, BEACHES, AND RECREATION AREAS

2 Brea Dam Recreation Area

🐾🐾🐾 (See Orange County map on page 138)

Dogs love to cool their heels in the stream that winds through this 250-acre park. While there are plenty of trails throughout the park, not one runs by the stream for any significant length. But it's fairly open land with only occasional thick brush, so it's not too tough to get around.

For dogs who like trees (and what canine isn't an arborist at heart?), you'll find oaks and California bay laurel galore. When Joe Dog used to visit, he liked to picnic under a shady oak and sleep on his back, all four legs pointed straight up to the sky.

Enter at the Fullerton Tennis Center area, at Harbor Boulevard and Valencia Mesa Drive. 714/738-6300.

🖪 Craig Regional Park

🐾🐾🐾 (See Orange County map on page 138)

This natural haven's undulating tiers of green slopes create an island of tranquility right next to the bordering Highway 57. A nature trail leads for 2.2 miles through the hills and flats of the park. Pick up a brochure at the ranger kiosk and learn about the multitude of plant and animal life that hides from civilization here.

For the humans in your crew, there are facilities for basketball, softball, volleyball, and racquetball. You can picnic with your pooch or have your dog help you watch your kids at the playground.

The parking fee is $2 per car on weekdays, $4 on weekends, $5 on major holidays. The entrance is on State College Boulevard, just south of Highway 90. 714/990-0271.

PLACES TO STAY

Fullerton Marriott Hotel: If you and your pooch need to stay near California State University, Fullerton, this is the place for you. Rates are $99–159. Dogs pay a $35 cleaning fee for the length of their stay, plus a $100 deposit. 2701 East Nutwood Avenue 92631; 714/738-7800.

Anaheim

Anaheim is the home of Disneyland and just a few miles from Knott's Berry Farm, Movieland Wax Museum, Medieval Times Dinner Tournament, and Wild Bill's Western Dinner Extravaganza.

These attractions may be fun and laughs for humans, but they don't exactly make a dog howl with joy. "Who cares?" say the dogs. If humans were banned, you'd feel the same way.

If someone in your party is sick of Disneyland and has just come along for the ride, he can take the dog around while you play. Several parks make life a little easier for the canines among us.

Otherwise, if you go to Disneyland and don't have a dog sitter, you can bring your dog to the Disneyland Kennel Club for the day. Rates are $10 per day (no dogs overnight). Bring your dog's favorite toy or blanket. (The Kennel Club supplies food and water, but you can bring your own food if you prefer.) You can take a break from Fantasyland, Tomorrowland, or any of the other incredible lands and take your pooch for a leashed walk in the kennel's tiny exercise area whenever you want. For details, call 714/781-7662 or 714/781-7290.

PARKS, BEACHES, AND RECREATION AREAS

◢ Boysen Park

😺😺 (See Orange County map on page 138)

Not only is this park attractive and green, it's also fairly close to Disneyland. Leashed dogs enjoy romping in the short grass, lounging under a big shade tree, and watching the kids ride in the faux rockets in the creative playground here.

From Harbor Boulevard around Disneyland, go north several blocks and turn right on Vermont Avenue. The park is on your right in about 1.5 miles. Park on the street, or turn right on State College Boulevard and make a quick right onto Wagner Avenue, which will take you to the parking lot. 714/765-5191.

◢ Pearson Park

😺😺 (See Orange County map on page 138)

This park is a straight shot north from Disneyland. Besides all the recreational facilities, which include tennis courts and a pool, there are plenty of trees and a ducky little pond. Leashed dogs like walking in the green, grassy fields here.

From Disneyland, continue north on Harbor Boulevard for a little more than 1.5 miles. The park will be on your right, at Cypress Street. If it's too crowded here, drive up the street another six blocks and take your dog to La Palma Park, a triangular park with a winding path and palm trees. 714/765-5191.

◢ Yorba Regional Park

😺😺😺 (See Orange County map on page 138)

If you like suburban-style parks, this one's for you. There are tot lots, ball fields, and plenty of picnic areas in this 166-acre park. You can also fish at the little lakes and connecting streams or ride your bike or hike around the trails here.

The park can get very crowded, so try to visit on a weekday. Dogs must be leashed. The parking fee is $3 per car weekdays, $5 weekends, $7–10 on major holidays. From Highway 91 in the far east reaches of Anaheim, exit at Weir Canyon Road/Yorba Linda Boulevard, drive north to La Palma Avenue, and follow the signs. 714/973-6615.

PLACES TO STAY

Many of Anaheim's zillion or so hotels now permit pooches. Don't be tempted to leave your dog in your room when you go out to play for the day. It's not good for your dog, your room, or any unsuspecting housekeepers. Disneyland's kennel is a decent option and a good deal if you're doing the Disney scene. (See above.)

We don't go into much detail on the hotels here because there are so many and we'd rather give you a wide selection in this area, since rooms here can be scarce at busy times. Every hotel below has a pool, which is nice for humans but makes water dogs ache with desire.

Anaheim Marriott Hotel: Rates are $129–159. Dogs are $50 extra for the length of their stay. 700 West Convention Way 92802; 714/750-8000 or 800/228-9290.

Anaheim Plaza Hotel & Suites: Rates are $59–139. Dogs require a $50 deposit and must stay in a smoking room. 1700 South Harbor Boulevard 92802; 714/772-5900 or 800/622-6415.

Anaheim Quality Inn: Dogs must be under 50 pounds to stay here, and they pay $25 extra per visit. Rates are $70–115. 2200 South Harbor Boulevard 92802; 714/750-5211.

Canyon RV Park: This is a really attractive park, with 700 acres of wilderness and 117 campsites. But you and your dog can only come to the park if you camp. Observe the leash law here, as they've lost a couple of dogs to coyotes in the past. Sites are $27–30. Dogs are $1 extra. Reservations are required mid-May–October. From Highway 91 in the eastern part of Anaheim, exit at Gypsum Canyon Road and follow the signs to the park. Since it borders the highway, it's just a couple of minutes until you're there. To reserve a campsite, call 714/637-0210.

Clarion Anaheim Resort: Dogs need to be under 60 pounds to stay here. Rates are $90–209. Dogs pay $25 for the length of their stay. 616 Convention Way 92802; 714/750-3131; www.choicehotels.com.

Coast Anaheim Hotel: This one rates high with our dog readers, whose people love the pool and the dog fee. (There is no fee.) Dogs must stay on the first floor, and they can peruse a grassy area on hotel grounds. Rates are $89–149. 1855 South Harbor Boulevard 92802; 714/750-1811.

Embassy Suites Hotel Anaheim North: This is one of the more attractive place to stay with a dog. The hotel's gardens, complete with waterfalls and koi pond, are a welcome relief to all the plasticized perfection of Disneyland. Rates are $119–159. Dogs are $50 extra per stay. 3100 East Frontera Street 92806; 714/632-1221.

Hilton Anaheim: This luxurious hotel will allow your dog, as long as you sign (and follow) a pet agreement. Dogs must be under 85 pounds. Rates are $79–399. Dogs require a $25 deposit. 777 Convention Way 92802; 714/750-4321 or 800/916-2221.

La Quinta Inn Anaheim: Rates are $90–140. 1752 South Clementine Street 92802; 714/635-5000.

Residence Inn by Marriott: You'll feel right at home in the comfy suites here. (And you won't be stuck eating Mickey Mouse–shaped pancakes. Each suite has a kitchen.) Rates are $109–139. Dogs pay a $60 fee plus $10 per day. 1700 South Clementine Street 92802; 714/533-3555.

Sheraton Anaheim Hotel: If your dog has a long face because she can't go to Sleeping Beauty's castle in Disneyland, then stay here: This big, sprawling hotel on 13 acres has a castle-like look to it. (The lobby even features a huge stone fireplace.) Rates are $110–230. Dogs are $25 extra. 900 South Disneyland Drive 92802; 714/778-1700; www.sheratonanaheim.com.

Staybridge Suites by Holiday Inn—Anaheim Resort: All the suites at this attractive hotel here have kitchens. You get a free breakfast buffet with your stay, too. Rates are $110–235. Dogs are $150 for the length of their stay. 1915 South Manchester Avenue 92802; 714/748-7777; www.hianaheimresort.com.

Orange

PARKS, BEACHES, AND RECREATION AREAS

No dogs are permitted in any City of Orange parks.

🐾 Santiago Oaks Regional Park

🐾🐾🐾🐾 (See Orange County map on page 138)

This 350-acre wildlife reserve is dominated by majestic coast live oaks and California sycamores. Santiago Creek, the main tributary of the Santa Ana River in Orange County, runs through much of this park.

Dogs love it here, but they have to be leashed. Boy dogs seem to have a special fondness for the park, no doubt because there are thousands of ornamental trees on the north side of the creek.

Bring your binoculars. The wildlife watching is terrific. More than 130 species of birds have been observed here. Coyotes, bobcats, and mountain lions have also been known to frequent the park. If you need any extra inspiration to keep your dog leashed, that should do the trick.

The parking fee is $3 per car on weekdays, $5 on weekends, $7–10 on major holidays. From Highway 55, take the Katella Avenue exit east about 4.5 miles to Windes Drive (Katella Avenue eventually becomes Santiago Canyon Road). Turn left on Windes Drive and follow its angular turns as it leads you north to the park entrance. 714/973-6620.

🐾 Irvine Regional Park

🐾🐾🐾🐾 (See Orange County map on page 138)

This 447-acre park is home to the Orange County Zoo, but since dogs aren't allowed at the zoo, they don't care much for it. They prefer to hike along the miles of equestrian and nature trails that run through the chaparral and forests of huge oaks and sycamores.

There's something for everyone here. You can rent a horse, a pony, a bicycle, or a paddleboat. You can walk by the creek, eat lunch at shaded picnic tables, play softball, throw horseshoes, or just do nothing and take a snooze with your dog under a big old tree. Dogs usually opt for the hike, the snooze, or both.

The parking fee is $3 per car weekdays, $5 on weekends, $7–10 on major holidays. If you walk in, there is no fee. From Highway 55, take the Chapman exit and head east for about five miles to the park entrance. 714/973-6835.

🟥 Peters Canyon Regional Park

🐾🐾🐾🐾 (See Orange County map on page 138)

Dogs love this park, and for good reason: It has 358 acres of coastal sage scrub, freshwater marshes, and grasslands. Trees such as willows and black cotton-woods line the 55-acre reservoir (no dogs in the water here!) and the creek (again, no paws, please). Our favorite trail, the Peters Canyon Creek Nature Trail, takes you and your leashed dog along the creek through lush groves of trees. Jake the Water Dog thinks this is peachy.

I almost decided not to include this park in the book because of some things a park ranger told me. He said too many people allow their pooches off leash here, and that this is jeopardizing the already fragile environment, in addition to the future of dogs in the park. "Peters Canyon is a biological hot spot, an area of exceptional biodiversity in a rapidly urbanizing landscape. Studies of at-large dogs in protected areas attest to increased reproductive failure, stress, and mortality in breeding avifauna." (Jake Dog looked up this word, and it means birds.) "At least two documented nest failures last spring were directly attributed to at-large dogs here."

I finally decided to include the park because I believe it's better that people know the risks and keep their dogs leashed than if they proceed blindly and hurt the environment and eventually get dogs banned from the park. If there are some folks out there who want to form an informal "watchdog" group to let folks know about leashes, that might be just what the park ranger ordered.

If all this doesn't convince you to leash up, maybe this will: Wildlife abounds here. Included in the mix: mountain lions, rattlesnakes, bobcats, and coyotes. There's poison oak, too. So grab a leash, head for the hills, stick to the trails, and everyone will be happy. End of lecture.

The park is in the far east end of Orange. From Newport Boulevard (a few blocks south of Chapman Avenue), drive east on Canyon View Avenue to the park entrance on the right. The parking fee is $3 per car on weekdays, $5 on weekends, $7–10 on major holidays; 714/973-6620.

PLACES TO EAT

Pickle's: This deli serves great sandwiches and fries at its outdoor tables. 312 South Main Street; 714/978-6071.

Fountain Valley

PARKS, BEACHES, AND RECREATION AREAS

10 Mile Square Regional Park

🐾 🐾 🐾 (See Orange County map on page 138)

The park has many miles of scenic trails that leashed dogs love to explore. The trails go through 200 acres of grass, trees, and picnic areas. If your pooch is a sports enthusiast, take her to the fishing lakes, soccer fields, or ball fields. She's even permitted to watch from a suitable distance as folks in the large hobby area play with model rockets, remote-control airplanes, and model cars.

This is a welcome expanse of green for folks in the dense residential developments that surround the park. The parking fee is $3 per vehicle on weekdays, $5 on weekends, $7–10 on major holidays. The park is at Edinger Avenue and Euclid Street. There are entrances on both sides. 714/973-6600.

Santa Ana

It's refreshing to see that a few farm fields still thrive in the midst of this governmental center of Orange County. The downtown area is a charmer, but there's not much for a dog to do, unless he feels like soaking up history on a walking tour of the renovated district. Call the Orange County Historical Society at 714/543-8282 for information.

PARKS, BEACHES, AND RECREATION AREAS

11 Prentice Park

🐾 🐾 🐾 (See Orange County map on page 138)

While your kids are visiting the adjacent Santa Ana Zoo, you and your leashed dog are free to wander around the attractive parkland surrounding it. Dogs like the grass and picnic tables, but they're often so intoxicated by the ripe animal odors emanating from the zoo that they notice little else.

Exit I-5 at the 1st/4th Avenue exit and follow the signs to the zoo. It's at Chestnut Avenue, a few blocks east of Grand Avenue. 714/571-4200.

12 Centennial Regional Park

🐾 🐾 🐾 (See Orange County map on page 138)

If you want a real treat, get here early on a cool morning and watch the steam from the park's lake rising up through the surrounding willows. As the sun's rays turn the vapors a golden-orange hue, you'll swear you've never seen such a beautiful sight.

The sign on the lake says "No Swimming," but the ducks just don't listen. You and your leashed dog should stay high and dry, though, no matter how tempting a little wade would be on a hot summer afternoon.

The park has many big green fields, most of which are sports fields. But if you visit during a non-athletic time, you'll just about have the whole place to yourself. Walkways run throughout the park, so you and your dog can cover lots of ground with ease.

The park's main entrance is at Centennial Park and Mohawk Drives. 714/571-4200.

PLACES TO EAT

The Green Parrot Café: You and your dog will love eating and relaxing at this restaurant's enchanting Spanish-style courtyard, which features a fountain and even has ivy growing along the large arches. (Not the Golden Arches, thankfully.) The menu here changes frequently, but you're pretty much guaranteed excellent California bistro cuisine no matter what the chef is cooking that day. Thirsty dogs get a bowl of water. 2035 North Main Street; 714/550-6040.

Morton's: The Steakhouse: I guess the restaurant's subtitle is so you don't confuse it with Morton's: The Salt. The house specialty is a 24-ounce porterhouse, but the 14-ounce double-cut filet is a smash hit with some beef aficionados we know. Your dog will want to cry for joy when you bring him to Morton's patio area for this to-drool-for dining experience. 1641 West Sunflower Avenue; 714/444-4834.

PLACES TO STAY

Motel 6: Rates are $40–48 for the first adult, $6 for the second. 1623 East 1st Street 92701; 714/558-0500.

Red Roof Inn: Rates are $55–70. 2600 North Main Street 92701; 714/542-0311.

Huntington Beach

Hey, dog dude! This is the surfing capital of the Orange coast. And you're allowed off leash here! Dogabunga!

PARKS, BEACHES, AND RECREATION AREAS

🔟 Dog Beach

🐾 🐾 🐾 🐾 🐕 (See Orange County map on page 138)

It was a tough fight, but Dog Beach has finally gone to the dogs! In the end, the courts made the final decision: A three-quarter-mile strip of beach here is now off-leash heaven! Your dog needs to be in the water or on wet sand (the courts said that this territory is federal land, and that the city—which was not being terribly cooperative—didn't have jurisdiction), but there's always enough room for a great walk. You'll have a wider berth if you visit during an outgoing tide, but as Stu Black, information director for Huntington Dog Beach told us, "There is plenty of room for lots of dogs on the wet sand at all times."

Dog Beach is on the Pacific Coast Highway between 21st Street and Seaport Street. You'll recognize it by all the blissed-out dogs running around the golden sand and jumping into the surf. Be sure to bring plenty of quarters, because the parking here is all meters. At a quarter for 10 minutes, an hour here will cost you $1.50. Hours are 5 A.M.–8 P.M. every day. Be forewarned: If you stay at the parking lot past 8 P.M., you are very likely to get a ticket. The phone number for more beach info is 714/536-5281.

Until relatively recently, dogs had been in danger of losing even their leashed pooch privileges here, because too many owners seemed to think their dogs had poop privileges. The poop on the beach was getting out of hand. The problem was actually that it was never getting *into* hand, or at least into poop bags. When the city made noises about banning dogs here, a group of responsible, energetic dog people got together and formed the Preservation Society of Huntington Dog Beach. Their motto: "To preserve, protect and pick up."

Their clean-up rallies and increased signage, as well as casual spot patrols for scofflaws, started bringing dogs back into good graces with the city. At various rallies, hundreds of people came to help scoop the poop. Newspapers and TV stations got the scoop and gave the group lots of coverage. "All my life I've done important things and haven't had a lot of public notice," says society chairman Martin Senat, a dapper English gent. "All of a sudden I'm picking up dog feces and the world is watching."

The graces weren't quite good enough to convince the city, so the courts ended up making the final—and wonderful—decision. To find out what you can do to help with Dog Beach, call 714/841-8644 or check out the Dog Beach website at www.dogbeach.org. This is a very active group, with fundraisers and fun items for sale to benefit beach maintenance. Dogs around California wish to thank Martin Senat and the rest of the crew for a job very well done. Three arfs for you all!

14 Best Friend Dog Park

🐾🐾🐾🐾 🐕 (See Orange County map on page 138)

Pooches here can let down their hair and run around like the dogs they were meant to be—happy and leash-free, sniffing anywhere they want to sniff without their people getting embarrassed. The dog park is two acres within 350-acre Central Park, with mulch ground cover (for mud-free romping), fledgling trees, running water, benches for people, poop bag dispensers (they go through more than 52,000 bags a year!), and even an ocean breeze. You can see the ocean from parts of the park.

Small dogs love it here, because they have their own little fenced area. Of course, most small dogs think they're really huge dogs, so they don't need their own park. But for the more timid tiny pooch, this "park within a park within a park" offers a feeling of security.

There's even a **Doggy Walk of Fame** here. The sidewalk from the parking lot to the park's front gate is covered with more than 800 12-inch-squares of cement on which dogs have impressed their own paw prints and people have written something about their dogs. Kind of a Mann's Chinese Theatre of the canine world.

The dog park is in the west side of the park, on Edwards Street, a little north of Ellis Avenue and south of Slater Avenue. Call the Best Friend Park hotline for info on dog park activities: 714/536-5672.

Best Friend Dog Park is in beautiful Central Park. Unless you visit the park on a sunny weekend day, it isn't hard to find a peaceful place where you can be away from people and just have a restful picnic with your favorite person, your favorite book, and your favorite dog. There are lots of trees, rolling hills, and all the natural settings dogs dig.

Central Park is divided in half by Golden West Road. It's almost as if there are two separate parks. Each half even has a truly wonderful restaurant chock-full of outdoor tables (read about and then visit Alice's Breakfast in the Park and the amazing Park Bench Cafe, a must-visit for dogs). Enter the east half of the park by heading east on the entry road, just across from Rio Vista Drive. The west half is accessible by driving west on Ellis Avenue. The dog park is on Edwards Street, at Talbert. 714/848-0690.

15 Farquhar Park

🐾🐾 (See Orange County map on page 138)

This is a beautiful park just north of the dog-friendly strip of restaurants on Main Street. It's not very big, but the lush green grass and thickets of healthy palm trees create a charming place for even the most discriminating dog to lift a leg.

The park is on Main and 11th Streets. 714/536-5486.

PLACES TO EAT

Alice's Breakfast in the Park: Many folks bring their dogs to this enchanting restaurant during a Sunday morning stroll. It's in the western half of Central Park, and it has plenty of outdoor tables. The cinnamon rolls are great. 6622 Lakeview Drive; 714/848-0690.

Dwight's at the Beach: This isn't the part of the beach that allows dogs, but it's OK if dogs grab a bite at this beachside hot dog/burger/ice cream stand. (Try the cheese strips. They're superbly decadent.) 201 Pacific Coast Highway; 714/536-8083.

Ibiza Bistro: You can eat tasty Mexican cuisine here at the patio dining area with your pooch at your side. Dogs can order a bowl of fresh, cool water. 209 Main Street; 714/536-7887.

Park Bench Cafe: This extremely dog-friendly eatery warrants a write-up in the *Los Angeles Times*. It deserves to be featured on NBC *Nightly News*. The BBC could even do a nice piece on it. In fact, these news organizations and many others have been drooling over this place since owner Mike Bartusick created a dog menu and added some picnic tables just for dogs and their people in 1994.

Now dogs can drool just like the media, thanks to some snout-watering culinary treats for dogs only. The motto here is "Every Dog Has His Day at the Park Bench Cafe." On weekends, the place is jammed with dogs having their days. "It's crazy busy," says Bartusick. "I love it." With Central Park's leash-free pooch park just a bone's throw away, this place is almost always hopping.

The Canine Cuisine menu items include the Hot Diggity Dog (a plain all-beef hot dog, sans bun, cut up in doggy-size bites), the Wrangler Roundup (a juicy lean turkey burger patty, again bun-free), and Anabelle's Treat (four chopped strips of bacon). As you can see, the dog menu is much like the human menu, only with the focus more on meat, less on accessories. All pooch items are served on disposable dishes, so don't worry about finding dog slobber on your plate when you're downing your own food here.

The Park Bench Cafe, located in the shade of pine trees at the edge of Central Park, has been a dog-friendly eatery for years. Thirsty canine cruisers were invariably offered a big bowl of water when their people stopped by for a bite during a long walk through this beautiful park. Bartusick saw that many of the people were also ordering food items for their pooches. "Eventually I thought, why not have a menu where dogs are as welcome as people?" he says. "It's very California, but hey, what's wrong with that?"

The café is conveniently located at the entrance to the east side of Central Park. 17732 Golden West Street; 714/842-0775.

Super Hero's: You won't find Wonder Woman or Batman here, but these super heroes are even better: You can eat them with your dog. This is something you can't really say about Spiderman or Superman. (Unless your dog has very big jaws.) "The Godfather" is a big hit here: It's made of pastrami, salami, pepperoni, and provolone cheese, and it comes with all the delectable fixings a true Italian hero should. (Please don't say Italian hero is an oxymoron. That would hurt me in my Italian roots.)

Dogs get treated like heroes here (not the edible kind, thankfully) and get water if they're thirsty and attention if it's not too busy. Dogs enjoy the grassy area outside, where they can dine with their humans. A server told us they're thinking about giving dogs some kind of extra-special treatment, but they hadn't figured out just what. 714 Adams Avenue; 714/536-1188.

PLACES TO STAY

Unless you're a very tiny dog, you'll have to find your overnight digs elsewhere. The only dog-friendly hotel is the Hilton Waterfront Beach Resort, and all dog guests must weigh less than 10 pounds. Yipes and yips! Meanwhile, if you feel like camping, try this one:

Bolsa Chica State Beach: Your dog can come mighty close to the beach here if she joins you for a night of camping at one of the 60 sites. Fees are $25–39. The camping area turns into a parking lot by day, so don't be expecting to lounge around.

There's a small paved trail where you and your dog can go for a stroll. Sorry, pooches, but you can't set a paw on the beach itself. Fortunately, just down the sand a bit is Huntington's Dog Beach.

The state beach is on Highway 1, about three miles north of the main section of Huntington Beach. For information, call 714/846-3460. For reservations, phone 800/444-7275.

Costa Mesa

PARKS, BEACHES, AND RECREATION AREAS

16 Bark Park/TeWinkle Park Dog Run

🐾🐾🐾🐾🐕 (See Orange County map on page 138)

I met a woman who has trained her dog, Nadine, to go to the bathroom on command. The magic word is "Tinkle." It's not dignified, but it works just about every time. When she first took her dog to TeWinkle Park, a few people were talking about "TeWinkle," and sure enough, Nadine went tinkle just about every time.

Dogs can tinkle in TeWinkle, but they can also do plenty of other fun things. Now that this 50-acre park has three acres fenced for dogs, they can cavort about the dog run sans leash for hours on end. After a heated battle with the city over whether to cover the park with 12–18 inches of mulch (making life for small dogs rather difficult) or replant grass, the park users won out, and green grass is everywhere. The park is at Arlington Drive and Newport Boulevard. 714/754-5300.

17 Fairview Park

🐾🐾🐾 (See Orange County map on page 138)

The poop bags here are handsome, and the city offers them free to all dog owners. But if you need a better reason to visit the park with your pooch, try this one: It's a big, mostly undeveloped park, with dirt trails that wind through grassy, weedy areas. Your dog will have a good time sniffing around. The farther back you go, the less likely you are to run into other people.

Traveling north on Placentia Avenue, the entry road is on your left. 714/754-5300.

PLACES TO EAT

Brooklyn Pizza: This is about as close to it gets to authentic New York pizza in this neck of the woods. If you prefer juicy calzone, they've got a killer one here. The pizza chef has an exhibition kitchen and is happy to let people watch him do his craft, but your dog needs to stay outside with the other humans in your party while you watch him toss the dough like a real New Yorker. Dine with doggy at the umbrella-topped outdoor tables. Got a thirsty pooch? They'll give her a bowl of water. 2278 Newport Boulevard; 949/646-9399.

California Wrap & Grill: You can get just about anything in a wrap here, including steak and potatoes, Thai chicken and veggies, and salmon. Next on the menu should be the Dog Biscuit Wrap. Why not? Dogs are welcome at the 20 partly shaded outdoor tables and would love a wrap to call their own. 250 East 17th Street; 949/548-4403.

Diedrich Coffee: This is a happening place for dogs. "We get lots of good dogs. They're the best," one server said. On pleasant days, the big windows here are wide open, so if you don't want to find an outdoor seat for you and your pooch, you (the human) can sit inside by a window and pat your outside dog on the head. (It helps if you order him a really buttery pastry.) 474 East 17th Street; 949/646-0323.

Gypsy Den Café: Located at the wonderfully different Lab Anti-Mall, the Gypsy Den serves up some great veggie food as well as "light carnivorous cuisine," as one employee puts it. Dine with your dog at the many outdoor tables, which come with heat lamps when needed. 2930 North Bristol Street; 714/549-7012.

DIVERSION

Take Your Lab to The Lab: Dogs are welcome to cruise around with you as you peruse **The Lab Anti-Mall** in Costa Mesa. The Lab is kind of the flipside of malls. It's mellow. It's artsy. It's cutting edge. It's a dog's kind of place. "You're never going to see as many people with tattoos and pierced body parts as you'll see here," says Mary Bavry, who has frequented The Lab for years with her sweet dogs. "But dogs sure do feel welcome."

The stores are not what you'd find at the Fashion Island mall. The Lab has hipster and progressive clothing stores, edgy gift stores, and Dr. Freeclouds, a popular underground electronic music store. Many stores will let your pooch inside to shop with you. The **Gypsy Den** café permits pooches at its outside table.

The Lab is at 2930 North Bristol Street; 714/966-6660; www .thelab.com.

Ruby's Diner: This small local chain has good old-fashioned, somewhat greasy, delicious diner food. Dine with your doggy on our favorite, "frings" (a combo of fries and onion rings for the indecisive) and grilled cheese, at the four umbrella-topped tables near the entrance. 428 East 17th Street; 949/646-RUBY (949/646-7829).

Side Street Cafe: Want to dine on decadent, delectable food with your dear dog? Come to this café's four umbrella-topped tables for breakfast and order the stuffed French toast. "Cheapskates welcome," says a server. The prices are indeed good for what you get. 1799 Newport Boulevard; 949/650-1986.

PLACES TO STAY

Best Western Newport Mesa Inn: Rates are $160–180. Dogs are $25 extra. 2642 Newport Boulevard 92627; 949/650-3020 or 800/554-2378.

La Quinta Motor Inn: Dogs must be under 25 pounds to stay here. Rates are $91–111. 1515 South Coast Drive 92626; 714/957-5841.

Ramada Inn: Stay here with your little dog (25 pounds and under only) and you get a complimentary continental breakfast, a free *USA Today* (my alma mater), a heated pool and spa, a fitness room, and a pleasant guest room. This is all fine and dandy with your dog (at least the muffins at breakfast are of some interest), but what dogs really enjoy about this place is that there's a Trader Joe's adjacent to it. If you can't figure out why your dog might be pawing you to go in Trader Joe's direction, I'll give you a hint: Dog treats are delicious and plentiful at TJ's, and inexpensive too. Grab a bag of rawhides or a box of peanut butter biscuits, and your stay at this hotel will be one your dog will look back on fondly. Rates are $79–129. 1680 Superior Avenue 92627; 949/645-2221 or 800/272-6232; www.ramadalimitednewport.com.

Vagabond Inn: Rates are $59–80. Dogs are $5 extra. 3205 Harbor Boulevard 92626; 714/557-8360.

Westin South Coast Plaza Hotel: The rooms are spacious and well-appointed, the beds are heavenly (truly—the Heavenly Bed is the cornerstone of the hotel's luxury comfort reputation), and the luxury amenities are top-rate. But what small-to-midsize model dogs (40 pounds or less is the rule here) dig most is that they get the royal treatment: Guest dogs receive treats upon check-in, plus use of dog bowls and the pooch equivalent of the Heavenly Bed: the Heavenly Dog Bed. After a restful night on the king of dog beds, your dog can stretch his gams at a park across the street. Rates are $109–209. 686 Anton Boulevard 92626; 714/540-2500; www.westin.com.

Newport Beach and Corona del Mar

If your dog enjoys the water-dog lifestyle, he's sure to love Newport Beach. Between the beaches, bays, and boats, many watery adventures await any dog who doesn't get seasick while watching you fill the bathtub.

The city encompasses several communities, including Balboa Island, Corona del Mar, and Mariners Mile. Balboa Island has its own section in this chapter.

PARKS, BEACHES, AND RECREATION AREAS

18 Upper Newport Bay Regional Park

🐾🐾🐾 (See Orange County map on page 138)

Upper Newport Bay is surrounded by shopping centers and suburban sprawl, but fortunately, this large park preserves the remaining sanctity of the once-pristine bayside. The myriad dirt trails in this open, hilly area provide you and your leashed dog with a great way to get around. Dog footprints are embedded in the trails—evidence of happy pooches on muddy days.

The park is made up of tall grasses and twiggy weeds. No trees get in the way of the bird-watching here. Bring your binoculars and try to ignore the tall office buildings in the distance. You can also do some excellent, up-close bird-watching from Back Bay Road, on the east side of the bay. But it's easier to get to the regional park section, and it's less stress for the birds if you keep

DIVERSION

Go Island Shopping: Dogs are a normal part of the scene at **Fashion Island,** Newport Beach's huge open-air shopping mall. There's plenty of walking room and even some grassy areas where your dog can rest her weary paws. Some of the mall's 200 stores permit pooches inside, but since they do it on a case-by-case basis, we'll let you explore for yourself. (FYI, should you be looking for lingerie, Victoria's Secret allows any well-behaved dog. "We've had our share of mishaps, but we still welcome dogs here," says a manager.)

Be sure to stop by the concierge desk with your dog. Most concierge staff love dogs and will supply your dog with a treat. As an added bonus, the mall is just a bone's throw away from Upper Newport Bay Regional Park, a great place to drop after you shop. Fashion Island is on the Pacific Coast Highway (Highway 1), between Jamboree Road and MacArthur Boulevard (Veterans Memorial Highway). 949/721-2000.

DIVERSION

A Three-Minute Tour: The historic **Balboa Pavilion/Balboa Fun Zone** in Newport Beach is where you and your dog can embark on nautical adventures on two unique boat lines. This is one of our favorite places to go with pooches because they're so welcome on these vessels. It's easy for your dog to feel like one of the family here. Best of all, pooches go for free on both excursions.

The smaller of these boats is the **Balboa Island Ferry,** which is open-hulled and fits only three cars and a few passengers at a time. The trip from Newport Beach to lovely Balboa Island takes only a few minutes, but it's a good way to test if your dog is up for a longer journey on the other dog-friendly boat line here. Fees range from 35 cents for a walk-on passenger to $1 for a car and passenger. The ferries run every few minutes during daylight hours.

Dogs with a more nautical bent can join you for a howling good time on a cruise of Newport Harbor—one of the nation's finest yacht harbors. The **Fun Zone Boat Company** offers a couple of grand tours. On one, you'll see the homes and yachts of celebrities and learn the history of the area. On the other tour, you'll cruise up to the haunts of the vocal, local sea lions. "The sea lions are fascinated by the dogs, and the dogs are fascinated by the sea lions," says Captain Mike. "It's quite a sight." Each tour is 45 minutes long and costs $7 per adult and $2 per child. Or take a 90-minute tour that combines both of the shorter jaunts. It costs $9 per adult and $2 per child. Call 949/673-0240.

your dog far from them. The poor birds have enough on their minds with the onward march of malls and suburban subdivisions.

Traveling north on Irvine Avenue, turn right on University Drive. About the equivalent of a block down the road, turn around and park on the other side of the street (there's no parking on the south side), then walk back across the street and to the park entrance. 949/644-3151.

🔟 Balboa Beach

🐾🐾🐾 (See Orange County map on page 138)

Balboa Beach is wide and sandy enough for a dog to forget that it's a dog's life. The only reminders here are the mandatory leash attire and the restricted dog-access hours. Dogs are permitted year-round these days (a big improvement over the previous ban on dogs in summer), 6–9 A.M. and after 5 P.M.

The beach runs from around Main Street to the West Jetty area. You can enter the beach at the ends of many of the streets. 949/644-3047.

DIVERSION

Swimwear Optional: Visit the **Three Dog Bakery,** and you may find dogs in bathing suits (or naked—gasp!). Or they may be wearing board shorts. Or wacky Halloween costumes. Anything is possible. The bakery's owner, Sandy, and her labs Storm and Jag, think up all kinds of fun events for their dog customers. Pool parties (three wading pools in the parking lot, a pet psychic, and a toenail-painting groomer were among the attractions at a recent pool party attended by 200 dogs), luaus, and various seasonal parties are the norm here. And now, once a month, the bakery is home to a pet adoption fair. On the best day so far, 21 lucky dogs and cats and an iguana found new homes.

The fresh-baked dog goodies at this bakery are so good, and the service so doggone dog friendly (read: they get a free treat), that dogs have been known to tear into here, leaving their people scratching their own heads about the location of their canine. They always sniff them out, though. And once your dog enters, you may be hard-pressed to get her to leave. Sandy says that sometimes a dog's people have to bribe the stubborn (and smart) pooch out with dog delicacies.

The bakery is in Newport Beach's upscale Corona del Mar Plaza, 924 Avocado Street; 949/760-3647.

20 Corona del Mar State Beach

🐾🐾🐾 (See Orange County map on page 138)

Fear not! Although this is a state beach, dogs are permitted to peruse the place. That's because the city of Newport Beach maintains it and makes most of the rules. Dogs can sample the sandy life daily 6–9 A.M. and after 5 P.M.

If you happen to be east of the eastern jetty at the entrance to Newport Harbor, you'll be happy to know that this large and popular beach also permits leashed pooches. The beach starts at the eastern jetty at the entrance to Newport Harbor. 949/644-3047.

21 Newport Beach

🐾🐾🐾 (See Orange County map on page 138)

This beach starts out quite narrow at the northern border of Newport Beach and widens as it continues south to around Main Street. You'll have fun watching the surfers surf and the sun worshippers sizzle to a golden brown.

The only problem is that during the times when dogs are allowed, there's not a whole lot of sun to worship. Dogs, who must be leashed, can enjoy the beach daily 6–9 A.M. and after 5 P.M.

Many dogs, including Jake, enjoy hanging out by the pier area and grabbing a bite from the nearby restaurants. Your dog will, too. (Jake asked me to write that on behalf of his pooch friends in the area.) 949/644-3047.

22 Peninsula Park

 (See Orange County map on page 138)

It's 9:01 A.M. and your dog is looking at you with those "I really need to go for a walk" eyes. You've narrowly missed the dogs-OK hours at the nearby beaches (6–9 A.M.), and your dog can't cross his legs until the beaches become dog friendly again (5 P.M.). What to do? One option is to sniff out this square-block park. It's nothing special, but dogs don't care about special when their next chance for a walk is eight hours later.

The park is west of Ocean Front Avenue, just south of the Balboa Pier. It's flat and grassy, with a band shell, baseball diamonds, a playground, and picnic tables. There's not much shade, but the ocean breeze usually cools things off enough. 949/644-3047.

PLACES TO EAT

Alta Coffee: The large gazebo outside the restaurant is a terrific place for you and your pooch to sip the great coffee and dine on the café's tasty soups, pastas, and pastries. In fact, the gazebo is packed with lucky dogs every weekend, according to a manager. We've also heard it's a great place to sniff out potential romance (with your dog first introducing you to someone else's dog, and then, of course, the dog's person). If your dog is thirsting for something more quenching than love, a bowl of water will be provided on request. 506 31st Street; 949/675-0233.

Bibi Anna's: "We get a lot of dogs here," a personable server told us. "Just yesterday this woman ordered pancakes for herself and an extra order for her dog. That dog looked real happy." Dogs and their people are welcome to dine at the lovely white-tablecloth-topped shaded sidewalk tables. The cuisine is traditional American with a flavorful, fairly healthful bent. In other words, I suppose, California cuisine. (Try the blackened ahi with teriyaki peanut sauce, and a grilled artichoke appetizer. The parmesan-crusted chicken is also delicious.) Bibi Anna's is on the Balboa peninsula, at 205 Main Street; 949/675-8146.

Bluewater Grill Seafood Restaurant & Oyster Bar: Dine with your salty dog at this classic New England–style seafood house on the waterfront. The mesquite-charbroiled seafood is truly droolworthy. Your dog can join you at the patio tables, and if she's thirsty, she'll get a bowl of water. 630 Lido Park Drive; 949/675-3474.

Bruegger's Bagel Bakery: If you don't have a dog, you may feel positively naked here. This terrific bagelry is so doggone dog friendly that on weekends, you can find up to a couple dozen dogs at a time hanging out on and around

Bruegger's wraparound porch. Dogs love it here, not only because they get to chat with each other and socialize with other humans, but because Bruegger's treats dogs like kings: Dogs who visit get a free bagel! And not even a day-old bagel—a fresh one. The bagels are delicious, so your dog will be a lucky dog indeed if he gets to accompany you here. George Dog and his person JoAnna Downey told us about this place. A big thanks to them! (George Dog is the one with the poppy seeds stuck between his teeth.) Dogs also get fresh water. This is a four-paw, must-visit destination. 2743 East Pacific Coast Highway; 949/723-4485.

Sabatino's Sicilian Restaurant: The Sicilian cuisine here is *fantastico.* Jake highly recommends the sausages, although the lasagna is to drool for, too. Dogs get to dine very close to you, but they have to be tied on the other side of the shrubbery "railing." Plus they can't join you for dinner because of the crowds. But the lunches here are *delizioso.* If your dog's snout looks dry, they'll likely offer him a bowl of cool water. 251 Shipyard Way; 949/723-0621.

PLACES TO STAY

Your dog has to be a wee one to stay at the only two dog-friendly hotels here. The hotels are lovely, but if you have a medium or large dog, sniff around somewhere else for your lodgings.

Four Seasons Hotel Newport Beach: This glorious five-diamond hotel rolls out the plush red carpet for dog guests, who must be under 25 pounds: They get a little welcome card when they arrive and receive doggy biscuits,

even doggy dishes with their names on them. This sumptuous hotel is a breathtakingly luxurious urban oasis for humans, but since the size limit rules out most dogs reading this book, we won't devote more space to the details. You can find out more at www.fourseasons.com/newportbeach. 690 Newport Center Drive 92660; 949/759-0808.

The Sutton Place Hotel: Dogs must be under 25 pounds to stay at this large hotel, and they pay $50 extra for the length of their stay. Rates are $135–180. 4500 MacArthur Boulevard 92660; 949/476-2001; www.suttonplace.com.

Irvine

PARKS, BEACHES, AND RECREATION AREAS

23 Central Bark

😊😊😊😊 🐕 (See Orange County map on page 138)

With a whopping three acres of off-leash romping room, Central Bark is one of the largest dog parks in Southern California. It's a big fenced field with a smaller fenced area for small or shy dogs. There's not much in the way of trees here, but in the summer people bring a tarp and canopies for shade.

Central Bark is a very popular spot, and it includes all the dog-park accoutrements, including doggy fountains, lights, poop bags, and even faux fire hydrants. If your dog isn't the only one who has to lift a leg while you're at the park, you'll be happy to know that restrooms are available for humans, too.

The park is open every day except Wednesday, when it's closed for maintenance. It can get mucky and muddy here in the rainy months, and if it's bad enough, the park will close for the day or a few days. If in doubt, phone 949/724-MUDD (949/724-6833) for updates on park closures. The park is at 6405 Oak Canyon, one driveway past the Irvine Animal Care Center. 949/724-7740.

24 William R. Mason Regional Park

😊😊😊 (See Orange County map on page 138)

If you're a local University of California dog and you need to get away from campus for a few hours, tell your owner about this county park. Three miles of hiking and biking trails wind through the park's eastern wilderness. It's a great escape from the urban realities lurking just outside the park's perimeter.

The park has the usual human recreational facilities, as well as one unusual one: a Frisbee golf course. It's a good thing dogs have to be leashed, or it would be pure, unbridled, ecstatic mayhem among the retrieving pooches here.

The parking fee is $3 per car on weekdays, $5 on weekends, $7–10 on major holidays. You don't have to pay a thing if you walk in. The park is at University and Culver Drives. 949/923-2220.

25 Turtle Rock Park

🐾🐾 (See Orange County map on page 138)

During the week, this 20-acre park gets little use. That's what makes it so comfortable for dogs. Leashed pooches can walk around the hills and flats of the park with little danger of getting hit by a foul ball.

The park is on Turtle Rock Drive at Sunnyhill, between the suburbs and the San Joaquin Hills. 949/854-8144.

PLACES TO EAT

Britta's: Interestingly, we have a Brittany spaniel to thank for telling us about this super-dog-friendly spot. "My mom thought maybe it was named after me. You know, Britta-Brittany?" writes Brenda, an alliterating Brittany who adores Britta's. Dogs who visit Britta's partly shaded patio get pooch biscuits, and if thirsty, water. People who come here get terrific food. For breakfast, try the hot granola brulée. It's snout-lickin' good. 4237 Campus Drive; 949/509-1211.

Champagne French Bakery Cafe: The quiches, croissant sandwiches, French onion soup, and salad Niçoise are delectably Franco-American (not in the Uh-Oh Spaghettio sense), but you'll also find a big variety of non-French foods here. If you're in the mood for a decadent pastry, look no further. The sweets are divine. Thirsty dogs get water when you dine at the patio. The café is at Woodbridge Center, at 4628 Barranca Parkway; 949/653-6828.

PLACES TO STAY

Candlewood Suites: If your dog needs plenty of room, the spacious suites here will fill the bill. There's even a walking trail around the hotel's property. Rates are $80–150. Dogs must be under 70 pounds and are $75 extra for a stay of up to two weeks, and $150 extra for more than two weeks. 16150 Sand Canyon Avenue 92618; 949/788-0500 or 800/946-6200; www .candlewoodsuites.com.

Hilton Irvine/Orange County Airport: Rates at this attractive hotel are $149–219. Dogs are $50 extra per visit. 18800 MacArthur Boulevard 92612; 949/833-9999.

Irvine Marriott Hotel: This fancy hotel permits pups of every poundage. Rates are $80–160. 18000 Von Karman Avenue 92715; 949/553-0100.

La Quinta Inn: Some of the rooms here are architecturally fascinating—one of the buildings used to be a lima bean silo! Really. You must see this place for yourself. Rates are $89–99. 14972 Sand Canyon Avenue 92718; 949/551-0909.

Residence Inn Irving Spectrum: Stay in a suite and you can cook for yourself and your dog in a nice little kitchen. Rates are $140–200. Dogs pay $60–80 per stay plus $10 extra daily. 10 Morgan Street 92618; 949/380-3000.

Laguna Woods

PARKS, BEACHES, AND RECREATION AREAS

26 Laguna Woods Dog Park

🐾🐾🐾🐕 (See Orange County map on page 138)

This is a pretty little dog park with some shade trees (hey, it's Laguna Woods, after all) that provide welcome relief from the summer sun. Dogs are provided with water and poop bags. The list of rules on the park's website says that dog tags must be "worm and visible," which I hope is a typo.

If your big dog is a morning dog, you'll have to take her elsewhere for her early constitutional: The park is open only to small dogs 8 A.M.–1 P.M. Small and large dogs can run about here 1–7 P.M. The park is on Ridge Route between Moulton Parkway and Avenida de Carlotta. 949/452-0600.

Mission Viejo

PARKS, BEACHES, AND RECREATION AREAS

27 Wilderness Glen Park

🐾🐾🐾 (See Orange County map on page 138)

At certain times of year, a creek rushes through this narrow, two-mile-long wooded park and provides a refreshing escape from the surrounding suburbs. This is a hidden, unmarked park that most people just drive past without realizing it's there. It's in a narrow canyon, surrounded by lush foliage. A trail follows the creek, so you and your leashed dog can have a waterside sojourn. You can even dip all your feet in the water to cool off on a warm afternoon.

The park is bordered by Los Alisos Boulevard on the east side. You can enter the park at many points by turning left on any street that runs into the park. Our favorite is Via Noveno. Park around Atomo Drive and walk down the wooden stairs into the park. 949/470-3000.

28 O'Neill Regional Park

🐾🐾🐾🐾 (See Orange County map on page 138)

So close to suburbia, and yet so far, this is the paws-down favorite Orange County park for dogs who like wilderness. Dogs are not permitted in the county's true wilderness parks, but for some reason, this 1,700-acre piece of lush land doesn't fall into that category.

Dogs love to hike along the 6.5 miles of trails that go past streamside oak and sycamore woodlands. They have to be leashed, which is something the mountain lions here don't appreciate. Besides the woodlands, you can peruse grassy meadows and shrub-covered hillsides. And if you're in a hungry mood, the area near the entryway has plenty of picnic tables. You supply the food and the park will supply the ambience.

Camping is available along the creek and in the higher elevation Mesa Camp area. There are 90 campsites, all first-come, first-served. Fees are $15–17. Camping pooches are $2 extra. If you're just here for the day, you'll be charged a parking fee of $3 per car on weekdays, $5 on weekends, $7–10 on major holidays.

Follow El Toro Road (in the city's northernmost reaches) northeast. It eventually turns into Live Oak Canyon Road and veers to the south. About three miles past where the road changes names, you'll come to the park's main entrance. It's just south of the Rama Krishna Monastery, on the right side of the road. 949/923-2260.

29 Oso Viejo Park

 (See Orange County map on page 138)

It can get mighty crowded here on days when the sports fields are jammed with ball players. But you can almost always find an escape by heading to the creek that runs along the northwest side of the park. There, you'll find some trees, shrubs, and enough room for you and your dog to sit down and read a good book. Make sure to keep your dog on leash, because rattlesnakes and mountain lions have been seen here.

The park is on La Paz Road at Oso Viejo, just east of Marguerite Drive. 949/470-3000.

PLACES TO STAY

O'Neill Regional Park: See O'Neill Regional Park, above, for camping information.

Balboa Island

This small Newport Harbor island is a bayfront wonderland. You can drive here from the mainland, but dogs prefer to take the ferry from Newport Beach. The island isn't exactly replete with big parks, but dogs enjoy strolling down Bayfront to the Grand Canal and back. When you've worked up a big hunger, head for the dog-friendly Park Avenue Cafe, not far away.

PLACES TO EAT

Park Avenue Cafe: Dogs are welcome to dine at one of the two tree-shaded patios with you, and boy do they like it here. It may have something to do with the thick steaks, steaming racks of lamb, and other assorted goodies. (Just a hunch.) 501 Park Avenue; 949/673-3830.

Wilma's Patio: This homey, attractive, family restaurant is beloved for its breakfasts. You and your happy pooch will drool over the Balboa Belly Bomber, a warm French roll stuffed with an egg. ("This woman bought herself one and her dog one the other day," a server told us. "The dog ate his in, like, five seconds.") Dogs can't actually eat at the namesake patio at Wilma's Patio, but they can join you for a meal at the two shaded front tables. 203 Marine Avenue; 949/675-5542.

Laguna Beach

Exclusive but friendly, Laguna Beach has an unmistakable Mediterranean feel, thanks to the mild seaside climate and all the fine art galleries and outdoor cafés. Dogs are happy here, especially because of a fine off-leash dog run.

PARKS, BEACHES, AND RECREATION AREAS

30 Bark Park/Laguna Beach Dog Run

🐾🐾🐾🐾 🐕 (See Orange County map on page 138)

People come from many miles away to take their dogs to this fenced-in dog-exercise area in the canyon. During dog rush hour, it's not uncommon to see dozens of leashless, grinning dogs running and tumbling around in great joy.

Although there's no shade, there's plenty of doggy drinking water. Picnic tables add a dimension of comfort for the park's humans.

The park has to close periodically because of the danger of mudslides, so if you're traveling a long way to get here, call the city first to check on the situation. In addition, we've heard that there was quite the problem with poop. The city had to come in and haul it out in huge barrels. Park people have apparently been doing a better job of scooping since that ugly day.

From Highway 1, go north on Broadway/Laguna Canyon Road. The park will be on your right in 2.6 miles, just before the GTE building. 949/497-0706.

31 Heisler Park

🐾🐾 (See Orange County map on page 138)

The landscaping is lovely and the view is just as good. This small, palm-filled park sits on a bluff just above Picnic Beach. Dogs must be leashed, but they enjoy cruising around here during the times they're restricted from the beaches.

The park runs from Canyon Drive to Broadway/Laguna Canyon Road, just west of Cliff Drive. 949/497-0706.

32 Laguna Beach Beaches

🐾🐾🐾 (See Orange County map on page 138)

Leashed dogs can peruse the beaches, but June–mid-September, their visiting times are limited. During that period, pooches aren't allowed on the beach 8 A.M.–6 P.M.

Main Beach is a long, sandy beach with a playground and basketball courts. A good entry point is just south of the Heisler Park area (see above). If you want to get away from people, you may be better off at any of the pocket beaches dotting the city's coast. There are also several small, rocky pocket beaches you can reach via walkways off Cliff Drive. 949/497-0706.

PLACES TO EAT

A La Carte: You and your dog are welcome to dine on the patio of this pink restaurant. With 16 different entrées (not to mention numerous salads and desserts), it's likely that no one will go away hungry. And your dog surely won't go away thirsty, because if she asks for a bowl of water, they'll be happy to bring her one. 1915 South Coast Highway; 949/497-4927.

Cafe Zinc: This place is just one outdoor table after another. At times, reports café regular Mary Bavry, "there's a dog at every table." Don't trip, and try the apple spice muffins. (Thirsty dogs can get a big bowl of fresh water.) 350 Ocean Avenue; 949/494-6302.

Cottage Restaurant: As long as you and the pooch sit on the outer rim of the patio, the folks here will be happy to see you. 308 North Coast Highway; 949/494-3023.

Subway: There are plenty of benches for you and the hungry pooch. 1350 South Coast Highway; 949/376-1995.

PLACES TO STAY

Carriage House: Only the most well-behaved dogs are welcome here, and only if you call ahead of time and get the OK. After all, it's not every day a dog gets to stay in a 1920s bed-and-breakfast that's a historic landmark. You'll get a carafe of wine, some fresh fruit, and other taste treats when you check in. The courtyard here is lovely and relaxing, but no leg lifts, please. Rates are $140–175. Dogs are $10 extra. The friendly folks here will help you arrange a pet sitter if you find yourself in need of some pooch-free time. 1322 Catalina Street 92651; 949/494-8945 or 888/335-8945; www.carriagehouse.com.

Casa Laguna Inn: The Casa Laguna is an enchanting, romantic Spanish-style bed-and-breakfast that overlooks the mighty Pacific Ocean. Its 15 rooms, four suites, Mission House, and charming cottage are set on a terraced hillside. Surrounding the lodgings are luscious tropical gardens that include such goodies as banana and avocado trees and bougainvillea. Well-behaved dogs and their people love to relax on the aviary patio, beneath a family of glorious queen palms.

There are many little nooks and gardens to discover at the Casa Laguna, and your dog will enjoy helping you find them all. As the day ends, watch the sun set over Catalina Island.

Dog guests feel very welcome here: Upon check-in they get a doggy food bowl and a water bowl, some pooch treats, and a list of nearby dog-friendly parks. Rates are $130–350 and include an extensive buffet breakfast and afternoon wine with hors d'oeuvres. Dogs are $25 extra. 2510 South Coast Highway 92651; 949/494-2996 or 800/233-0449; www.casalaguna.com.

Vacation Village: Dogs love staying at this vacation oasis, because they're allowed on the beach, which is right behind the hotel. Leashed pooches can peruse the beach here anytime it's open to dogs (see Laguna Beach Beaches, above, for dog-OK times). Humans like the fact that there's full beach service, complete with towels and lounge chairs. Usually, however, sunbathing and dogs don't mix. The hotel's restricted dog times (they're not allowed in from the last week of June through Labor Day) certainly decrease the temptation to get tan with your dog.

If you (the human in your party) want to swim but find the surf a bit rough, the hotel has two pools for your paddling pleasure.

Rates are $85–349. There's a $10 pooch fee per visit. 647 South Coast Highway 92651; 949/494-8566 or 800/843-6895; www.vacationvillage.com.

Laguna Niguel

PARKS, BEACHES, AND RECREATION AREAS

33 Aliso/Wood Canyons Regional Park

🐾 🐾 (See Orange County map on page 138)

Since dogs aren't permitted in county wilderness areas, they're banned from the Wood Canyon section of this 2,500-acre park. But because Aliso Canyon isn't considered wilderness, leashed dogs are welcome. The good news is that about two-thirds of the acreage is in Aliso Canyon. The 13-mile-long Aliso Creek Trail takes you and your pooch through some very scenic areas, but unless you're both in extraordinary shape, you won't want to tackle the whole thing.

The "eh" news is that Aliso Canyon is brushy and scrubby, with none of the wonderful trees that grace Wood Canyon. One school of thought behind the contrasting landscapes is that back around 1776, when Father Junípero Serra was building missions, his men may have denuded this canyon to create the San Juan Capistrano Mission. The county is considering reforesting the canyon, but it's an expensive task.

The parking fee is $3 per car on weekdays, $5 on weekends, $7–10 on major holidays. There's an entrance to the park off Alicia Parkway, just west of town. Call 949/923-2240 for directions to specific parts of the park.

34 Crown Valley Community Park

🐾 🐾 🐾 (See Orange County map on page 138)

It's so peaceful here that it's hard to believe you're in a community park. The park is fairly large, with green hills, lots of trees, and trails that wind through all this splendor. You and your leashed dog will enjoy the tranquility here.

The park is on the west side of Crown Valley Parkway, just north of Niguel Road. 949/362-4350.

35 Laguna Niguel Regional Park

👣👣👣 (See Orange County map on page 138)

A big chunk of the accessible land here is devoted to a lake where you and your leashed dog can fish for rainbow trout from shore. It's a fun pastime, but dogs can get bored just watching you cast and reel in all day.

If your dog needs a hiking break, the equestrian trail here isn't a bad place for a walk. Parts of it are too close to La Paz Road for traffic-free ambience, but other sections (especially the trail far west of the lake) are more secluded. You'll be shaded by eucalyptus trees and acacias as you hike up and down the rolling hills.

From Crown Valley Parkway, turn northwest on La Paz Road and follow the signs to the entrance. The parking fee is $2 per car on weekdays, $4 on weekends, $5 on major holidays. If you walk in, it's free. 949/831-2791.

36 Pooch Park

👣👣👣🐕 (See Orange County map on page 138)

It's only a bit over one acre, and it has only three small trees, but to dogs who long to run unfettered by a leash, this fenced park is poochy paradise.

Pooch Park is gobs of fun for dogs on the go. It's at the top of a canyon, and it's got the coolest dog-watering area yet. If your dog is Lassie, or a Lassie wannabe, she can press a lever with her paw and drink the water as it streams several inches into the air. Or she can let the water fill a strategically placed water bowl. Of course, if she's like Joe Dog was, she can accidentally step on the paw-activated fountain, get splashed in the face, and have the heebie-jeebies for the rest of the afternoon.

No longer grassy, the park is filled with wood chips. It can be a little tough on tender paws, but it's easier to maintain than grass, and it's not as splintery as it sounds. Humans enjoy the shaded sitting areas under attractive canopies and sun umbrellas on hot days. Dogs do, too.

The park is on the west side of Street of the Golden Lantern, between Beacon Hill Way and Chapparosa Park Road (closer to Beacon Hill Way). My faithful correspondent "Three-Dog-Dave" Hepperly tells me there are now signs stating "Dog Park Parking," which make the entrance easier to find than it used to be. 949/362-4350.

Dana Point

PARKS, BEACHES, AND RECREATION AREAS

Dogs are not allowed in any beaches here or at any Dana Point city park. The city's adventure-loving namesake, Richard Henry Dana Jr., who wrote the high-seas novel *Two Years Before the Mast*, probably wouldn't have liked Dana Point's attitude. But he's been dead for more than a century, so there's little he can do about it.

37 Lantern Bay Park

 (See Orange County map on page 138)

Since this is a county park, pooches are permitted. It's a beautiful stretch of grass and trees set high above the ocean. Paved walkways meander throughout and there are picnic tables galore. Leashed dogs love to sniff the sea breezes and watch the gulls.

From Highway 1, turn toward the beach on Harbor Drive and make a right onto Lantern Street. 949/248-3530.

PLACES TO EAT

Hennessey's: Dogs who come to this fun tavern and eatery "get water always, get treats sometimes, and get lots of attention from the staff if we're not too busy," says a friendly manager. Drink and dine with your happy dog at the partly covered tables outside. 34111 La Plaza; 949/488-0121.

PLACES TO STAY

Doheny State Beach: Dogs can't go on the long sandy beach here, but if you camp with them at one of the 122 sites, they can hang out on the grassy area of the park. They can pay a whopping day-use fee of $10 (per vehicle) to explore for a few hours, but it's better to make a real vacation of it and camp here. Some campsites border the beach. Rates are $21–31. From Highway 1, turn toward the beach on Harbor Drive and make a left onto Lantern Street. Call 949/496-6171 for information, or call 800/444-7275 for reservations.

Laguna Cliffs Marriott Resort and Spa: The rooms at this spectacular hotel are very attractively appointed, with a fresh, colorful decor that even an artful dog could appreciate. Some overlook the shining Pacific. (Even if your room doesn't, the two pools do.) You can bring any size dog here "as long as it isn't noisy or yappy," says a front desk employee. Rates are $250–415. Dogs are $75 extra per stay. 25135 Park Lantern 92629; 949/661-5000.

St. Regis Monarch Beach Resort & Spa: Oh, to drool for! This five-diamond ultra-luxury resort hotel has everything you could want in a sumptuous seaside vacation, from to-die-for rooms to a private beach club to pampering spa treatments. There's no size limit for humans, but alas, dog guests here are limited to 30 pounds. Little dogs get treated well here and are provided with a doggy bed, cute little dishes, and bone treats. Rates are not cheap, with rooms starting at $410. Dogs are $75 for the length of their stay. One Monarch Beach Resort 92629; 949/234-3200 or 800/722-1543; www.stregismb.com.

San Juan Capistrano

The rebuilt version of the mission that was constructed by Father Junípero Serra in 1776 attracts some 300,000 visitors annually. Around March 19 every year, the swallows arrive from Argentina to nest in the valley. They used to flock to the mission, but with recent noisy renovations and hordes of visitors, they've taken to other parts of the valley. "They've gone to the suburbs, just like humans," says one docent.

Dogs aren't allowed on the grounds of the mission, but you can watch this annual migration from just about anywhere in town. It's not as dramatic as Alfred Hitchcock's *The Birds,* but it's still a great way to pass a lazy afternoon in one of the parks here.

PARKS, BEACHES, AND RECREATION AREAS

38 C. Russell Cook Park

🐾🐾🐾 (See Orange County map on page 138)

Big old trees line the perimeter of this park, where you and your leashed dog may choose to amble along the shaded path near the creek bed.

If your dog likes his paws to hit green grass with every step, hang out on the greenbelt area. You'll find ball fields and playgrounds, but you'll also find some open areas where you can get away from other folks.

The park is on Calle Arroyo and stretches for several blocks between Calle del Campo and Avenida Siega. 949/493-5911.

39 Acu Park

🐾🐾 (See Orange County map on page 138)

This park is about 11 blocks long but only a couple of blocks wide. When the park isn't packed with people, you and your leashed pooch can cruise through the soccer fields, play in the open areas, or picnic at the many tables here. Trees surround the park, but there's not much shade in the heart of the park.

The park is between Connemara Drive and Camino Las Ramblas and Kinkerry and Pescador Lanes. 949/493-5911.

PLACES TO EAT

Cedar Creek Inn: You and your history-loving dog can dine at the lovely, big, tree-shaded patio that faces Mission San Juan Capistrano. The fresh fish is delicious, as are the house-made desserts. 26860 Ortega Highway; 949/240-2229.

PLACES TO STAY

Best Western Capistrano Inn: "Smallish" dogs only, please. The hotel offers a complimentary breakfast to humans on weekdays. (Actually, it's a breakfast voucher for Denny's.) Rates are $70–130. Dogs are $25 extra. 27174 Ortega Highway 92675; 949/493-5661.

San Clemente

San Clemente has become a very dog-friendly place. Dogs have now an off-leash park to call their own. And they can also set paw in three city parks (Calasia Park, Mira Costa Park, and Verde Park)—a feat their feet had never known. City park decisionmakers were considering allowing leashed dogs in all parks; call 949/361-8264 for updates on this great development.

PARKS, BEACHES, AND RECREATION AREAS

40 Rancho San Clemente Ridgeline Trail

🐾🐾🐾 (See Orange County map on page 138)

The views from this three-mile trail are to drool for: At certain points you and your leashed dog can see the mighty Pacific, Catalina, and even some parts of San Diego. If you venture to the highest parts of the park (a 700-foot elevation), you can even see Los Angeles County, in all its smoggy splendor. You'll hike through brush and grass, with not much in the way of shade trees. Bring plenty of water.

Mountain bikes share the trail, so keep your eyes peeled and your leash ready to reel in your dog. There are several entrance points, including one at Avenida Salvador, from Avenida Presidio or East Avenida San Juan, and

one at Calle Cordillera, off Calle Amanecer. If you happen to be going to the dog park and want to get a little exercise yourself, you can start at a fire road behind the dog park. 949/361-8278.

41 San Clemente Dog Park

🐾🐾🐾🐕 (See Orange County map on page 138)

When it first opened, this fenced dog park got a lot of publicity about being a park for canine senior citizens. Everyone from national radio stations to the *Los Angeles Times* called it a "gerontological dog park," where 80-year-old dogs could sniff around and not have to roughhouse.

Well, it's kind of true, but really a media-induced exaggeration of something many of the new breed of dog parks have: a separate section for small dogs or dogs who just don't want to race around with the big ones. The main part of the park is for any good dog; the smaller is for little, shy, or older dogs.

The park is a terrific little gem with all the good dog-park amenities, including benches, some shade, water, and poop bags. It's not terribly big, but dogs—young and old—have a great time here. It's at Calle Extremo and Avenida La Pata; 949/361-8278.

PLACES TO EAT

Antoine's Cafe: Dine on tasty French and American food (mostly American, with some Frenchish offerings like quiche) at several umbrella-topped sidewalk tables. Thirsty dogs get a bowl of water. 218 South El Camino Real; 949/492-1763.

Beach Garden Cafe: The views from the outdoor tables are gorgeous, and the breakfast and lunch fare is just as delectable. 618$^{1}/_{2}$ Avenida Victoria; 949/498-8145.

Pacific Taste: If your dog is dying for sweet and sour pork or spring rolls, take her to the two patio tables here and partake in some tasty Chinese food. 223-A Avenida Del Mar; 949/366-0809.

PLACES TO STAY

Holiday Inn San Clemente: If you're lucky, you might get a room with an ocean view here. Rates are $159–225. Dogs are $10 extra. 111 South Avenida de Estrella 92672; 949/361-3000.

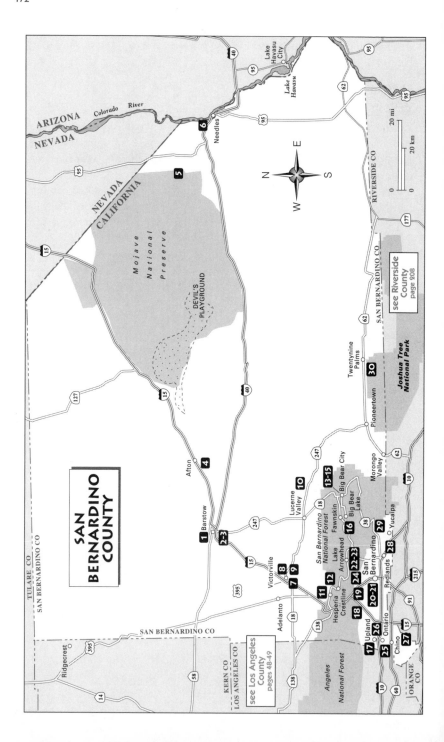

CHAPTER 4

San Bernardino County

This is the Texas of California. It's just plain big. In fact, it's the biggest county in the nation, weighing in at more than 20,000 square miles.

That means you'll find a lot of variety here. This is where dogs can do just about everything they ever imagined a dog could do. They can ride the rails through a ghost town, roam around off leash on millions of acres of land, herd goats in Chino, take a horse-and-buggy ride in Big Bear, ride a rented boat around Big Bear Lake, and stay in some of the most wonderful cabins and resorts this side of the Rockies.

Try to visit the San Bernardino Mountains at sunset, when occasionally they play an optical trick. A few of the mountains will turn purplish pink, while others stay the same sandy brown and forest green. Then everything fades into a surreal orange mist. For people, it's a stunning sight. If dogs really do have black-and-white vision, they're probably not quite so thrilled.·

PICK OF THE LITTER—SAN BERNARDINO COUNTY

BEST OFF-LEASH HIKING
San Bernardino National Forest (page 174)
Rainbow Basin Natural Area, Barstow (page 176)
Stoddard Valley Open Area, Barstow (page 177)

BEST DOG PARK
Wildwood Dog Park, San Bernardino (page 194)

MOST DOG-FRIENDLY PLACE TO EAT
Wolfgang Puck Café, Ontario (page 200)

MOST DOG-FRIENDLY PLACES TO STAY
Cienaga Creek Ranch Mountain Cottages, Big Bear Lake (page 189)
Eagle's Nest Bed & Breakfast Lodge, Big Bear Lake (page 189)
Arrowhead Tree Top Lodge, Lake Arrowhead (page 197)
Rimrock Ranch Cabins, Pioneertown (page 206)

MOST WELCOMING STORE
Big Dogs Sportswear, Lake Arrowhead (page 196)

BEST LIVE "THEATER"
Pioneertown Posse's Old West skits, Pioneertown (page 206)

NATIONAL FORESTS

The National Forests and Wilderness Areas resource at the back of this book has important information and safety tips on visiting national forests with your dog and has more information on San Bernardino National Forest.

San Bernardino National Forest

Much of the southwest corner of San Bernardino County is San Bernardino National Forest land. So far, dogs are allowed off leash in most parts of the forest, except for several times when they meet up with state parks. (Dogs aren't even allowed there *on* leash.) Unfortunately, local national forest rangers are facing the question of whether off-leash rules are appropriate in the forest. Complaints about dogs running up to frightened humans or fighting with each other have led to this dilemma. So make absolutely certain your dog is Mr., Mrs., or Ms. Obedience before taking off that leash.

On the way up to Big Bear Lake via Highway 38, you'll find numerous forest trailheads and picnic areas that make great rest stops on a long journey. See the Big Bear Lake section in this chapter for more on this popular resort area.

NATIONAL PARKS

Joshua Tree National Park
🐾🐾🐾

Although most of this 794,000-acre park is in Riverside County, Twentynine Palms is where you'll find the visitor center and the gateways to some of the most beautiful areas in the park. (See the Twentynine Palms section later in this chapter.)

This is amazing land, with striking granite formations rising around dramatic desert plants and wildlife. In spring, it becomes a showcase of brilliant wildflowers. The giant Joshua tree plants are in the higher western half, and they're definitely worth a visit.

Dogs can be walked on paved and dirt roads, but not on hiking trails. They're permitted to wander on leash up to 100 yards from the road, and there are plenty of small dirt roads where you'll be far from most traffic. Leashes are the law here, but they're also a very good idea because of critters like mountain lions and bobcats. A bigger danger than those cats is actually the cactus. Dogs sometimes rub up against the prickly plants or try to bite them and end up with a major problem. One last warning: The ground here can get really toasty—sometimes too toasty for your dog's paws. If you wouldn't want to walk barefoot here, neither would your dog. Rangers report several cases of paw pad injury each year because of the hot ground. Come when it's cooler and you'll be better off.

There's a $10 entrance fee, and if you want to camp without water, it's $5. Otherwise, sites are $8–10. There are 492 sites available on a first-come, first-served basis. However, the 100 sites at Black Rock Canyon require reservations. Always bring lots of water on your hikes here, and make sure your dog gets her fill. It doesn't usually get nearly as hot as in other parts of the desert, but don't take a chance. From I-10, exit at Highway 62 and drive northeast for about 39 miles to the town of Twentynine Palms. The visitor center is on Utah Trail, just south of the highway about a mile east of town. 760/367-5500.

Barstow

This is a mighty dog-friendly town. In fact, it's just the place for a bruised canine ego to go after stepping on one too many threadbare doggy welcome mats. The folks here generally like dogs at least as much as they like people.

PARKS, BEACHES, AND RECREATION AREAS

1 Rainbow Basin Natural Area

🐾🐾🐾🐾🐾 (See San Bernardino County map on page 172)

If you and your dog like bones, faults, sediment deposits, or leash-free walks, don't miss this geological and anthropological wonder. Fossils of ancient animals are everywhere in the colorful sedimentary layers of the canyon walls (once a lake). Mastodons, camels, three-toed horses, rhinos, and dog-bears are among the animals whose remains have been discovered here. As you hike around, you'll see insect fossils that are among the best-preserved in the world. You and your dog need to keep your paws off these fossils so they remain undisturbed for others to enjoy.

The geology of the place is also fascinating. Rainbow Basin's sediment deposits are textbook examples of folds, faults, and other disturbances of the earth's crust. If you're studying geology in school, this is the place to visit if you want to get the big picture.

Unfortunately, your dog probably doesn't give a hoot about bones she can't eat and sediment she can't wallow in. She knows what's important—being able to be at your side, off leash, while you peruse the area. The Bureau of Land Management, which operates the park, has some of the most lenient, dog-friendly rules in the state for obedient pooches.

The best place to take an off-leash dog is any flat area where she won't have much chance of disturbing this national natural landmark. There are no developed paths or trails, but since the place is nearly devoid of trees and thick underbrush, it's easy to navigate a course almost anywhere here. Be aware that you may run across desert kit foxes and bobcats. If you can't control your dog with critters like these around, keep her leashed. And make sure she goes nowhere near desert tortoises, the California state reptile (bet your dog didn't know that). Tortoises are easily traumatized, and contact with people or dogs could lead to their death.

For your pet's sake, don't visit in the summer. Our favorite time to hike here is in late autumn, when it's crisp but not freezing. Leashed dogs are allowed to camp with you at the 22-site Owl Canyon Campground (no hookups). The fee is $4 per vehicle. No reservations are necessary.

From Highway 58 in Barstow, drive 5.5 miles north on Fort Irwin Road and turn left on Fossil Bed Road. It's a rough dirt road, and it will seem like an

DIVERSION

Go West, Young Pup: How many dogs can say they watched an Old West shootout on a dusty saloon-packed street? How many can brag they rode aboard a train through a ghost town?

Your leashed dog can be that lucky dog, if you take her to **Calico Ghost Town.** Calico thrived during the 1880s silver boom, and you can still roam around silver mines and stroll along wooden sidewalks on Main Street.

If you're a fan of this era, spend the night. Camping costs $18–22. There are about 260 campsites. Reservations are recommended in spring and fall. Or rent one of the six cabins in town. They're not haunted, but the price is so low you'll howl for joy: $28 for up to four people. A $25 deposit is required.

Admission to Calico Ghost Town Regional Park is $6, $3 for children ages 6–15. Train rides are $2.50, $1.25 for children. Dawgs are a buck. From Barstow, drive about six miles east on I-15 and exit at Calico Ghost Town/Ghost Town Road. Drive north three miles. When you see a yellow wagon, you'll know you're there. 760/254-2122; www.calico.com.

eternity of bouncing before you reach your destination, but it's actually just three miles. 760/252-6060.

❷ Foglesong Park

🐾🐾 (See San Bernardino County map on page 172)

This is a decent-sized city park with plenty of shade for those searing summer days. The kids will like the playground, and the dogs are sure to enjoy the open grassy fields. Enter at Avenue G, just north of Nancy Street. 760/252-4800.

❸ Stoddard Valley Open Area

🐾🐾🐾🐾🐕 (See San Bernardino County map on page 172)

Is your dog tired of those five-acre parks where leashes are a must? Does she long for wide-open desert ranges where she can tear around without a care in the world (except rattlesnakes and their friends)?

This 52,000-acre parcel of land just southeast of Barstow could be the answer to her poochie prayers. Not only are there mountains and endless open areas, there are also plenty of fascinating rock formations for you and your dog to explore.

To enter at the northern end, where there's a campground, exit I-15 at Sidewinder Road and drive the only way the road takes you. The campground has no developed sites, and no reservations or permits are required. The public land here is interspersed with private land, but Bureau of Land Management folks say unless an area is fenced off, posted, or developed, it's probably OK for hiking. 760/252-6060.

PLACES TO EAT

Foster's Freeze: The soft-serve ice cream here is to drool for. Dine on tasty frozen treats and basic burger cuisine at the outdoor tables. 1580 West Main Street; 760/256-8842.

PLACES TO STAY

There's no shortage of dog-friendly lodgings in Barstow.

Best Motel: Rates are $30–40. 1281 East Main Street 92311; 760/256-6836.

Econo Lodge: Rates are $35–55. Dogs are $5 extra. 1230 East Main Street 92311; 760/256-2133.

Executive Inn: Rates are $27–35. Dogs are $5 extra. 1261 East Main Street 92311; 760/256-7581.

Gateway Motel: Rates are $36–55. Dogs are $10 extra. 1630 East Main Street 92311; 760/256-8931.

Quality Inn: The folks here really like dogs. But because of guests' allergies, you'll have to stay in a room designated for smokers. Rates are $50–110. 1520 East Main Street 92311; 760/256-6891.

Rainbow Basin Natural Area: See Rainbow Basin Natural Area, above, for camping information.

Stoddard Valley Open Area: See Stoddard Valley Open Area, above, for camping information.

Afton

PARKS, BEACHES, AND RECREATION AREAS

🐾 Afton Canyon Natural Area

🐾🐾🐾🐾 (See San Bernardino County map on page 172)

Wow! Woof! How does 42,000 acres of land sound to you and your canine companion? If you don't demand lush green meadows to be part of your elysian ideal, this can be heaven on earth.

Afton Canyon is one of only three places where the Mojave River flows above ground year-round, so not only has it attracted visitors throughout history, it's also a water dog's delight. If you don't expect fine fishing here, no one will be disappointed.

Keep in mind that hundreds of bird, mammal, and reptile species call Afton Canyon their home, or at least their migratory hotel. It's a great place for wildlife watching, and you need to keep leashed.

Camping here isn't the prettiest, but it's a convenient place to spend the night. Sites (there are no hookups) are $6. There are 22 sites available on a first-come, first-served basis.

Afton is about 40 miles east of Barstow. From I-15, exit at Afton Canyon Road and drive three miles south to the park. 760/252-6060.

PLACES TO STAY

Afton Canyon Natural Area: See Afton Canyon Natural Area, above, for camping information.

Needles

Named for the sharp peaks at the southern end of the valley, this Colorado River town is surrounded by some of the most fascinating desert landscapes in the world.

If all the wide-open territory near Needles makes you and your dog feel like insignificant specks in the universe, try a side trip to London Bridge, just down the road a bit in Lake Havasu City, Arizona. This is the same London Bridge that was sinking into the Thames River in 1962, until developers of this town bought it for $2.5 million and shipped it to the United States—granite block by granite block. Your dog can go back home and tell all his buddies that he visited London Bridge, and they'll be impressed (most of them think it's still in London). English springer spaniels get a misty, faraway look when they come here.

PARKS, BEACHES, AND RECREATION AREAS

🐾 Mojave National Preserve

🐾🐾🐾🐾 (See San Bernardino County map on page 172)

The next time your dog gives you one of those sideways glances that says "I gotta get outta the city," you might want to consider spending a few days exploring a desert environment that seems to go on forever. It actually does go on forever, or at least for 1.5 million acres to the west and north of Needles, whichever comes first.

Within this gigantic swath of land are volcanic cinder cones, booming sand dunes, old mines, new mines, mysterious petroglyphs, and dramatic cliffs. If you're a newcomer to desert life, you'll find the wildflowers, cacti, and yucca fascinating.

Dogs must be leashed here, now that the once leash-free land has been transferred from the dog-loving Bureau of Land Management to the National Park Service. Fortunately, the Park Service designated it a preserve rather than a park, so dogs are still allowed in many areas. They can join you for a jaunt along the many miles of old mining roads, but they're not permitted on the trails. And they're not allowed in the designated wilderness area unless they're hunting with you, and then they may hunt off leash. (Hunting just doesn't work well with leashes.)

Keep in mind that nearly 300 species of animals live here, including coyotes and Mojave green rattlesnakes. Since these rattlers are more aggressive than most other rattlers, and since dogs have been known to be a coyote delicacy, it's extra inspiration to keep your dog close at paw.

Camping ranges from no cost for wilderness camping to $12 for regular sites. Dogs must be leashed at the campgrounds. There are 65 campsites available on a first-come, first-served basis. The preserve can be entered at several points along I-40 and several points along I-15. Call 760/733-4040 to find out which entrance would best suit your travel plans.

6 Moabi Regional Park/Park Moabi

🐾🐾🐾 (See San Bernardino County map on page 172)

If your dog likes the water, tell her that the Colorado River runs through this park. If she's a landlubber, let her know that most of the park is lawns and desert land. There's something for most tastes at this 1,025-acre county park, but it's not always the quietest place in the world. Anglers can become frustrated with all the personal watercraft and fast boats that cruise around here. To have the run of the lake, try renting a houseboat from the park's marina. It's loads of fun, and all your dog has to do to go for a swim is hop out the back door.

There's a $6-per-vehicle day-use fee. Camping at the 130 sites is $12–25 (the pricier sites are on the river). Dogs are $1 extra. The park is at the intersection of I-40 and Park Moabi Road. 760/326-3831.

PLACES TO EAT

Burger Hut: Sure, you can get their traditional beef burgers, but vegetarians will be happy to know that they also serve a mean veggie burger here. 701 Broadway; 760/326-2342.

Jack-in-the-Box: It's so refreshing to find a dog-friendly link in a restaurant chain. This one allows pooches to dine at the 12 outdoor tables, and they'll even supply your dog with water. 221 J Street; 760/326-4746.

PLACES TO STAY

Best Western Colorado River Inn: Enjoy the hotel's heated indoor pool, the sauna, and a small exercise room (without your dog, of course). Dogs have to stay in the smoking rooms here, which is convenient if your dog smokes. Rates are $63–70. Pooches pay a $25 deposit. 2271 West Broadway 92363; 760/326-4552.

Moabi Regional Park: See Moabi Regional Park, above, for camping information.

Mojave National Preserve: See Mojave National Preserve, above, for camping information.

River Valley Motor Lodge: If your dog is small and has short hair, the management here will be mighty accommodating. Otherwise, you'll find there's no room at the inn. Rates are $25–40. Dogs are $5 extra. 1707 West Broadway 92363; 760/326-3839.

Victorville

PARKS, BEACHES, AND RECREATION AREAS

7 Center Street Park

🐾🐾 (See San Bernardino County map on page 172)

While it's only a couple of blocks long, this park is Victorville's most attractive municipal park. It's full of trees, so there's plenty of shade and plenty of places for your leashed dog to sniff. And it's usually quiet, except when there's a ball game going on at one of the playing fields.

Exit I-15 at Mojave Drive and go east a little more than a mile to Hesperia Road. The park is on your right. 760/955-5257.

8 Eva Dell Park

🐾 (See San Bernardino County map on page 172)

This park is literally on the other side of the tracks. Just a couple of blocks from the railroad tracks, it's not in the most desirable part of town. Nor is it the most desirable park. It's got a rough, dusty feel. But if you find yourself in this part of town with a pooch who's got to go, the fenced-in ball fields aren't bad. Keep in mind that dogs are supposed to be leashed.

Eva Dell Park is just above the Mojave River (tough access, though). Take D Street to 6th Street and drive northeast, following the signs to the park. 760/955-5257.

⑨ Mojave Narrows Regional Park

🐾🐾🐾   (See San Bernardino County map on page 172)

This 840-acre park is by far the largest park in the area. It's kind of triangular, bordered on the left by railroad tracks and on the right by the Mojave River. The rangers tell that to people hiking with dogs, lest they get a little lost in their eagerness to get back to nature.

There are plenty of fields here, but the best place for walking around with your leashed dog is the more forested part of the park. If you're an angler with a dog who likes to cheer you on as you cast for supper, you'll be happy to know there's fishing year-round for $3 per day.

Camping costs $10–17. Dogs are $1 extra. There are approximately 65 campsites available. Reservations are recommended, and there's a $2 reservation fee. The park's day-use fee is $3 per vehicle, $1 per dog. From I-15, take the Bear Valley Cutoff exit and drive east for five miles. When you come to the railroad track overpass, turn left at Ridgecrest Road. Drive three miles north to the park. 760/245-2226.

PLACES TO STAY

Mojave Narrows Regional Park: See Mojave Narrows Regional Park, above, for camping information.

Ramada Inn: The Ramada website says that this big Ramada is the only full-service hotel "in the High Dessert" with indoor corridors. Yum, I've always wanted to spend a night or two in a dessert. But I suppose that "desert" is the real word, alas. The rooms are standard motel/hotel fare, but the outdoor pool is a real plus, as is the free continental breakfast. Rates are $75–90. Dogs are $20 extra. 15494 Palmdale Road 92392; 760/245-6565.

Red Roof Inn: This motel is conveniently close to Mojave Narrows Regional Park. Rates are $55–79. 13409 Mariposa Road 92392; 760/241-1577.

Lucerne Valley

PARKS, BEACHES, AND RECREATION AREAS

🔟 Johnson Valley Open Area

🐾🐾🐾🐾🐕 (See San Bernardino County map on page 172)

If city life has your dog tied in knots, a visit to the Johnson Valley Open Area is bound to unkink him. There's nothing like 250,000 acres of leashless terrain—including mountains, scrubby desert, dry lakes, sand dunes, and rock formations—to take the "d" out of "doldrums" and put it back in "dog."

While you may not run into any other people during your visit, keep in mind that much of this land is OK for off-highway vehicles to cruise. If you hear one of these loud beasts coming, make sure your dog is close by. Some dog owners like to put something bright orange on their dog just in case. Also be aware that coyotes are not unheard of around here. Don't let your dog wander far from you.

There are many access points to this huge acreage. One good bet is to exit Highway 247 at Bessemer Mine Road and drive north a few miles. Big signs will show you the way. The public land here is interspersed with private land, but Bureau of Land Management folks say unless an area is fenced off, posted, or developed, it's probably OK for hiking. 760/252-6000.

Hesperia

PARKS, BEACHES, AND RECREATION AREAS

1️⃣1️⃣ Hesperia Lake Park

🐾🐾🐾 (See San Bernardino County map on page 172)

Most people visit this 200-acre park to nab a trout or catfish out of the seven-acre lake. But since dogs aren't allowed on the lake bank, or in the lake, it's probably not the activity of choice if you're looking for something you can do with your pooch at your side.

The park has plenty of trees for shade and leg lifts, plus sports fields and playgrounds for the humans in the family. Look for the small waterfall, which feeds a meandering rock-lined stream that eventually leads to the lake. It's a great spot to stop for a picnic.

While there's no day-use fee, you'll be charged $10 to fish. Camping is $20–25, and dogs are $2 extra. The 58 campsites are set near the lake. The campsites can be reserved, but are available on a first-come, first-served basis. Although there's a sign for this park from the Bear Valley Cutoff exit of I-15, don't be fooled into thinking it's just off the highway, especially if your dog is getting that glazed look that tells you he can wait no longer. The park is actually several miles southeast of the exit. The route is complicated, but the signage is excellent, so follow the brown signs all the way. 760/244-5951.

12 Silverwood Lake State Recreation Area

🐾🐾🐾🐾 (See San Bernardino County map on page 172)

Got a water dog? This is a fine place for a little dog paddle. The park used to ban dogs from being in the water, even on a boat. But now pooches can swim or join you on your boat while you fish or putter around the 1,000-acre lake. They're supposed to be leashed, but at least they can get their paws wet.

Landlubbing dogs are happy to know 2,500-acre park has 13 miles of paved hiking/biking trails. You'll go through high chaparral country here, with all the bushes and trees a boy dog could ever dream of claiming for himself. And if that's not enough, you can head over to the national forest land on the lake's east side and hike forever.

Dogs must be leashed at Silverwood Lake. There are coyotes and bobcats and bears, oh my. Camping costs $20 a night. There are 131 sites available on a first-come, first-served basis. (Reservations are required in the summer.) Call 800/444-7275 for reservations. The day-use fee for the park is $8 per vehicle. From the Crestline area, 10 miles north of San Bernardino, take I-15 to Highway 138 and drive east about 11 miles on Highway 138 to the park. 760/389-2281 or 760/389-2303.

PLACES TO STAY

Days Inn Suites—Hesperia/Victorville: Fill your belly at the free extended continental breakfast and out you go for a day of adventuring with poochface. Rates are $65–110. Dogs are $7 extra. 14865 Bear Valley Road 92345; 760/948-0600.

Hesperia Lake Park: See Hesperia Lake Park, above, for camping information.

Mojave River Forks Regional Park: This 1,100-acre patch of high desert land has 80 campsites and five group areas available. Sites are $8–15. Dogs are $1 extra. If you camp here, you can hike, explore the often-dry Mojave River, and have access to the nearby Pacific Crest Trail. Be sure not to miss the Santa Fe Mormon Trail, complete with ruins. The park is on Highway 173 between Silverwood Lake and Hesperia; 760/389-2322.

Silverwood Lake State Recreation Area: See Silverwood Lake State Recreation Area, above, for camping information.

Big Bear Lake

This lakeside mountain resort community isn't exactly Lake Tahoe, but that's part of its charm. It's generally more rustic, more natural, and far less crowded. The crisp, clean alpine air is a godsend any time of year.

The town's old-fashioned honesty and lack of smooth public relations pros is evident as soon as you approach the old village section. There, you'll see a road sign for skiing, with an arrow pointing to the left. Immediately below that is a sign for the hospital, with an arrow pointing to the right. It's not a joke.

This is a very dog-friendly community, complete with incomparable off-leash hikes, great restaurants, and charming lodgings where dogs are as welcome as their chauffeurs. Check out the old Big Bear Lake village. It gives a new meaning to old-style charm.

PARKS, BEACHES, AND RECREATION AREAS

Although this book doesn't normally go into detail on specific trails in national forests, we're mentioning a few here because they're so integral to your pooch having a doggone good time in the Big Bear Lake area. (Sadly, these used to be off leash, but leashes are now the law.)

DIVERSION

Whatever Floats Your Boat: A great way to explore **Big Bear Lake** with your dog is to do it by boat. A couple of marinas will rent you and your dog a variety of boats, with the proviso that you try not to let your dog have any little accidents on board. (Take frequent land breaks if your dog has a small bladder or has just eaten.) Pontoon boats are probably the most fun for dogs, because they're big, slow, and stable. Aluminum fishing boats are an option for fairly calm dogs who won't wriggle themselves into the drink with excitement when you land a big one. Very mellow dogs can even find out the answer to the age-old question: Can you canoe? (If your dog isn't a swimmer, she should wear a doggy life jacket on any boat. Even if she is a swimmer, it's not a bad idea, especially on a tippy canoe ride.)

Holloway's Marina (398 Edgemoor Road; 909/866-5706 or 800/448-5335; www.bigbearboating.com) rents fishing and pontoon boats. Big Bear Marina (500 Paine Road; 909/866-3218; www.bigbearmarina.com) rents fishing boats, pontoon boats, pedal boats, and canoes. You could also rent a Wave Runner water scooter with your dog, but don't.

DIVERSION

Get Hitched, with Your Dog's Help: The Big Bear **Hitching Post Wedding Chapel** is a dog's kind of marriage sanctuary. It's got a mountain/Western theme and no overly frilly froufrou.

Owners John and TraCee Green have played host to canine ring bearers, canine bridesmaids, and canine best men. A former owner said once he even helped a dog sign a marriage certificate (not the license, though). "We just put his paw on the ink pad, then stamped the certificate. He was a smart dog, but his penmanship wasn't good enough to sign his name," he said.

The Greens ask that dogs attend only midweek weddings. On busy days like Saturday, they don't have enough time to vacuum up dog hairs, and a few people visiting after dogs participated have complained about their allergies flaring up.

The fee for getting hitched here is $95 and includes the chapel and a donation for the minister. Licenses are extra. For more information, call 909/584-1030 or 800/828-4433 or write them at P.O. Box 1583, Big Bear Lake, CA 92314; www.bigbearweddings.com.

13 Cougar Crest Trail

🐾🐾🐾🐾 (See San Bernardino County map on page 172)

This two-mile trail goes through a mixed conifer section of San Bernardino National Forest. It's full of juniper, Jeffrey pine, and pinyon. Obedient dogs used to be able to go leash-free, but no more.

We like it best here in late autumn, when a dusting of snow rests on the pine needles and the air is crisp. We've never run into another person on the trail during this time of year. Cougar Crest Trail eventually connects with the Pacific Crest Trail, which traverses 39 miles of the Big Bear area. The scenery is outstanding.

From Big Bear Lake village, cross the lake at the Stanfield Cutoff and turn left on Highway 38. As you drive west, the trail is just over a half mile west of the ranger station, on the right side of the road. There's plenty of parking. 909/866-3437.

14 Pedal Path

🐾🐾🐾🐾 (See San Bernardino County map on page 172)

Here's one way to hike the Big Bear Lake area without roughing it too much. This six-mile paved path allows you and your leashed, lake-loving dog to hike along the scenic north shore of Big Bear Lake.

Sometimes bikers think they own the trail (it is called Pedal Path, not Four-

DIVERSION

Catch a Stagecoach: If you and your little varmint have a hankerin' to be part of the Old West, hanker no longer! Michael Homan and his trusty **Bear Valley Stage Lines** in Big Bear Lake will take you and your dog and up to 12 other people on a 15-minute ride around town in a stagecoach so genuine it looks like John Wayne ought to be at the reins. Dogs will want to sit up front with Homan, who wears Western clothes. But it's not Homan they want to be near. It's the horses. Actually, the horses' rears, to be exact.

Enough of that. Adults are $8, children are $4. Dogs don't pay a cent. Homan says you'll need to be able to lift your dog up 3.5 feet to get him inside the stagecoach (it's a high entrance). The stagecoach stand is on Village Drive across from Chad's Place. No reservations needed. Homan also can hitch a beautiful carriage to some beautiful horses, should you care to go on a more elegant, intimate ride. You'll need to make special arrangements for that, but dogs are also welcome. 909/584-2277; www.stagelines.com.

Paw Path, after all), so make sure your dog is close to you. The trail starts at the north end of the Stanfield Cutoff. 909/866-3437.

15 Woodland Trail

🐾 🐾 🐾 🐾 (See San Bernardino County map on page 172)

This 1.5-mile nature trail in San Bernardino National Forest has 20 stops where you and your well-behaved, leashed dog may learn about the flora and fauna of this mountainous region. It's especially glorious in an early-morning mist.

The trail rarely gets crowded, so it's a sure escape from the madding crowd. From Big Bear Lake village, cross the lake at the Stanfield Cutoff and turn left on Highway 38. Shortly after you turn, the trail is on your right. 909/866-3437.

PLACES TO EAT

Most of the restaurants listed below are in the old-style alpine village in the heart of Big Bear Lake. Whenever you visit here, you'll feel like it's Christmas.

The Log Cabin: You can eat on the deck here, which is three feet above the lawn, where your dog has to be tied. Tie your dog securely under a shady tree and hover above her as you eat the German-American food here or sip any of the 10 beers on tap. 39976 Big Bear Boulevard; 909/866-3667.

The Mandoline Bistro: The food here is delectable and so diverse it's like choosing from the menus of several different restaurants. Entrées include Caribbean salmon (with grilled banana, lemon Dijon and chutney sauce, and sticky rice), cashew-crusted chicken breast (with wild mushroom bread pudding and tomato chutney), and filet mignon (with garlic mashed potatoes). The bruschetta appetizer is really wonderful, according to Tapper Dog, who sniffed this place out for us, but the menu warns that it's not for first dates. (In other words: Garlic City!) Dine with your dog at the umbrella-topped patio tables. 40701 Village Drive; 909/866-4200.

Mozart's Restaurant: This place looks like a huge alpine cottage, with a big wooden deck where dogs may watch their people dine. 40701 Village Drive; 909/866-9497.

Pine Knot Coffee House & Bakery: Mmm. Come here on a cool autumn afternoon and try the hot pot pies or mulligan stew while sitting on the small deck. 535 Pine Knot Avenue; 909/866-3537.

Sonora Cantina: This delightful restaurant boasts the best Mexican food in Big Bear. You can dine with your furry friend at the patio, where thirsty dogs get a nice bowl of *agua*. If you're very, very, very hungry, try the "Big Juan Burrito." If you can finish it in under 45 minutes, you get a T-shirt proclaiming your triumph. (No cheating by sharing it with your dog—you'd be sorry later, with the burrito's four meats, beans, and onions interacting in your dog's digestive tract.) 41144 Big Bear Boulevard; 909/866-8202.

PLACES TO STAY

Big Bear Lake is one of the best places in the entire state to spend the night with your dog. There are so many lodgings that accept dogs that you'll have a hard time choosing.

Bear Claw Cabins: These homey cabins are a quarter mile from the lake and skiing. Rates are $99–129, and dogs can stay in all rooms except the ones with Jacuzzis. 586 Main Street 92315; 909/866-7633.

Big Bear Frontier Cabins & Hotel: If your dog wants to splash around the lake, this is a great place to stay. Most of the 33 cabins and 22 motel rooms are on the lakefront or just across the street. Dogs and humans can wet their paws at the private beach here, and humans (sorry, dogs) can also enjoy the lodging's heated pool and large hot tub. The lodgings are cozy, and even the motel rooms have beautiful wood paneling that's so shiny you could practically ice skate on it if gravity weren't an issue. All but a couple have wood-burning fireplaces.

It sounds like it's far off the beaten track, but Big Bear Frontier is just one block from the dog-friendly village of Big Bear Lake. Rates are $70–300. Dogs are $15 extra. (As for pet rates, the website also mentions that "birds fly free. Call about mules or horses." I asked if they really get mules and horses, and a front desk clerk cheerfully told me, "No, but we love animals, so maybe we could work something out.") 40472 Big Bear Boulevard 92315; 800/457-6401; www.big-bear-cabins.com.

Big Pine Flats Campground: This is one of the more out-of-the-way campgrounds in the Big Bear area. You and your dog can hike around the area and be fully enveloped by ravishing Mama Nature. Or you can drive a few miles and be in the heart of Big Bear Lake. There are 19 sites available on a first-come, first-served basis. The campground closes in winter. Sites are $16. From Fawnskin, follow Rim of the World Drive (its name will change) for seven miles to Big Pine Flat Station. The campground is on your right. 909/866-3437.

Black Forest Lodge: Everything here is Swiss chalet–style, from the cute motel to the cabins to the real chalets. A few of the cabins date back to 1895! These log beauties have been gutted, and couple of the old ones even have Jacuzzi baths inside. Many accommodations are graced by fireplaces, and all are clean and attractive. The lodge's property has lots of trees for your pooch's perusal. Rates are $45–150. (And up to $225 for a chalet that sleeps 10.) Dogs pay a $25 flat fee. 41121 Big Bear Boulevard 92315; 909/866-2166 or 800/255-4378; www.blackforestlodge.com.

Cienaga Creek Ranch Mountain Cottages: The five upscale-yet-rustic cottages here are set on 50 acres of forest where well-behaved dogs can say sayonara to their leashes. As if that's not enough, this tranquil acreage is surrounded by thousands of acres of dog-friendly national forest land. It's enough to make a grown dog cry with joy. And the giant pines, firs, and junipers that blanket the land are another dream come true for many boy dogs. Combine this with some pet treats at the beginning of your visit, and you'll surely have a dog who thinks he's found canine heaven on earth.

It's pretty heavenly for people, too. Everything is solar powered, so ubiquitous utility lines don't mar the landscape. The cottages combine the rustic (log beds, log trim, wood wainscoting) with the divine (featherbeds, artisan tile, and marble in the spacious kitchen and bathroom). All have fireplaces; some have Jacuzzi spas. They're 100–200 feet away from each other, so there's plenty of privacy, too. And the little extras, including high-end toiletries and super-plush towels and robes, help guests feel extra pampered in the wilderness. Rates are $119–299. Dogs are $10 extra. There's no street address. P.O. Box 2773 92314; 888/336-2891; www.mountaincottage.com.

Cozy Hollow Lodge: This lodge deserves its name, since the simple cabins here have fireplaces and are definitely on the cozy side. It's a great place to stay after a long day on the slopes. In summer, a stream runs through the woods behind the lodge. Rates are $59–159. There's a $100 deposit for dogs and an additional $10 fee for each pooch. 40409 Big Bear Boulevard 92315; 909/866-8886; www.cozyhollowlodge.com.

Eagle's Nest Bed & Breakfast Lodge: Dogs are warmly welcomed here with a pet basket full of goodies including treats, a doggy toy, food and water bowls, and a towel for drying off wet paws. (The latter two are loaners.) They can stay at a charming two-room cottage suite with a fireplace or in the Highland Cabin, an absolutely wonderful, cozy, two-bedroom cabin with a wood-burning fireplace and even a deer head on the wall. (Jake is scared of it. This

is embarrassing.) The cabin is rustic yet beautifully appointed. The exterior looks like it's straight out of a fairy tale in some woodland setting.

But dogs don't care about the decor or the storybook charm. What they want to know is: 1) Where can I go sniff out some nature and check out some trees? 2) What do I do while the humans are just sitting around reading and talking and watching TV? The answers will put a wag in any dog's tail: 1) The dog-friendly San Bernardino National Forest surrounds the cabin, and 2) You can curl up by the wood-burning fireplace or hang out in your completely fenced backyard. And don't forget to eat the treats they give you. Rates are $99–165. Dogs are $10 extra. 41675 Big Bear Boulevard 92315; 909/866-6465 or 888/866-6466; www.eaglesnestlodgebigbear.com.

Golden Bear Cottages: There's an unmistakable bear theme going here. Most of the 28 cabins sport bear names. (Little Bear, Honey Pot, Snuggle Bear Manor, and Grizzly's Den are but a few of the cabins.) The pawprints on the lodging's literature seem like dog paw prints at first glance (at least to the dog-oriented among us) but are actually bear prints. You and your dog will have a beary good time at the interesting assortment of rustic cabins strewn over five acres. The prices are quite bearable too. Rates are $79–229. Dogs are $10. 39367 Big Bear Boulevard, Highway 18 92315; 909/866-2010 or 800/461-1023; www.goldenbear.net.

Grey Squirrel Resort: These charming cottages are a half block from the lake, on 4.5 acres. Several of the cottages have fireplaces. For those achy muscles fraught with post-skiing-stress-disorder, the resort has a heated pool, which is enclosed in the winter (but pooches can't paddle here). Rates are $85–170. There's a $100 deposit for pets and an additional $10 fee per pooch.

The cabins are on Highway 18, just west of town at 39372 Big Bear Boulevard 92315; 909/866-4335 or 800/381-5569; www.greysquirrel.com.

Pine Knot Guest Ranch: Love llamas? Bonkers for bunnies? Stay at the comfy housekeeping cabins at Pine Knot and you can interact with animals other than your traveling companion (the one with dog breath). The two-plus-acre property is home to llamas you can join for a stroll or bunnies whose huge cage you can enter for a close encounter of the rabbit kind. It's also home to eight cabins, five of which allow dogs. All but one cabin has a wood-burning fireplace, and they all feature spa tubs for two. They're great to come back to after a long day on the slopes or on the lake. Rates are $139–299. The people who run the ranch also have six vacation home rentals not far away. Call to inquire about these. 908 Pine Knot Avenue 92315; 909/866-6500 or 800/866-3446; www.pineknotguestranch.com.

Quail Cove: "Pets are always welcome!" exclaims the lodge's brochure. The six cottages here are in a wooded, park-like setting by the water. All have wood-burning fireplaces, knotty-pine paneling, and full kitchens. Rates are $79–229. Dogs are $15 extra and require a $100 deposit. 39117 North Shore Drive 92315; 909/866-5957 or 800/595-2683; www.quailcove.com.

Serrano Campground: If you like rustic campsites and good hot showers, this San Bernardino National Forest campground is worth the $24–34 fee. The 132 sites are close to Big Bear Lake and the solar observatory (which is open to the public during certain days in the summer). The campground is on the north side of the lake, about two miles east of Fawnskin. It's very close to the Cougar Crest Trail. Call 877/444-6777 for reservations or 909/866-3437 for more information. The campground is closed in the winter.

Shore Acres Lodge: Does your dog love to swim and hike? If so, Shore Acres is a great place to stay, because it has lake access and is near some fun trails. This two-acre property has 11 comfortable housekeeping cabins, each with a fireplace, sundeck, and barbecue grill. Humans who enjoy outdoor recreation can also swim in the pool during warmer months, fish from the lodge's property, or embark on a boat trip from the lodge's own dock. Little humans enjoy the playground here. Soak in the year-round hot tub at the end of a long day of fun. Rates are $105–245. Dogs are $10 extra. 40090 Lakeview Drive 92315; 800/524-6600; www.bigbearvacations.com/lodge.htm.

Timberline Lodge: Like woods? You're in a little foresty area here. Like being close to the village? Stay here and you will be. How about lake views from cozy housekeeping cabins? The views are terrific. And the active life? The lodge has a seasonal heated outdoor pool, a children's playground, and volleyball, basketball, horseshoes, and tetherball (for humans only). The folks behind the front desk can tell you some fun nearby hikes your dog. "We love our puppy dogs up here!" says friendly manager Dave. Dogs dig Dave, too. Rates are $79–200. Dogs are $10 extra. 39921 Big Bear Boulevard 92315; 909/866-4141; www.thetimberlinelodge.com.

Wildwood Resort: When we inquired about whether dogs could stay at this wonderful four-acre resort, we were immediately and enthusiastically told "Oh, yes!" The woman we spoke with belongs to a Newfoundland dog club (actually, her dogs do), and she said that when the resort played host to the club's 50 Newfies, not a single pile of poop remained after their visit. It's stories like this that give dog people a good name and make dogs more welcome at other lodgings.

The resort has 25 sweet cabins that permit pooches. All have full kitchens, and most have fireplaces. You'll like it here. Rates are $100–205. Dogs are $10 extra. 40210 Big Bear Boulevard 92315; 909/878-2178 or 888/294-5396; www.wildwoodresort.com.

Fawnskin

This little town is near several dog-friendly lodgings and surrounded by the San Bernardino National Forest. (See the National Forests and Wilderness Areas resource at the back of this book for more on this wooded wonderland.) But in case you're hankering for a more civilized park, we've sniffed out a sweet one for you.

PARKS, BEACHES, AND RECREATION AREAS

16 Dana Point Park

🐾🐾🐾 (See San Bernardino County map on page 172)

Swimming dogs adore this county park. It's along the north side of Big Bear Lake's Grout Bay, so it's somewhat off the beaten track. It's a fairly small park, but it has some romping room for leashed dogs, as well as a picnic area for hungry dogs and their people. Bird-watching is one of the big activities here, so be sure to bring your binoculars. November–March, you might see bald eagles roosting and feeding.

The park is just off the main part of this charming old village, on the south side of Highway 38. 909/866-0130.

Twin Peaks

PLACES TO STAY

Arrowhead Pine Rose Cabins: This five-acre property is three miles from Lake Arrowhead. Dogs like the fact that they can walk around the spacious land here and check out all the sweet-smelling pines. About half of the 17 cabins permit pooches. Some cabins have back patios where your dog can relax in a quasi-outdoor atmosphere without escaping.

Pet blankets are provided. If your dog makes himself at home on human furniture, please cover it with the blanket. Rates are $59–450. Anything above $200 is in the three-bedroom-plus category, so you probably won't need to worry about that price. Dogs are $10 extra, and there's a $100 pooch deposit. 25994 Highway 189 92391; 909/337-2341 or 800/429-PINE (800/429-7463); www.lakearrowheadcabins.com.

Upland

PARKS, BEACHES, AND RECREATION AREAS

🖤 Baldy View Dog Park/Upland Dog Park

🐾🐾🐾🐾🐕 (See San Bernardino County map on page 172)

This fenced dog park is five grassy acres of fun, with lots of trees for your pooch's perusal. Small dogs have their own little area. Humans get to repose on benches. It's the de rigueur dog spot in Upland.

The people here know how to party. If they're not entering their dogs in the local Christmas parade, they're partaking in Valentine's festivities with their furry friends or hosting a "spring fling" party for them. You can get an idea of some of the events by checking out www.uplanddogpark.com.

The park is on 11th Street between San Antonio and Mountain Avenues. 909/931-4280.

Rancho Cucamonga

PARKS, BEACHES, AND RECREATION AREAS

🖤 Rancho Cucamonga Dog Park

🐾🐾🐾🐾🐕 (See San Bernardino County map on page 172)

This is one of the more attractive fenced dog parks we've come across. The park is about 30,000 square feet of grass, with great views of the San Gabriel Mountains. It's shaded here and there by beautiful jacaranda trees. When they bloom, their purple flowers are stunning. Bring a camera, and see if you can get your pooch to hold still long enough to get a photo of her under a canopy of purple blossoms.

The park has all the usual dog park amenities, including water and benches. There's a separate area for shy or tiny dogs (or both rolled into one) to get away from it all. Many more amenities, including a dog wash, are in the offing. Dogs are not necessarily smiling about this last addition.

We're going to give you directions from the freeway, since this park is so close to a major freeway traveling dogs routinely find themselves on. Exit I-15 at Baseline Avenue and immediately take the option for heading north on East Avenue. The park, which is in Etiwanda Creek Community Park, is on your right within a few blocks, at the corner of Banyan Street and East Avenue. 909/477-2700.

San Bernardino

PARKS, BEACHES, AND RECREATION AREAS

19 Wildwood Dog Park

🐾🐾🐾🐾🐕 (See San Bernardino County map on page 172)

The grass is always greener on the other side of the fence here. That's because dogs use one side of this lush 3.5-acre park some days, and when the turf starts getting a little worn down, they switch to the other half to let the trampled half recover. It keeps it attractive and mud-free.

This is a super dog park in many ways. Small dogs have their own area, and there are restrooms, benches, poop bags, drinking fountains, lights, and even a building used for vaccination clinics. Enough trees provide shade to make some parts of the park more tolerable in summer.

The dog park is within 24-acre Wildwood Park, at East 40th Street and Waterman Avenue. If you feel like it's just your dog who gets exercise at the dog park (let's face it, it's not like humans get in great shape standing around talking and occasionally lobbing a tennis ball), you can pop on your dog's leash and head to the main park, where you can breeze along a fitness trail. 909/384-5233.

20 Glen Helen Regional Park

🐾🐾🐾🐾 (See San Bernardino County map on page 172)

This 1,425-acre park features two lakes that are regularly stocked with such goodies as trout and catfish. But if your leashed dog doesn't like to fish, she's sure to enjoy such goodies as the ecology trail and the grassy little hills that await her happy paws.

Rangers tell us that some dogs seem to get a kick out of watching kids zoom down the 300-foot, two-part water slide at the swim complex in the park's southeast corner. Dogs aren't allowed there, but the park has plenty of viewing spots for pooches and their people.

With all these activities, Glen Helen Regional Park is a great place for your dog to take the family. You can even camp here. There are 50 sites available on a first-come, first-served basis. The fee is $10, and dogs are $1 extra.

The day-use fee here is $5, plus $1 per dog. Fishing is $5 per person over six years old. Exit I-215 at Devore Road (just south of the I-15/I-215 junction) and follow the signs about 1.5 miles to the park. 909/887-7540.

21 Perris Hill Park

🐾🐾🐾 (See San Bernardino County map on page 172)

This park makes dogs happy, in part because there's dense shade almost everywhere. The trees providing this comfort are generally very big and very old. Although dogs must be leashed, they have smiles on their snouts when they gather during dog rush hour, around 5 P.M. or so.

The park is at Highland and Valencia Avenues. 909/384-5233.

PLACES TO STAY

Dog lodgings aren't exactly abundant here.

Glen Helen Regional Park: See Glen Helen Regional Park, above, for camping information.

La Quinta Motor Inn: Dogs are allowed to stay in this motel's smoking rooms. Fortunately, there's a little grassy area outside where they can get some fresh air. Rates are $69–85. 205 East Hospitality Lane 92408; 909/888-7571.

Motel 6: There are two of these pooch-friendly motels in town. Rates are $38–49 for the first adult, $6 for the second. In northern San Bernardino: 1960 Ostrems Way 92407; 909/887-8191. The other location is 111 West Redlands Boulevard 92408; 909/825-6666.

Lake Arrowhead

This attractive resort village in the mountains of San Bernardino National Forest has plenty for a dog to do. Dogs can lounge in lodges. They can hike the hillsides. They can do the dog paddle in the lake.

The Arrowhead district of the national forest has some terrific trails ranging in elevation 3,000–7,000 feet. Pooches are welcome to join you on a day hike or an overnighter. Contact the ranger station at 909/337-2444 for trail maps and advice on which hikes and campsites are better suited for your skill level and the time of year you'll be visiting. We've listed two of the more popular trails and campgrounds below, but there are plenty of smaller hike-in sites as well.

The lake itself is managed by an exclusive homeowners association, so public lake access is rather limited.

PARKS, BEACHES, AND RECREATION AREAS

22 Indian Rock Trail

🐾 🐾 🐾 (See San Bernardino County map on page 172)

If your dog's motto is "nice and easy does it," this trail will do it for him. It's an effortless half-mile hike through the San Bernardino National Forest to a former Serrano Indian encampment, where you'll still find the bedrock once used for grinding the area's abundant acorns into flour. (The stones were the answer to having to carry around heavy mortar and pestles.) Although this is national forest land, your dog should be leashed because it's a fairly well-used trail.

From Lake Arrowhead, drive north on Highway 173 to the Rock Camp Fire Station. The trail starts just east of the station. Parking is across the road. 909/382-2782.

DIVERSION

Sniff Out Some Cool Clothes: A clothing store with the name **Big Dogs Sportswear** that has a giant St. Bernard as its logo can't help but allow clean, well-behaved dogs to shop with their people. Most stores in the chain are dog friendly, but the folks at the Lake Arrowhead store go the extra mile and keep a bowl of fresh water handy for thirsty dogs, and even give biscuits to their canine customers. 28200 Highway 189; 909/336-1998.

23 North Shore National Recreational Trail

🐾🐾🐾🐾 🐕 (See San Bernardino County map on page 172)

This trail offers a variety of hike possibilities, depending on how your dog is feeling about a long hike versus a shorter, more gentle one. The trail itself is 1.7 miles, and the initial leg is pretty effortless, going gradually downhill through firs and pines to peaceful Little Bear Creek. Dogs love dipping their paws in the creek. You can get there and turn around, of course going gradually uphill on your way back. Or you can join up with Forest Road 3N34, which comes out about four hours later at Crab Flat, in Running Springs. It's a terrific hike, and if your dog is under good voice control, she can go off leash when away from the more popular parts of the trail. (Generally, off the initial portion of trail.)

From Highway 173 going north from Lake Arrowhead, go right (east) at Hospital Road and drive about five minutes. You'll see a hospital on your left and the North Shore Campground on your left. Park at the camp area and take the trail from there. Camping costs $16, and fear not: You won't really see the hospital from your site, and you're almost guaranteed never to hear an ambulance siren. 909/382-2782 or 909/337-2444.

PLACES TO EAT

Belgian Waffle Works: The waffles are crispy, the toppings are yummy, and you can enjoy them with your dog at the lakeside patio. The only hitch is that your dog needs to be on the other side of the fence. This isn't a big deal, since your dog can still be right beside you, but it's something Jake Dog thought you should know. The restaurant is dockside at the Lake Arrowhead Village, a cute little shopping area, at 28200 Highway 189; 909/337-5222.

Borderline Restaurant: This Mex-American restaurant offers two places where dogs can dine with their people: at a little two-table patio where you can dine side by side or in the solarium with your dog right outside and the doors open. (Barring bad weather or crowds.) "We bring them water and treat them good," a very pleasant waiter tells us. You can get shrimp, salmon, burgers, Mexican food, you name it. "The only thing we don't have is pizza," says the waiter. The restaurant is actually just a bone's throw from Lake Arrowhead, in the sweet town of Blue Jay, at 27159 Highway 189; 909/336-4363.

PLACES TO STAY

Arrowhead Tree Top Lodge: "We love dogs," says a kindly employee who also works for the local humane society. In fact, dogs get treats upon arrival.

Some of the rooms at this attractive lodge have kitchens and fireplaces, for that homey touch. The lodge is on five acres with a nature trail and creeks. Dogs dig that. It's a short walk to the village and to the lake from here. Rates are $69–179. Dogs are $8 extra. 27992 Rainbow Drive 92352; 909/337-2311 or 800/358-TREE (800/358-8733); www.arrowheadtreetop.com.

Dogwood Campground: This isn't one of the more secluded or rustic campgrounds in the area, but I mention it here because it's conveniently located one mile from the lake, and because my dog friends insist I list it due to its name. Dogwood is a privately operated national forest campground with 93 sites and all the amenities a camper could need, and then some ("then some" refers to things like laundry facilities). The camp is set along the lake's outlet.

The campground is open May–mid-October. Sites are $24–29. Dogwood is at Highway 18's Blue Jay turnoff. For information, call 909/337-2444. For reservations, call 877/444-6777.

North Shore Campground: See North Shore National Recreational Trail, above, for information on camping here.

Prophets' Paradise Bed & Breakfast: This bed-and-breakfast is a real charmer. You and your dog will drool over the cozy antique-filled living room, which is especially inviting in winter when the fireplace is roaring. Take a dog here at Christmas for the best present you could give him. (And speaking of Christmas, the "Prophet" in Prophets' Paradise is the last name of the innkeepers, not anything prophetic.)

The bed-and-breakfast is a five-level, 5,000-square-foot house on a hillside. Each room has its own floor. It's wonderfully private for a B&B. The pet rooms have decks and outside entrances. Rates are $120–185. 26845 Modoc Lane 92352; 909/336-1969 or 800/987-2231; www.prophetsparadise.com.

Saddleback Inn: Howard Hughes frequented this enchanting historic inn (although it wasn't quite so historic then, having been built in 1919), as did Charles Lindbergh and countless Hollywood icons, including Mae West.

In keeping with Mae West's famous line, now your dog can "Come up and see me sometime" at the Saddleback Inn. Many of the lovely cottages in back of the three-story inn welcome dogs. They're decorated in kind of a country-mountain cabin style, and most have gas log fireplaces and Jacuzzi tubs. All come with a little fridge and microwave, should your dog hanker for a midnight snack. There's a fun restaurant on the premises, but your dog will have to be content with leftovers, as there's no outdoor dining. What dogs and their people usually like best about Saddleback is the gorgeous setting overlooking Lake Arrowhead, in the midst of big pines and cedars. The cottages are surrounded by these arbors, and that puts a smile on any dog's face.

Rates are $109–218. Dogs are $8 extra. 300 South State Highway 173 92352; 909/336-3571; www.saddlebackinn.com.

Crestline

PARKS, BEACHES, AND RECREATION AREAS

24 Lake Gregory

🐾 🐾 🐾 (See San Bernardino County map on page 172)

Here's a county park the way we like to see them: free. It's rare, but it happens. Lake Gregory is an 86-acre lake in a park that has only about 20 acres of dry land. But the land is lush and forested, with ponderosa pines, sugar pines, and cedars everywhere.

A 2.75-mile path (complete with fitness stops) takes you around the lake, but alas, dogs aren't allowed in the water. They must be leashed at all times. At one point you'll come to a portion of the park that's popular with the pooch set. It's so green that signs warn "No Golf." It's also very popular with the ball-playing set, so keep away during game time.

From Highway 18, take the Crestline exit, which turns into Lake Drive. Follow the road into the park. For the hiking path, start at the south shore. The golf-green entrance to the park is at 24646 San Moritz Drive. The Rim of the World Recreation & Park District runs that area: 909/337-7275. San Bernardino County Regional Parks is in charge of the rest: 909/338-2233.

Ontario

PARKS, BEACHES, AND RECREATION AREAS

25 John Galvin Park

🐾🐾 (See San Bernardino County map on page 172)

Lazy leashed dogs like this city park. The big old trees seem like they were made for shading dogs whose main focus is sleeping. For a perfectly lazy afternoon outing, bring a book, lean against a tree, and revel in the sound of your snoring pooch. An open field in one section of this municipal park provides just enough room to roam should your mellow dog choose not to snooze.

Exit I-10 at Fourth Street and go west a couple of blocks. The park will be on your left. 909/395-2020.

26 Cucamonga-Guasti Park

🐾🐾🐾 (See San Bernardino County map on page 172)

The park's name may not exactly roll off the tongue, but there's something for dogs of every stripe (and spot) here. Dogs who enjoy dipping their paws in the water like the fishing lake, where anglers catch bass, catfish, or trout. (Pooches aren't permitted in the swimming lake.) Dogs who like lazing in the grass under gracefully shade-giving trees can snooze the afternoon away. And dogs who dig a good walk can amble along the park's lovely walking and bike paths.

The entry fee at this regional park is $5 per vehicle, except on holidays, when it's $7. If you walk in, it's $2 per person. Dogs are $1 extra whether you

walk or drive in. You can buy fishing permits at the entry. The park is just north of I-10 on the Archibald Avenue exit. 800 North Archibald Avenue; 909/481-4205.

PLACES TO EAT

Winston, a local little Jack Russell terrier who has a nose for fine food, helped us sniff out a couple of the fun eateries listed below. A big thanks to him and his human family, including Tera (who is not a terrier), for helping us out.

Casa Corona: Dogs can eat at the four outdoor tables next to some trees out front. Try the enchiladas. They're really tasty. Thirsty *perros* get a bowl of water. 401 North Euclid Avenue; 909/986-5200.

The Coffee Bean & Tea Leaf: You can have your coffee and your canine, too, when you sip at the two umbrella-topped outdoor tables here. The vanilla steamed milk is a great alternative if you feel like something more relaxing than a cuppa joe. In summer, you can cool off with a delicious ice-blended drink. 929 North Miliken Avenue; 909/481-5558.

Wolfgang Puck Café: This wonderful café's food is half the price of Puck's more upscale Spago restaurants, so it's a great place to take a dog who's on a budget. Puck's delicious wood-fired pizzas, as well as pastas, salads, and terrific rotisserie chicken, are to drool for. Best of all, dogs feel very welcome; they get water and treats when they visit. 1 Ontario Mills Circle; 909/987-2299.

PLACES TO STAY

Country Inn & Suites: Stay at this all-suites hotel and get a complimentary breakfast, plus take part in a social hour. Rates are $79–144. Dogs are $50 extra for the length of their stay. 231 North Vineyard Avenue 91764; 909/937-6000; www.countryinns.com.

Holiday Inn Hotel & Suites Airport: This is the best hotel for dogs who have to stay near the airport. Not only do you get a continental breakfast, but all the rooms are actually suites, complete with kitchenettes. And guess what else? Fire hydrants are pretty prominent outside the hotel. It's a boy dog's dream. People prefer the Jacuzzis, which grace half the rooms. Rates are $112–142. Dogs pay a $25 fee for their stay, in addition to a $50 deposit. 3400 Shelby Street 91764; 909/466-9600.

Residence Inn by Marriott: Staying in a one- or two-bedroom suite here is like staying at home, except you get regular maid service. It's a great place to stay if you like having a kitchen when you travel, along with a living room with a fireplace and access to a swimming pool (heated outdoor), whirlpool, and exercise room. The suites are comfortable, attractive, and located across from the Ontario Convention Center, which is convenient if your dog has an important convention to attend. Rates are $135–185. Dogs pay $100 "sanitation fee" per stay for a smaller suite, $150 for a larger suite, plus $10 extra each night, so try to stay for a few nights to make it worth your while. (Or at least eat a lot at the complimentary continental breakfast buffet.) 2025 Convention Center Way 91764; 909/937-6788.

Chino

PARKS, BEACHES, AND RECREATION AREAS

27 Prado Regional Park/Prado Recreation, Inc.

🐾🐾🐾🐾 🐕 (See San Bernardino County map on page 172)

This 2,200-acre park is actually in two sections. There's the regular old regional park, with lakes, huge manicured fields, and playgrounds, and the dog park, with 1,100 acres of land for dogs to go leashless.

The regular old park charges $5 per vehicle and $1 per dog. Dogs must be on leash. A day here makes for a pleasant family outing. Camping can be fun, too. Sites are $16–20. If you want to fish, it'll cost you $2–7, depending on your age.

The dog training park will cost you $10 per person or per couple per day (up to two dogs are included in the fee). Camping anywhere on the 1,100 acres costs $6. But don't get the idea that this place is just a heavenly area where your dog can run like a crazy California canine. This is a dog training area, and we're generally not talking about the old sit-stay stuff. We're talking hunting and herding. We're talking dogs who work for a living.

Prado Recreation is not for vegetarians or anti-hunting folks. Chances are good that you'll see some dead birds here. You'll even see people shooting and the dogs retrieving what they've shot. (If your dog spooks at gunshots, this is not a good place to take him.) As we drove through, we saw Labs and springers everywhere obeying hand signals in ponds and fields where there were bound to be birds.

People laughed at poor old Joe Airedale as we cruised through. "Ha ha ha" was all we could hear as they pointed at his dumbfounded, curly head. Somehow they could tell that his retrieval instincts stop where his nose starts. He was embarrassed, but he continued to stick his head out the window anyway. Mr. Yellow Lab, Jake, has not yet visited, but he'll fit right in here, even though the only hand signal he obeys is "Look, I've got a treat! Come sit down and you'll get it!"

Dogs who herd really can go to town here. On a mist-shrouded field, we saw an elderly gent walking with a long wooden staff. He would quietly whistle or give subtle hand signals to two very intense border collies who were keeping a couple of big goats in line. It was as if we'd been transported across the Atlantic. Aye, rarely have we seen a more lovely dog scene.

You'll need to bring along proof of your pooch's rabies vaccine to either part of the park. The regular section of Prado Regional Park is about seven miles south of Highway 60, on the left side of Euclid Avenue. Call 909/597-4260 for information or camping reservations. To get to the dog section, take the first left after Prado Regional Park. You'll be on a very bumpy dirt road for what may seem like a long time, but eventually you'll come to the park's office. Call the Prado Kennel at 909/597-6366 for more information.

PLACES TO STAY

Prado Regional Park: See Prado Regional Park, above, for camping information.

Redlands

Parts of this lush, resort-like town provide a breath of fresh air from smog-ridden and traffic-filled Southern California.

PARKS, BEACHES, AND RECREATION AREAS

28 Prospect Park

🐾🐾🐾 (See San Bernardino County map on page 172)

You'll be surrounded by exquisite views, towering palms, multitudes of orange trees, and flowers everywhere at this enchanting, verdant park. Prospect Park is out of a fairy tale. It's one big hill, with delicate wooden seats overlooking the surrounding orchards. At the top, you'll find an open-air theater, some peacocks, and a resident cat, so be sure to follow the rules and leash your dog.

This one's well worth the short trek from I-10. For the most scenic ride, exit the freeway at Orange Street and drive south, through the quaint downtown area. In about seven blocks, bear right at Cajon Street. The park is on your right in about one mile. Park on Cajon Street just after Highland Avenue (just past the orange grove and before the picnic area on your right). Walk back several feet to the wide paved path and embark on your wondrous journey. 909/798-7509.

PLACES TO EAT

Cafe Society: Dogs are welcome to help you dine on good sandwiches and tasty bakery items at the sidewalk and patio tables. 308 West State Street #1A; 909/798-5578.

PLACES TO STAY

Best Western Sandman Motel: With a name like this, it's got to be a good place to catch some winks. Enjoy the heated outdoor pool and hot tub. Room rates are $60–110. Dogs require a $50 deposit. 1120 West Colton Avenue 92374; 909/793-2001.

Yucaipa

PARKS, BEACHES, AND RECREATION AREAS

29 Yucaipa Regional Park

🐾🐾🐾🐾 (See San Bernardino County map on page 172)

This picturesque park is surrounded by the San Bernardino Mountains and Mt. San Gorgonio. But dogs who visit here have more important things on their minds than pretty scenery. First of all, they're not relegated to the usual six-foot leash—their leashes can be 10 feet long! Joy of joys. Then there's the size of this park—it's 885 acres, with enough grassy fields to tire even the friskiest hound dog.

Water-loving dogs enjoy accompanying their people to the three trout-stocked lakes, and water-loving kids get a kick out of the 350-foot water slides at the swim lagoon (no dogs allowed on the slides because they'd make the slides too hairy). Several campsites are available near the lake, so if you're in the mood for a little camping with your angling, you couldn't ask for a more convenient location. Sites are $13–22. There are about 35 campsites here. Reservations are recommended.

The day-use fee is $5 per vehicle. On major holidays, it's $7 per vehicle. Dogs are $1 extra. Fishing permits are $5 daily for anyone over eight years old, $2 for the little-kid set.

From I-10, take the Yucaipa exit and follow the brown signs for "Regional Park." It's about five miles from the freeway. 909/790-3127.

PLACES TO STAY

Yucaipa Regional Park: See Yucaipa Regional Park, above, for camping information.

Angelus Oaks

PLACES TO STAY

The Lodge at Angelus Oaks: One day I got a letter written in silver ink and very big, childish handwriting, and signed with paw prints by Jake Dog (not my Jake Dog; this was before he was even a twinkle in his mother's eye) and Sadie Dog. They were writing to tell me about this wonderful place, which they call "a hidden secret."

Jake and Sadie are very smart dogs, indeed, because the lodge is one terrific place to stay with a dog. It's made up of several homey wooden cabins and is set on some prime acreage in the San Bernardino National Forest. It was built in the early 1900s as a stagecoach stop for pooped-out travelers, and it really hasn't changed much since. Each of the 12 cabins has a kitchen, bathroom with shower, and one or two bedrooms. The main lodge/office is very cozy, with a stone fireplace, a library, and an antique billiards table. But what dogs dig most is that it has lots of fun things to do outside. There's a snowplay area (in winter) and a horseshoe pit and other fun non-snow recreational opportunities. Best of all, the San Bernardino National Forest is everywhere. Some prime trails start just a short car ride away.

Rates are $70–95. Dogs are $5 extra. 37825 Highway 38 92305; 909/794-9523.

Joshua Tree

An entry point into Joshua Tree National Park (see the Twentynine Palms section) is just down the road from here.

PLACES TO STAY

Joshua Tree Highlands House: You'll feel like Joshua Tree National Park is your very own backyard when you stay at this roomy, attractive vacation home on 10 acres. (The park is actually three short minutes away, but it looks like it's right here.) Dogs who like contemporary-yet-retro decor will brag to their furry friends about this clean, cool, sleek two-bedroom, two-bath home with a Jacuzzi tub, steam shower, full kitchen, and enclosed deck.

By day you get a jaw-dropping 360-degree view of the beautiful surrounding desert from this remote locale, and at night you get amazing stargazing. There's nothing like breathing in the sweet scent of desert night air while lying in your comfortable lounger looking up at Orion with your own down-to-earth Canis Major at your side.

The house's owners, Frederick and Jimmy, love dogs. In fact they have three of their own, and one regularly visits a children's ward at an L.A.-area hospital to give the kids a boost.

Rates for the house are $750 for a week, $350 for a weekend. Nightly rates are available. (A smaller, less expensive home is available as well, and it's just a bone's throw away.) Dogs are $35 extra. They don't give out the address until you reserve, but you can phone them to make arrangements at 760/366-3636 or 310/827-5144; www.joshuatreehighlandshouse.com.

Twentynine Palms

PARKS, BEACHES, AND RECREATION AREAS

30 Joshua Tree National Park

🐾🐾🐾 (See San Bernardino County map on page 172)

This town houses the headquarters and a good-sized swatch of this stunning park. See the National Parks section at the beginning of this chapter for details.

PLACES TO EAT

Foster's Freeze: Eating the cold, creamy treats here is the perfect way to end a day of exploring Joshua Tree National Park. Your dog will be indebted if you happen to drop a tad of vanilla on the ground. 73629 Two Mile Road; 760/367-9303.

PLACES TO STAY

29 Palms Inn: Set on 70 acres of beautiful desert, this rustic resort is just what the vet ordered for you and your pooch. It's a stress-free environment, with a peaceful spring-fed shaded pond for toe-dipping, a pool (with a cute little bar) and hot tubs for lounging, hammocks galore, phone-free bungalows and adobe cottages, and a view of the heavens you don't want to miss. You can get a massage in your room, on your sun patio, or even in the great outdoors. The cooks at the delightful restaurant can pack a picnic lunch that you and your dog will drool for. Take it on a hike in Joshua Tree National Park, which is just down the road.

The cottage and cabins are unique, with a down-home, Old West, nouvelle-desert feel. Some have a fireplace and a kitchen. They all have evaporative coolers for hot summer days and heaters for cool winter nights. They also have cable TV, but the TVs are small and most are black and white. The resort's brochure says this is to help guests focus on more important things, but Jake Dog thinks it's because televisions are expensive. I love the lack of big Sonys, though, and I believe the brochure. Besides, snazzy new TVs just wouldn't fit in.

Rates are $75–245. There's a $35 dog fee per visit. 73950 Inn Avenue 92277; 760/367-3505; www.29palmsinn.com.

Pioneertown

Everything on this town's "Mane Street" looked 100 years old from the moment it came to life in 1947. Pioneertown was built with two purposes in mind: as an Old West–style getaway for folks in the film business and a location for Hollywood Westerns. If it looks familiar, you may have seen it as a backdrop in a few Gene Autry films, including *On Top of Old Smokey* and *Whirlwind*. If you're a real buff of the genre, you may know it from lesser-known B-grade films such as *The Gay Amigo* and *The Daring Caballero*. (Gotta love those names.)

What separates this from your typical movie backlot is that it's a real town (albeit a tiny one). The false fronts aren't just propped up with lumber: They're the fronts of real working buildings, including the local post office.

P-town is a very cool place to visit with your dog, because dogs, like horses, fit in beautifully. Mane Street is unpaved, and as casual as it gets. In fact,

DIVERSION

Woof for the Good Guys: Dogs can boo the bad guys, cheer for the good guys, and laugh at the drunk guys as they watch some amusing **Old West skits** with you on Pioneertown's scenic "Mane Street." (The good guys always win.) A dozen or so members of a local Western reenactment ensemble perform these lively sketches in this seemingly historic old movie town at 2:30 P.M. Sunday April–November. The cost: free. You might even get to see some rope tricks and hear cowboy poetry. And you'll surely hear some loud gunfire (blanks, but loud; the opposite of silent-but-deadly). If your four-legged varmint is skittish of loud noises, it may be best to keep your distance. Afterward, you and your dog can have your photo taken with a gunslinger. For more information, phone the Pioneertown Posse at 760/228-0494 or check out www.pioneertown.com.

dogs who don't mind the sound of guns (shooting blanks) can watch some Old West skits here on Sundays (see the Diversion Woof for the Good Guys). For lots more details on this great, out-of-the-way place, check out www.pioneertown.com.

PLACES TO EAT

Pappy and Harriet's: What used to be a biker hangout (Harleys, not Schwinns) is now one happening restaurant and saloon. Its look fits right in with the Old West theme of Pioneertown, and so does the food (salads and veggie burgers notwithstanding). The steaks, chicken, and ribs are smoked and grilled over an outdoor mesquite fire, giving them a taste that will make your dog drool puddles. Dogs can join you at the picnic tables in the outdoor beer garden. "Horses, dogs, they're all fine with us," says friendly co-owner Robin. 53688 Pioneertown Road; 760/365-5956; www.pappyandharriets.com.

PLACES TO STAY

Rimrock Ranch Cabins: Like everything else in this pseudo–Old West town, the four cozy, spotless housekeeping cabins here were born in the 1940s as a place where the directors and stars of Western movies could kick off their boots and relax. Gene Autry and Roy Rogers were probably among the guests, say the owners, who are researching the history of the ranch. The cabins have a wonderfully funky charm, each with original knotty pine paneling, attractive antique/Western decor, artisan tile floors, a well-equipped kitchen, and a private patio with outdoor fireplace. Guests get use of the wonderful mineral-water swimming pool, too. It's a delightful treat, and it seems to do wonders for skin and hair.

What dogs love is that the cabins are on 35 acres, and this acreage is backed by hundreds of acres of fairly new wilderness preserve. This is beautiful, pristine land with lots of fun hiking. (Keep it pristine and bring your poop bags.)

Dogs come here and never want to leave. "We're very dog friendly," says Szu (pronounced Sue) Wakeman, who owns the cabins with her Texas-born husband, Dusty. (Great name for these parts.) Dogs get tasty biscuits when they check in, along with a doggy bed and food and water bowls during their stay. You'll be greeted at the gate by Yellow Dog, a canine you'll never forget. He's a sweet, shaggy dog with piercing ice-blue eyes. "People come here and want to take him home. He's our canine ambassador," says Szu. He's been in hundreds of guest photos (they send them to Szu), and he apparently endears himself to guests so much that some even end up letting him sleep on their bed. (Not that he's pushy; just cushy.)

Rates are $103–157, with a 20 percent discount in summer. Dogs are $10 extra. The mailing address is P.O. Box 313 92268; 760/228-1297; www.rim-rockranchcabins.com.

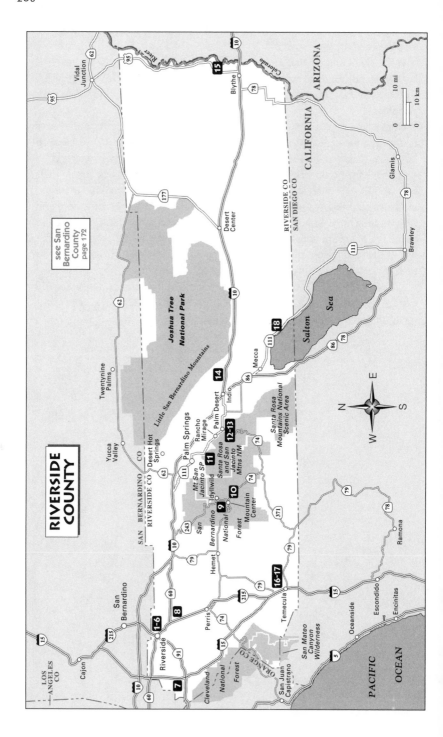

RIVERSIDE COUNTY

CHAPTER 5

Riverside County

Dogs are dancing with happiness in Riverside County these days, because they now have seven dog parks to call their very own and at least three more in the works. Dogs are no longer going to have to take to the desert to have a good time around here.

Actually, a trip to the desert during the more temperate months isn't a bad idea at all. In fact, dogs think it's a four-paws notion. But if it's hot or even warm outside, please forget it. The sand can be scorching even if the air isn't, and it can poach a pooch's paws.

Palm Springs has become quite the doggy destination of late. If you're in the mood for delectable desert oasis life, you'll find this resort town most amenable to dogs and their people.

The Bureau of Land Management (BLM) oversees millions of acres of desert and mountain land out in Riverside County, and dogs applaud the great job the agency does. On almost all the BLM land (except places like nature preserves), pooches are permitted to go leashless.

Our favorite BLM land in Riverside County is the Santa Rosa Mountains

PICK OF THE LITTER—RIVERSIDE COUNTY

BEST DOG PARKS
Pat Merritt Dog Park, Riverside (page 211)
Palm Springs Dog Park, Palm Springs (page 225)

MOST JUICY PARK
California Citrus State Historic Park, Riverside (page 212)

MOST DOG-FRIENDLY PLACE TO EAT
Sherman's Deli & Bakery, Palm Desert (page 231)

MOST DOG-FRIENDLY PLACE TO STAY
Caliente Tropics Resort, Palm Springs (page 227)

FRANK CAPRA'S MUSE
La Quinta Resort & Club, La Quinta (page 236)

BEST HOMAGE TO MAN'S BEST FRIEND
March Air Field's War Dog Memorial, Riverside (page 214)

BEST RIDE
Orange Empire Railway Museum trains, Perris (page 219)

National Scenic Area. It's rugged, desolate, and utterly pristine. It's also so sweeping that giving general directions is futile. It spans much of the area of the central county from I-10 south to the north border of the Anza-Borrego State Desert. Call the BLM's Palm Springs district office at 760/251-4800 for specifics.

County parks welcome leashed dogs, but be forewarned: Most of these parks charge $2 for adults, $2 for dogs, and $1 for kids. (I think this price structure means your dog had better act like an adult, not a child.)

NATIONAL FORESTS

The National Forests and Wilderness Areas resource at the back of this book has important information and safety tips on visiting national forests with your dog and has more information on the national forests listed below.

Cleveland National Forest
🐾🐾🐾🐾🐕

San Bernardino National Forest
🐾🐾🐾🐾🐕

NATIONAL PARKS

Joshua Tree National Park
🐾🐾🐾

Although the bulk of this huge desert park is in Riverside County, the large visitor center area with easily accessible hikes is north of the border in San Bernardino County. Please see the National Parks section of that chapter for details.

Riverside

If your dog loves trees (Jake's ears just perked up), a jaunt along beautiful Victoria Avenue is a must. The seven-mile-long historic avenue is lined with more than 4,000 trees of 95 species. Male dogs think they've died and gone to heaven when they stroll down the avenue's walking path, past tree after tree after tree. To get a brochure that will help you identify the trees you and your dog admire here, call the visitor center at 951/684-INFO (951/684-4636).

PARKS, BEACHES, AND RECREATION AREAS

1 Pat Merritt Dog Park
 (See Riverside County map on page 208)

Dogs are ecstatic when they see this lush, green, park—even if they can see only in black and white. The park is two terrific acres with great mountain views, and it's full of very happy dogs and their super-friendly people. The trees are merely glorified sticks at this point, but they'll grow. The fencing—something I don't usually mention except to note that a park is fenced—is some of the most attractive dog-park fencing I've seen. Chain-link be damned! Stylish black wrought iron is what you'll see here. (The Palm Springs Dog Park fencing beats it out, but it's Palm Springs. What else can I say?) The park features two sections: one for all dogs, one for small or timid dogs. It has all the usual amenities, including benches and picnic tables (sleek and modern), water, poop bags, and lights. A huge thanks to my intrepid correspondent "Three-Dog-Dave" Hepperly for the heads-up about this terrific park (and photos).

The park is at Limonite Frontage Road and Emery Street, about a half mile north of the Santa Ana River. 951/955-1151.

DIVERSION

Take Your Dog Out on a Date: Going to the **Van Buren Drive-In Theatre** in Riverside is a great way to catch a first-run movie and spare yourself the guilt of leaving your dog home alone. And it's cheap: Adults are $5 each, and kids 11 and under are free, as are dogs of any age. Of course, if your dog is like Jake, he'll want you to keep getting out of the car and going to the snack bar for one greasy item after another—and this gets expensive. During Jake's drive-in stints, he's been so busy staring at the floor in hopes of runaway popcorn that he hasn't even realized a movie's going on.

Drive-in theaters are a dying breed. Catch a flick here while you can. (Note: Dogs need to be walked before the movie, because management prefers that they stay in the cars. And no barkers allowed.) 3035 Van Buren Boulevard; 909/688-2360.

2 California Citrus State Historic Park

🐾🐾🐾🐾 (See Riverside County map on page 208)

Do you ogle oranges? Go ga-ga for grapefruit? Lust for lemons? If you're even remotely a citrus fan, this is a must-see park for your and your leashed dog. Dogs may not be as interested in citrus, but they love coming here anyway.

The park is a huge 377 acres, with a whopping 125 varieties of citrus trees. The citrus curious (and their canines) can learn more about these delights on a ranger-led or self-guided tour around the huge groves. Many of the trails are lined with palm trees, which add another level of that California Experience feel. In addition, there are miles of lush, landscaped trails and more rugged terrain. You'll learn so much about the history of oranges and their brethren that you'll never look at orange juice the same way again.

The people behind the park have big plans. They're now building a 6,000-square-foot visitor center, which will tell the story of California's earliest orange encounters. (The arrival of the orange in Southern California was like the gold rush in Northern California. These fruity beginnings led to the state's image as the Golden State—land of sunshine, opportunity, and plenty of sun-kissed eats.) The next phase of development involves the re-creation of a citrus-producing community circa 1880–1935. This will include an operating packing house, a workers' camp, a wealthy grower's home (which may serve as a restaurant), and an early citrus settlement with all kinds of neat old buildings.

Regular visitor Wendy and her dog Molly say they adore this park, and they inform us that dogs are not the only critters who visit here. "I have seen pet raccoons and pot-bellied pigs bring their owners to the park," says Wendy.

Those animals have good taste! And unlike most dogs, they're not averse to a little citrus.

Bring a picnic and enjoy lounging on the park's large grassy lawn (complete with barbecue grills). Now orange you glad you took the time to read this? (Joe Dog made me write that.) The entry fee is $4 per vehicle. The park is in the heart of Riverside, one mile east of Highway 91, at Dufferin Avenue and Van Buren Boulevard. 951/780-6222.

🐾 Carlson Dog Park

🐾🐾🐾🦴 (See Riverside County map on page 208)

This one-acre pooch park is in a really pretty spot, at the base of Mt. Rubidoux along the Santa Ana River. The dog park is fenced, with green grass, big shady trees, water fountains at human lip level and dog-slurping level, and poop mitts.

My wonderful correspondent "Three-Dog-Dave" Hepperly keeps me up to date on the goings on of this pooch park and other parks in the region, where he adventures with his dogs. He tells me there have been some problems with less-than-savory types drifting to the park's parking lot after they're kicked out of the adjacent Fairmount Park at night. The park folks are working on a remedy, but in the meantime Dave and I wanted to let you know that nighttime may not be the right time for a visit until things get cleaned up.

The park is one mile west of downtown Riverside, on the east bank of the Santa Ana River, at Mission Inn Avenue near the bridge. 951/826-2000.

🐾 Mount Rubidoux

🐾🐾🐾 (See Riverside County map on page 208)

The views from the top of this isolated granite outcrop are well worth the hike to get here. From its 1,364-foot elevation, you and your dog will see the surrounding mountains, the Santa Ana River, the city of Riverside, and probably a few other happy, peppy, leashed pooches.

There's not a lot of shade on the way up, so make sure you go when it's not hot. You and your dog should be in good shape to make this hike. If you have any doubts, go to Carlson Park (see above) and let your dog off leash to romp at a more leisurely pace.

A bit of history, courtesy of Patty Tambe of the city's parks department: In 1907, one of the park's founders put a cross at the hill's summit. The first Easter sunrise service here was held two years later, and that service is said to have inspired a cycle of outdoor Easter services across the country. Apparently, this was the granddaddy of these Easter events. So now you know. It's kind of fun to think about while you're at the summit.

The most convenient entrance to Mt. Rubidoux is at the small parking lot at Carlson Park. (See above for directions.) 951/826-2000.

DIVERSION

Pay Tribute to War Dogs and See Planes, Too: Back in the Vietnam War, thousands of specially trained dogs accompanied troops to the front lines in South Vietnam. Because their acute senses could detect danger in the form of ambushes, hidden trip wires, and explosives, and because of their dedication to their handlers, these amazing dogs are attributed with saving the lives of 10,000 soldiers. Nearly 300 dogs were killed in combat, and tragically, the rest were euthanized after the war because the military thought they'd be too dangerous to return to civilian life.

These dogs are gone, but far from forgotten, at least by the veterans who accompanied them on their one-way trip. On a rainy afternoon in February 2000, some 2,000 people, many of whom were veterans from across the United States, attended a dedication of the **War Dog Memorial** outside the **March Air Field Museum.** Tearful veterans patted and hugged the bronze German shepherd depicted with his soldier in the striking 18-foot statue. The vets referred to their dogs as "America's forgotten heroes." They placed dozens of flowers at the statue's base.

Now you and your civilian dog can pay homage to these war dogs. Since the statue is outside (in the museum's front courtyard, to be exact), the folks at the March Air Field Museum say it's perfectly OK to bring your dog with you to visit. (Bringing a dog has provided at least one visitor with a convenient excuse about being a bit misty-eyed here: "I told my date sometimes I'm allergic to my dog," says the man, who was a hair too young for the war. "I don't think she bought it.") To find out more about the War Dogs association, call 877/WAR-DOGS (877/927-3647); www.war-dogs.com.

While you're at March Air Field, you can have a more uplifting experience if you expand your visit to include the outdoor section of the museum's aircraft exhibit. About 40 historic aircraft are "parked" outside, and leashed dogs can accompany your exploration. You'll see everything from the Lockheed SR-71 Blackbird to the B-17 Flying Fortress and the B-25 Mitchell bomber. If you're an airplane buff, put this place on your must-see list. It's a good idea to take your dog for a thorough walk before your visit, because you really don't want him making his mark anywhere here.

If you're visiting with another human, you can switch off between being outside with the pooch and going inside to see more fascinating aircraft and related artifacts. The museum is a nonprofit organization, and a $7 donation ($3 for children 5–11) is requested. It's just off I-215, at the Van Buren exit. Its orange-and-white checkerboard roof is visible as you approach from the freeway. 22550 Van Buren Boulevard, Riverside; 951/697-6602; www.marchfield.org. (A special thanks to my invaluable correspondent "Three-Dog-Dave" Hepperly for helping me sniff out this wonderful place.)

5 Rancho Jurupa Regional Park

🐾🐾🐾🐾 (See Riverside County map on page 208)

This huge county park encompasses a few others, including the Hidden Valley Wildlife Area. Stretching east to west for almost 10 miles, it more than makes up for all those smaller city parks that say "no way" to dogs.

Depending on which section you visit, you and your leashed dog can see lots of wildlife, fish for your supper, hike through fields and woods, or relax on the manicured grass of a shaded picnic area. Since our tastes are sometimes dictated by money, we like to go where we can avoid driving in and paying the $2 per person and $2 per pooch fee—especially if we just need to stretch our legs. We've found a wonderful spot next to the park's nature center, where many interesting hikes originate.

To reach this fee-free area, exit Highway 60 at Rubidoux Boulevard, drive southwest a few blocks, and turn right on Mission Boulevard. In about six blocks, turn left on Riverview Drive/Limonite Avenue. In just a little more than a half mile, there should be a sign for a county park. That's where River-view Drive veers to the left (Limonite continues straight). Follow Riverview for about another 1.5 miles. It will be smaller and more rural than the previous road. The park is on your left. Park in the lot near the nature center. Look for a trail and have yourselves a great hike.

If camping is your bag, you'll have to go to the fee area at Rancho Jurupa. From Highway 60, exit at Rubidoux Boulevard and drive south to Mission Boulevard. Turn left and drive about a half mile to Crestmore Boulevard. Follow Crestmore as it curves around the north side of the park. In about 1.5 miles, you'll be at the gate. Sites are $18. Dogs are $2 extra. There are approximately 70 sites available. For camping information, call Rancho Jurupa at 951/684-7032. For camping reservations, call 877/444-6777.

6 Box Springs Mountain Park

🐾🐾 (See Riverside County map on page 208)

I'm not sure how this place got its name, but I found that, like a box spring mattress, it's not all that comfortable by itself. You need a little padding to enjoy it. Lots of people bring their horses here, but a dog will do. When you decide to take a break from hiking the many trails, you can lie down and rest against your reposing pooch.

This hilly park has little shade, so it may not be an ideal place to take a dog (don't take her if it's hot). The day use is $2 for adults, $2 for dogs, $1 for kids. Driving east on Highway 60, exit at Pigeon Pass Road (about five miles east of town) and drive north to the park. 951/955-4310.

PLACES TO EAT

Check out the attractive pedestrian mall along Main Street for some doggone friendly eateries and some interesting history. These restaurants are a bone's throw from the Mission Inn, the city's premier historic and architectural landmark, located at 3696 Main Street. You can't go inside with your dog, but you can gawk from the outside.

42nd Street Bagels: "We're dog friendly here," one of the servers told us. "We really like dogs." Dogs do feel welcome. The people are friendly, but I think it's the cream cheese that makes dogs feel particularly at home. Slather a bagel with shmear and share it with your dog at the outdoor tables. 3737 Main Street; 951/274-9445.

Gram's Mission BBQ Palace: Dogs who visit the six outdoor tables here drool with delight at being so close to mouthwatering Cajun-style barbecued ribs, chicken, and other meaty delights. Thirsty dogs get a bowl of water. (And who wouldn't be thirsty after all that drooling?) 3527 Main Street; 951/782-8219.

Mario's Place: Trixie, Omar, and Hannah are dogs with impeccable taste. When they rave about a restaurant, you know it's a winner. And do they ever rave about this downtown Riverside gem. They're impressed by the lovely, long, narrow patio area that allows good dogs, and by the white tablecloths on the patio tables, and especially by the food: It's some of the best Italian food in the region. Try the butternut squash ravioli, the pear-gorgonzola wood-fired pizza, or if you're more adventurous, the grilled ostrich (it comes with celery root puree, sun-dried tart cherries, and crispy sage in a red wine sauce). If you give your dog a bite, she'll surely think it's beef. 3646 Mission Inn Avenue; 951/684-7755.

Mission Inn Coffee Co.: The coffee here is delicious, as are the tasty pastries and the sandwiches. Dine at the outdoor tables with your favorite dog. 3600 Main Street; 951/341-6789.

Riverside Brewing Co.: Thirsty dogs can enjoy a bowlful of water while you enjoy a stein full of fine house brew at the outdoor tables. Wash it down with a tasty burger or salad. 3397 Mission Inn Avenue; 951/784-2739.

Simple Simon's: This bakery and café in the old mission district is a great place to lunch with your pooch. There's plenty of outdoor seating. 3639 Main Street; 951/369-6030.

Upper Crust Sandwich Shoppe: Dogs delight in this place because the folks here seem to delight in dogs. The meatloaf sandwich is one of the bigger draws, for humans and dogs alike. Dine with your dog at this downtown eatery's outdoor tables. Dog patrons get a big bowl of water. 3573 Main Street; 951/784-3149.

PLACES TO STAY

The county seat is not flush with places to stay, especially places of the dog-friendly variety. Here are your choices, should you need to bunk here overnight.

Best Western of Riverside: Rates are $75–150. Dogs are $10 extra and can't be "too huge." 10518 Magnolia Avenue 92505; 951/359-0770.

Dynasty Suites Riverside: Here are two hoops your dog must jump through to be allowed to stay here: 1) He needs to weigh less than 25 pounds and 2) "It has to be a AAA member," says a front desk clerk. I hope she meant that the dog's people must be members of AAA, because I don't know too many card-carrying canine members of this auto club. Rates are $60–80. Dogs are $10 extra. 3735 Iowa Avenue 92507; 951/369-8200.

Motel 6: Rates are $39–53 for the first person, $6 extra for the second person. 1260 University Avenue 92507; 951/784-2131.

Rancho Jurupa Regional Park: See Rancho Jurupa Regional Park, above, for camping information.

Desert Hot Springs

This little community is known for its naturally hot mineral water—and it doesn't smell like rotten eggs! Folks with aches and pains come to soak in pools and tubs full of the stuff, and they swear by it. Dogs do some swearing of their own around here, but for a different reason: Pooches aren't permitted in any city parks.

PLACES TO STAY

Sky Valley Resort: If you have an RV and a hankering to soak in water that's good for you, come here. Sky Valley Park has nine naturally heated mineral Jacuzzis, as well as four large swimming pools. The RV resort is on 160 acres, with eight fishing ponds and lots of grassy areas and palm trees for leashed pooches to sniff out. It's also surrounded by the desert, so you can get a taste of the area's natural environment, too. If you're bored traveling around in your RV, the park also offers 10 shuffleboard courts, horseshoes, a huge clubhouse, tennis courts, and a hobby court with lapidary, stained glass, and ceramic equipment. Sky Valley Park has a sister RV park where only seniors are permitted, but all ages are welcome here. Rates are $37–38. 74-711 Dillon Road 92241; 800/800-9218; www.skyvalleyresort.com.

Corona

PARKS, BEACHES, AND RECREATION AREAS

7 Butterfield Dog Park

🐾 🐾 🐾 🐕 (See Riverside County map on page 208)

The dog people here worked hard for almost five years to make this fenced park a reality. The park's size, under an acre, is nothing to bark home about. But with its big old shade trees, cool green turf, benches, poop bag dispensers, and friendly people and dogs, it's been a smash hit with dogs who dig the leash-free life. It's at 1886 Butterfield Drive. Exit Highway 91 at North Maple Street and follow it as it parallels the tracks for the Atchison, Topeka & Santa Fe (the railroad, not the song). Maple dead-ends into North Smith Street. Turn left on Smith, and go about three blocks to Butterfield Drive, where you'll go left again. The park is on your right, within the Butterfield Stage Trail Park. 951/736-2241.

PLACES TO STAY

Dynasty Suites Corona: Dogs need to be under 25 pounds to stay at this motel, and they're $25 extra. Rates are $65–79. 1805 West 6th Street 91720; 951/371-7185.

Motel 6: Rates are $40–46 for one adult, $6 extra for the second. 200 North Lincoln Avenue 92882; 951/735-6408.

Perris

Dogs love Perris in the springtime. Dogs love Perris in the fall. Dogs love Perris in the winter, when it drizzles. Dogs don't love Perris in the summer, when it sizzles. Other than summertime, Perris is a favorite place for dogs. Not, as with the Paris song, because their love is near, but because the Orange Empire Railway Museum is here.

DIVERSION

Chug It Out with Your Dog: Dogs and railroads go together like love and marriage—or maybe even better. The **Orange Empire Railway Museum** is a great place to take a pooch. Jake Dog and I want to thank reader Marsden Chew MacRae for opening our eyes to this fun place. "On one memorable day, my golden retriever and I rode every single running exhibit, including the steam engine," writes Marsden Chew MacRae. (I use his three names again because he has such a great name.) "I also noted a rail fan with an attending German shepherd, who was much better trained than my dog and could actually get on and off without being lifted! Many dogs find the steps confusing and can't or won't navigate them, so bringing a dog small enough to lift might be important." That's some good advice from a man who knows his railroads. (He's traveled to many of the state's railroads with his faithful pooch.)

Leashed, well-behaved dogs can visit the museum's collection of streetcars, trolleys, a steam engine, and several diesels. They're not allowed in the buildings, but that's OK because the trains are much cooler. Speaking of cooler, it can get really hot here in summer, and this place can roast, so it's a good idea to bring your pooch here during other times of year.

Trolleys and trains operate Saturday and Sunday and major holidays 11 A.M.–5 P.M. Special events are held throughout the year. An all-day ride pass is $8 for adults, $6 for children 5–11. Dogs and little kids don't pay a penny. Call or write for details. 2201 South A Street, P.O. Box 548, Perris, CA 92572-0548; 951/657-2605 or 951/943-3020; www.oerm.org.

PARKS, BEACHES, AND RECREATION AREAS

8 Lake Perris State Recreation Area

😺 😺 😺 (See Riverside County map on page 208)

When people talk about this park, they generally focus on the lake. Comments I got when I asked friends about the park included the following: "You can catch some world-class fish there." "We had a great time swimming at the beach." And "I like to stand on the edge and watch for birds."

Great. Well, dogs, if you're into any of the above activities, forget it. You can't go near the lake, much less in it or on it. In fact, pooches have to stay at least 50 feet from the lake's edge. But fortunately, you are allowed to wear a leash and hike the trails. You'll be in sage scrub countryside, and there's not much shade, so go somewhere else if it's a hot day.

The day-use fee is $8 per vehicle. Camping costs $15–28. There are 167 tent-only sites and 265 RV sites. To reserve, phone 800/444-7275. From Highway 60, exit at Moreno Beach Drive and drive south a little more than three miles to the park. 951/657-0676.

PLACES TO STAY

Lake Perris State Recreation Area: See Lake Perris State Recreation Area, above, for camping information.

Idyllwild

This sweet, year-round mile-high resort is great for dogs on the go or for dogs who just like to sniff around artsy shops. Outdoorsy dogs can check out some marvelous hiking and cross-country skiing opportunities at nearby San Bernardino National Forest (see the National Forests and Wilderness Areas resource at the back of this book). Indoorsy dogs can putter around the quaint alpine community's lovely village area.

With its myriad art galleries, visual art events, and music, dance, and theater productions, Idyllwild has been named as one of the 100 Best Small Art Towns in America. Dogs are invited into some galleries and little shops on a case-by-case basis, so we won't go into specifics here. Just let your terribly cute and well-behaved dog sniff toward the door of one of these establishments, and she may well get an invitation to come in and help you select some merchandise.

If you and your pooch want to experience small-town types of events in this quaint alpine community, there's plenty to keep you busy. Dogs and their well-behaved people are invited to everything from outdoor pancake feasts (always benefiting a good local cause) to the July 4 parade (complete with a greyhound contingent). The Idyllwild Chamber of Commerce website lists these and other to-do's: www.idyllwildchamber.com; 951/659-3259.

PARKS, BEACHES, AND RECREATION AREAS

🐾 Idyllwild County Park

🐾 🐾 🐾 (See Riverside County map on page 208)

In the morning, the cool mountain air is delicately scented with fresh pines, and you may find yourself so invigorated that you actually want to get out of your tent and start the day early.

This is an attractive park, with scenic self-guided nature trails for you and your leashed pooch to peruse. Better yet, there's easy access to the wonderful, off-leash trails of San Bernardino National Forest. But you must check with a ranger before venturing out, because you could easily find yourself in the middle of Mount San Jacinto State Park—a major no-no for four-legged beasts of the domestic persuasion.

The day-use fee is $2 for adults, $2 for dogs, $1 for kids. Campsites cost $15, with dogs being charged the usual $2 county fee. Reservations are accepted for the 96 sites from April 1 through October 24. The rest of the year they're available on a first-come, first-served basis. The park is one mile north of Idyllwild, at the end of County Park Road; 951/659-2656. For reservations call 800/234-PARK (800/234-7275).

PLACES TO EAT

Cafe Aroma: Your schnozzle may not be as sensitive as your dog's, but come anywhere near here and you'll find that the Cafe Aroma really lives up to its name. The place smells simply *mahvelous!* The cuisine is a mixture of coffee-house and Italian. Cafe Aroma is famous around here for its morning scones and coffee. Later in the day, the café is full of wonderful garlicky, saucy, rich smells. Evening diners get to eat on white tablecloth-covered tables. It's lovely, but a bit perilous for the life of the tablecloth when you're downing your penne in spicy red sauce or your meatball pie! Dogs can join their people on the deck. (That sound you may hear is just your dog fervently praying for you to drop a chunk of that meatball pie.) 3596 North Circle Drive; 951/659-5212.

Oma's European Bakery & Restaurant: The salmon mousse, veggie sandwiches, and soups are tasty, but if you're hankering for something really different, try Oma's Famous Wurst Platter, a heavy-duty dish with three "European links," red cabbage or sauerkraut, and German potatoes. Get a soft pretzel on the side, and you'll be doing the polka all the way home. Dine with your drooling dog under the magnificent pines at Oma's big outdoor section. Thirsty dogs get water. 54241 Ridgeview; 951/659-2979.

PLACES TO STAY

Fireside Inn: The seven duplex cottages here are oh-so-cozy. (Please don't let "duplex" conjure images of ugly 1970s-style housing units. The wood cottages here are just partnered together, but they're not cheap-looking. Of course, even if they were, your dog wouldn't care.) Each cottage has its own fireplace, a private bath with shower, a sitting room, and color cable TV complete with VCR. Real wood, stained in a warm golden hue, flanks cabin walls. Most cabins have kitchenettes, and a few have patios. All are nonsmoking. Rates are $65–135. Dogs pay a $20 flat fee. 54540 North Circle Drive, P.O. Box 313 92549; 951/659-2966 or 877/797-3473; www.thefireside-inn.com.

Idyllwild County Park: See Idyllwild County Park, above, for camping information.

Knotty Pine Cabins: Dogs are welcome to stay at three of the eight wonderfully cozy, unique, well-appointed cabins here. (If you didn't already guess by the name, knotty pine figures heavily into the design schemes.) The cabins back up to a hill that's a fun place to give your dog some exercise.

Although the cabins are within walking distance of Idyllwild village, this is a peaceful place to vacation with your dog. In addition to the usual pines, oaks, and other flora, the grounds are blessed with lilac bushes! The scent of these glorious flowers is well worth planning a spring vacation around. Rates are $59–135. Dogs are $20 extra for the length of your stay. 54340 Pine Crest 92549; 951/659-2933; www.idyllwild.com/knotty.

Tahquitz Inn: Here's a dog rule you don't hear every day: No peeing on the totem pole! The eagle-topped totem pole here is a tempting target for many a boy dog, so steer clear. There's plenty of room on the grounds for a good walk, and plenty of trees for dogs who want to lift a leg. Most of the 16 cabins that make up the inn are attached in sort of a stepped pattern. This arrangement looks very much like a giant shallow staircase that winds around the inn's small pool. The cabins are pretty basic and somewhat motel-like inside, but they all have kitchens, and most have kind of funky fireplaces, so it's not so bad. The inn is 400 yards from Idyllwild's village. Rates are $85–110. Dogs are $10 extra. 25840 Highway 243 92549; 951/659-4554; www.tahquitzinn.com.

Mountain Center

While in town, stop by the Living Free animal sanctuary and see just how beautiful and livable an animal rescue facility can be. Living Free occupies 160 acres of scenic mountain country at the edge of the San Bernardino National Forest. You and your dog can visit together, and while you're on tour finding out about the many wonderful programs here, your dog will be cared for in a special pen. Your dog is guaranteed tender loving care while you learn about ways to help other animals get the same kind of love. For more information, call 951/659-4684.

🔟 Hurkey Creek Park

🐾🐾🐾🐾 (See Riverside County map on page 208)

At an elevation of about 4,500 feet and surrounded by 7,000-foot peaks, this meadow-like park stays cool even in the summer. Hurkey Creek flows through here, attracting lots of critters, so be sure your dog is leashed.

There are a couple of hiking trails and dogs love them. They'd really like to be able to sneak into the adjacent San Jacinto Wilderness, but it's one of the few national forest wilderness areas that doesn't permit pooches (because of its intermingling with a state park that bans dogs).

The day-use fee is $2 for adults, $2 for dogs, $1 for kids. Camping is $15, with dogs paying $2 for the privilege. The park is four miles south of Mountain Center off Highway 74. There are 130 campsites available. For camping reservations, call 800/234-PARK (800/234-7275). The park phone number is 951/659-2050.

PLACES TO STAY

Hurkey Creek Park: See Hurkey Creek Park, above, for camping information.

Palm Springs

First, the warning, straight from Esther M. W. Petersen, of the Palm Springs Animal Shelter: "Our area can be quite warm (HOT!!!!) all year-round, so please, please, please be sure to warn travelers about the dangers…. Our visitors don't seem to realize how hot it is. With our low humidity, it doesn't feel as hot as it really is, and pets can't handle the hot cement sidewalks, hot desert sand, and hot asphalt without getting burned pads."

Petersen knows her stuff. She has seen too many dogs whimper their last breaths because of heatstroke and other heat-related horrors. The municipal code forbids dogs to be left unattended in enclosed vehicles, no matter what time of year. The law is a good one. Since it was enacted in 1988, not a single pet has been lost to this disastrous practice.

Believe it or not, the entire posh desert playground city of Palm Springs is a wildlife preserve. You can routinely spot coyotes, bobcats, raccoons, snakes, lizards, and migratory birds around town. Occasionally, mountain lions and badgers have been sighted. Make sure your dog is leashed and that you hold the leash securely at all times.

For many, many years, dogs were not allowed to set paw in any of the city's parks. But tails are wagging fast and furiously around here these days, because dogs now have a spectacular park of their own. Palm Springs is also home to a few natural areas around town where you can take your pooch for a good walk. In addition, you can also take your dog to some fun, if *un*natural, places.

Several spectacular lodgings (and several not-quite-so-spectacular ones) welcome well-behaved dogs. Many Palm Springs restaurants permit dogs to dine outside with you. And many of the shops on Palm Canyon Drive let pets shop with their people. If you want your dog's opinion on a new bangle or beaded dress, you can even bring him to Saks Fifth Avenue. Just make sure he doesn't do a leg lift on the merchandise.

PARKS, BEACHES, AND RECREATION AREAS

If you want to feel the desert in your paws when you and your dog go out for a walk, you'll be happy to know that Palm Springs is surrounded by land run by the Bureau of Land Management. Call 760/251-4800 for information on fun places to hike during the cooler months.

Dog owners in town frequently use the many local "wash" areas (dry streambeds) to run on leash with their dogs. You'll see them on the outskirts of town and beyond, but with the new park opening, you might not see them as much as you used to.

DIVERSION

Make Tracks to Saks: Need a frock for that special occasion and just can't bear to leave your furry friend behind? Good news! If she's clean, flea-free, well-behaved, leashed, and promises not to leave puddles, you can bring her with you to shop at **Saks Fifth Avenue** in Palm Springs. The woman we spoke with at Saks says that "maybe you wouldn't want to bring a St. Bernard here." If you do bring a fairly large dog, please be sure to ask an employee if it's OK before starting your shopping spree. 201 North Palm Canyon Drive; 760/327-4126.

You can also take your leashed pooch to a nearby hiking area for an interesting desert romp. The Carl Lykken Hiking Trail starts at the extreme west end of Ramon Road. Don't forget your water. (There's some talk about banning dogs from the trail, so don't be surprised if you see one of those horrible signs with a slash through a dog silhouette during a future walk.) Unfortunately, our other favorite area for dogs, the 27,000-acre Indian Canyons, no longer allows dogs because of some very bad incidents with pit bulls and their people.

11 Palm Springs Dog Park

🐾🐾🐾🐾🐕 (See Riverside County map on page 208)

Dogs of Palm Springs are panting, but not because of the heat (they all live in air-conditioned quarters, after all). They're panting with joy, because their dog park is so wonderful. This isn't just any ordinary dog park. Lest you've forgotten, this is Palm Springs, after all.

This 1.6-acre park is a real work of art, complete with an iron fence and double gates designed by sculptor Phil Evans. (How many dog park fences have dog paws and faces carved into them?) It's big compared with many dog parks, and it has everything a dog could want—and a lot more: It's grassy, with some trees, awnings for extra shade, a separate fenced area for pups or tiny dogs who are overwhelmed by the big dogs running around the main area, drinking fountains that have two levels so humans and their pooches can slurp together, picnic tables, lights at night, and plenty of poop bags. For your boy dog's aiming pleasure, the park also features *11* fire hydrants. Of course, these aren't your run-of-the-mill hydrants. These hydrants are of the beautiful antique variety. Your dog will do leg lifts in style.

The park is directly behind City Hall, at 222 Civic Drive North; 760/322-8362.

DIVERSION

Who Needs Hollywood?: You and your dog can sniff out the sidewalk-embedded stars of more than 70 celebrities who have "lived, loved, and played" in Palm Springs. The **Palm Springs Walk of Stars** includes stars for Ralph Bellamy, Elizabeth Taylor, Frank Sinatra, Bob Hope, Ginger Rogers, Marilyn Monroe, and Marlene Dietrich. The Walk of Stars is on Palm Canyon Drive in the beautiful central village. You can get a complete list of celebrities and their stars' locations by visiting www.palmsprings.com/stars.

PLACES TO EAT

Palm Springs is full of fine restaurants with outdoor areas where dogs are welcome.

Blue Coyote Grill: You and your dog can't exactly eat together here, since she must remain tied up just outside the railing while you sit just inside it. But she'll still be close enough to drool over the Southwestern delights on your dish. 445 North Palm Canyon Drive; 760/327-1196.

Hair of the Dog: As long as you don't find anything resembling this English pub's name floating in your appetizers or your beer, you'll enjoy it here. People can sit at a half dozen outdoor tables with their pooches. 238 North Palm Canyon Drive; 760/323-9890.

Native Foods: "A most outrageous vegetarian restaurant" is how regular diners Hannah the Human and her dogs Gracie and Petey describe this comfortable and dog-friendly restaurant. "It's the best place of all for your book." It's certainly right up there, especially if you're a vegetarian or vegan. Native Foods offers all kinds of tasty dishes—so tasty, in fact, that even avid omnivores enjoy plowing through the menu's offerings.

Co-owner Tanya Petrovna is a dog lover through and through. She makes sure canine guests get a big bowl of water. (This distracts doggies, who are then less likely to beg for your delectable veggie wrap or cheesecake—at least for a minute.)

Native Foods has one of Palm Springs' more pleasant patio areas for pooches and their people. Misters keep things cool, or at least tolerable. We're talking mister, as in a device that provides a cool mist, not mister as in Mister Rogers. (Although come to think of it, he always keeps things cool, too.) 1775 East Palm Canyon Drive; 760/416-0070.

Peabody's Coffee Bar & Jazz Club: You won't find Mr. Peabody here, but all other dogs, brainy or not, are welcome to dine and drink with you at the patio. (The listing for Sherman's, below, is pure coincidence. Either that, or

---

DIVERSION

My Fair Laddy: On Thursday evenings 7–10 P.M., well-behaved, leashed pooches may accompany you to Palm Spring's glamorous Palm Canyon Drive, where an old-fashioned **street fair** will charm the spots off your dog. Musicians, food, arts and crafts vendors, and a certified farmers' market make this street even more charming than it normally is. The fair takes place between Tahquitz Canyon Drive and Baristo Road. Parking is best behind the Desert Inn Fashion Plaza. Call 800/34-SPRINGS (800/347-7746) for more information.

---

someone's hiding a Wayback Machine somewhere in the desert.) 134 South Palm Canyon Drive; 760/322-1877.

Pomme Frite: The French and Belgian cuisine here is snout-licking good. Try the braised coq au vin for a traditionally delicious dish. If you're a mussel fan, you'll be happy to know that mussels are prepared nine different ways and always accompanied by crispy versions of the restaurant's name. Yum! Your dog can join you at the large, covered back patio. 256 South Palm Canyon Drive; 760/778-3727.

Sherman's Deli & Bakery: Dogs are welcome to join their people at the shaded tables in front of this New York–style eatery. And if your pooch is thirsty, she'll even get a big bowl of water. "We're dog friendly!" reports an equally people-friendly server. The pot roast dinner is to drool for. A lunch that's no lighter on the meat is the double-combo pastrami sandwich that includes another meat of your choice. (Yes, it's filling.) Breakfasts are a delight, too. 401 East Tahquitz Canyon Way; 760/325-1199.

Spencer's at the Mountain: Dogs go ga-ga when you order the delicious pecan-crusted chicken, but the drool really flows when they sniff out the steak and lobster dishes Spencer's is known for. (The liver and bacon sets their noses aflutter too, but that combo sounds too much like canned dog food varieties for us.) Dine next to the trees at one of two patios here. Thirsty dogs get a bowl of water. 701 West Baristo Road; 760/327-3446.

PLACES TO STAY

Palm Springs has oodles of quality canine accommodations. It used to be that they allowed only the itsy-bitsy-est of dog-ettes. Now most welcome any size good dog.

Caliente Tropics Resort: If you like campy, retro, fun, attractive, super-dog-friendly accommodations, look no further than this fully renovated 1960s Polynesian-style motel. The rooms are tiki-boutique-y, tiki torches flank the pool and the grounds, and the signage is delectably 1964.

You and your dog can sniff out tiki god statues and other Polynesian artifacts throughout the resort. There's a tall, cylindrical, angry-looking god head outside that can scare the daylights out of more sensitive dogs. One pooch wrote to tell me he had a little accident when he sniffed it out, thinking it was a tree at first until he saw its glowering eyes and fierce mouth. He fluffed up, cowered two steps back, and "suddenly my owners found themselves wishing they had a pooper-scooper." This dog asked that I not use his name because he is embarrassed about this incident. Poor Frank. (Oops! Sorry, Frank.)

With the exception of a few rare incidents like Frank's, dogs absolutely adore this place. It's one of the more dog-friendly lodgings in this book. Dogs who come here get gourmet treats shaped like tiki heads, water and food dishes, blankets, poop bags, and cushy dog beds. Best of all, there's a fenced grassy area by the pool where well-behaved dogs are welcome to trot around leash free. In fact, there's even a fledgling Pet Star Walk of Fame right there.

In case you or your dog is interested in a little celeb history, you should know that long ago the Caliente had a private underground supper club where Elvis, the Rat Pack, and other big celebs could relax in peace. It was beautiful, with the popular colors of the time—purple and white—on the leather banquettes, white tablecloths, and a stage. Alas, a former owner concerned about earthquake proofing filled it with cement.

Rates are $65–225. Dogs are $20 extra. 411 East Palm Canyon Drive 92264; 760/327-1391 or 866/HOT-9595 (866/468-9595); www.calientetropics.com.

Casa Cody Country Inn: Dogs love this quaint, quiet historic country inn almost as much as their peace-seeking people do. Past canine visitors have caused some problems because irresponsible owners have left them alone in the room. Don't even think of doing this. Rates are $49–199. Dogs are $10 extra for the length of your stay. 175 South Cahuilla Road 92262; 760/320-9346; www.casacody.com.

Doral Resort: This attractive hotel is set on a golf course. Some of the rooms have great views. Dogs up to 50 pounds can stay here. Rates are $69–219. Dogs pay a $50 flat fee. 67-967 Vista Chino 92234; 760/322-7000; www.doralpalmsprings.com.

Hilton Palm Springs Resort: "We are delighted to have dogs as guests. They find it very entertaining here," a vivacious, dog-loving staffer tells us. "That's why all the rooms have balconies. Dogs like to look out and see what's going on." From one side of this very comfortable, attractive hotel, dogs can look out at the mountains. From the other, they can look down at the swimming pool. Ask the concierge about nearby places to walk with your dog. "Lots of folks bring their pets here, and we've got some great places for them to walk," another staffer said. Rates are $130–400. Dogs require a $100 deposit, and they pay a $20 flat fee. 400 East Tahquitz 92262; 760/320-6868 or 800/522-6900; www.hiltonpalmsprings.com.

Motel 6: There are three of these motels in Palm Springs. Rates are $40–58 for one adult, $6 extra for a second adult. Phone 800/466-8356 for information and reservations.

Musicland Hotel: "Any pooch under 200 pounds is OK," says a dog-friendly staffer. Rates are $33–99. Dogs are $5 extra. 1342 South Palm Canyon Drive 92264; 760/325-1326.

Palm Springs Riviera Resort and Racquet Club: If you like recreation, you'll love this large, gorgeous resort. The Riviera boasts Palm Springs' biggest pool, plus an 18-hole lighted putting course and several lighted tennis courts. (It's home of the Billie Jean King World Team Tennis Finals, if that tells you how nice the courts are.) You can also play basketball and volleyball here, and the workout room is more than adequate.

Dogs don't care about all this, because they can't really do much other than lounge in the room and stroll the palm-festooned grounds with you. But the rooms are beautifully appointed in relaxing earthy hues, and the grounds are 24 acres of fun (no golf course jaunts with dogs, please), so there's plenty to keep a pooch happy. If you want to live it up, stay at one of the poolside suites. They're exquisite. Rates are $79–349. Dogs are $20 extra and require a $200 deposit. 1600 North Indian Canyon Drive 92262; 760/327-8311; www.psriviera.com.

A Place in the Sun: This is a fun place to stay if you like your immaculate room or larger bungalow surrounded by greenery and palms, backed by mountains. The two-bedroom bungalows (the largest accommodations) have a patio and fireplace, as well as a full kitchen. The pool and Jacuzzi are blissfully chorine free! They're actually filled with mild salt water (advertised as being only half as salty as your own teardrops). And yahoo! There's no longer the former size limit of 20 pounds. Any size good dog can stay here. Rates are $79–309. Dogs are $15 extra. 754 San Lorenzo Road 92264; 760/325-0254 or 800/779-2254; www.aplaceinthesunhotel.com.

Quality Inn Resort: Rates are $49–189. 1269 East Palm Canyon Drive 92264; 760/323-2775 or 800/221-2222.

7 Springs Inn & Suites: Dogs and their people adore staying at this charming, affordable boutique hotel. The 50 rooms and suites are relaxing and beautifully designed, with tranquil earth tones, 500-thread count sheets (the last motel we stayed at seemed to have 25-thread count sheets; ouch!), goose-down pillows, marble floors, granite countertops, and views of the inn's little pool and garden area. Rates are $69–259. Dogs are $15 extra. 950 North Indian Canyon Drive 92262; 760/320-9110 or 800/883-0417; www.palm-springs-hotels.cc.

Super 8 Lodge: If you're traveling with more than one dog, this is a good place to bunk for the night: You can have up to three dogs per room, and the cost is only $10 extra per room. Room rates are $45–85. 1900 North Palm Canyon Drive 92262; 760/322-3757.

Villa Rosa Inn: It's trees, trees everywhere at this lovely motel/inn, where all six accommodations are poolside. Dogs love the trees, and they enjoy the spacious Southwest-meets-Pier-1-Imports-style rooms and suites. Especially comforting to hot dogs are the cool terracotta tile floors. Built in 1948, this inn is just as immaculate and crisp as the day it was born. (Except the flowers and arbors are a lot bigger now.) Rates are $89–169. Dogs are $20 extra and shouldn't be too big. "We try to keep them not major size," says an innkeeper. 1577 South Indian Trail 92264; 760/327-5915; www.villarosainn.com.

Palm Desert

This desert resort town's motto, "Where the sun shines a little brighter," could use an addendum these days. We think it should read, "Where the sun shines a little brighter and dogs smile a little wider." See why below.

PARKS, BEACHES AND RECREATION AREAS

You may think nothing grows in the desert, but two dog parks have recently popped right up out of the ground like miraculous desert flowers. Actually, it was a lot more work than just popping out of the ground. But the success of these dog parks has paved the path for more in the future. A city councilman told the *Desert Sun* newspaper that he doesn't foresee any parks being built in Palm Desert without having some kind of dog park facility. Oh, what a wonderful place to be a dog!

🐾🐾🐾🐕 Civic Center Park Dog Park

🐾🐾🐾🐕 (See Riverside County map on page 208)

This luscious canine oasis is grassy, with trees, shaded seating, double gates, a beautiful iron fence, a separate area for small dogs who would rather not mess with the big guys, poop bags, and a big fire hydrant. The hydrant is so popular we've even heard about dogs lining up to make their mark.

The park is less than an acre, but dogs take advantage of their leashless freedom. They run and run, drink some water, run and run, sniff a newcomer, run and run, head for the hydrant, and run and run some more. Meanwhile, people have a grand old time socializing with each other. The park is within the attractive Civic Center Park, where there's a nice playground and lovely landscaping. It's at Fred Waring Drive and San Pablo Avenue, near College of the Desert. 760/346-0611.

🐾🐾🐕 Country Club Dog Park

🐾🐾🐕 (See Riverside County map on page 208)

No, you won't see dogs clad in white golf outfits showing off their pedigrees here. Any breed or mutt is welcome at Country Club Dog Park, and they can be stark naked, too. They don't even have to wear leashes at this fenced park. The reason for the exclusive-sounding name is because the park is in the Palm Desert Country Club neighborhood.

The park is less than half the size of the Civic Center dog park, but it has many of the same amenities, including grass, benches, water, poop bags, shade cover, and even a fire hydrant. It's set in a newish community park (which also has "country club" in the name) at Avenue of the States and California Avenue. 760/346-0611.

PLACES TO EAT

Sherman's Deli & Bakery: If you like New York–style deli food, this place is a must-visit. For something delectably different, try the corned-beef sandwich with potato pancakes instead of bread. It's a house specialty. The house-baked goods are tasty, too. Best of all, dogs get water and doggy biscuits here. (Jake Dog likes these, but his sweet tooth makes him quiver for Sherman's wonderful cheesecakes.) Sherman's is in the Plaza de Monterey Shopping Center, at 73161 Country Club Drive. 760/568-1350.

PLACES TO STAY

Desert Patch Inn: Dogs who dig quiet digs will enjoy this small inn. The rooms are spacious, and while not super stylish, they're clean and have fridges and microwaves. The grounds are lovely, with palms, a pool, and loads of greenery. An extensive continental breakfast comes with your stay. Rates are $47–130.

73-758 Shadow Mountain Drive 92260; 760/346-9161 or 800/350-9758; www .desertpatch.com.

The Inn at Deep Canyon: You and your dog can feast your eyes on the motel's palms, garden, pool, and hydrotherapy spa from most rooms here. You'll get a continental breakfast, too. Rates are $47–261. Dogs are $10 extra. 74-470 Abronia Trail 92260; 760/346-8061 or 800/253-0004; www.inn-adc.com.

Indio

It may look flat and boring, but this dry old town has the distinction of being the king of the only region in the United States that grows dates. And we're not talking a few trees—we're talking 4,000 acres' worth, making a semi-oasis out of an otherwise blah, depressing area.

PARKS, BEACHES, AND RECREATION AREAS

14 Miles Avenue Park

🐾🐾 (See Riverside County map on page 208)

If you're dropping someone off at the adjacent Coachella Valley Museum and Cultural Center, your dog might appreciate a little pause at this grassy, meadowy park. It looks like a golf course, but miraculously enough in this golf-inundated land, it's not. There are some deciduous trees, as well as palms, for the benefit of the boy dogs in the crowd.

The park is on Deglet Noor Street and Miles Avenue, about three blocks north of Highway 111. 760/342-6580.

PLACES TO EAT

Andy's Restaurant: The outdoor seating area is not huge, but that won't make your dog drool any less over the burgers, pastrami, and hot dogs you can eat here. Breakfast is also available. 83-699 Indio Boulevard; 760/347-1794.

PLACES TO STAY

Best Western Date Tree Motor Hotel: Rates are $60–120. Pooches are $10 extra. 81-909 Indio Boulevard 92201; 760/347-3421; www.datetree.com.

Palm Shadow Inn: This motel is truly a desert oasis. Its three acres of green grounds are ripe with flowers and date trees. There's a pool and hot tub, too. Not much here says "desert" except the sweet, dry air. Some of the rooms come with kitchens, which can make life easier when traveling with a pooch. Rates are $84–129. Dogs are $5 extra. 80-761 Highway 111 92201; 760/347-3476 or 800/700-8071; www.palmshadowinn.com.

Royal Plaza Inn: You'll get a heated pool and a spa when you stay here, but no pooches in the *agua*, please. Rates are $44–129. Dogs are $10 extra. 82-347 Highway 111 92201; 760/347-0911.

Blythe

If you're traveling from the east on I-10 and vow that you'll stop in the first California town you hit, get ready to brake. Blythe isn't an exciting town, but it's a welcome sight if you've traveled across the country with the Golden State as your goal.

PARKS, BEACHES, AND RECREATION AREAS

15 Mayflower Park

(See Riverside County map on page 208)

This park covers only 24 acres, but because it backs up on the refreshing Colorado River, it seems much bigger. The folks here are pretty laid-back about dogs when it's not crowded. Pooches should be leashed, but you can still let them do a little wading in the water. Just watch out for those pesky boats.

Mayflower Park is an excellent place to stop if you've been driving all day and feel like fishing for stripers or catfish, cooking your catch for dinner, and then camping by the river.

The day-use fee is $2 for adults, $2 for dogs, $1 for kids. Camping costs $15–16, with dogs costing $2 extra. There are 180 sites available. The park is six miles northeast of Blythe, just north of 6th Avenue and Colorado River Road. Sites are first-come, first-served. For park info, call 760/922-4665.

PLACES TO STAY

Best Western Sahara Motel: Rates are $59–109. 825 West Hobson Way 92225; 760/922-7105.

Legacy Inn: Rates are $45–62. Small pooches are preferred, and they need to stay in smoking rooms. 903 West Hobson Way 92225; 760/922-4146.

Hidden Beaches: This is one of the many camping resorts along the Colorado River. Sites are $22–27 per day, and pooches cost $2 extra. There are 92 sites available. Reservations are recommended in the summer. 6951 6th Avenue 92225; 760/922-7276.

Mayflower Park: See Mayflower Park, above, for information.

McIntyre Park: Dogs can stay here only in the winter (November–March). The camping fee is $20–25 per car or RV. There are sites to accommodate approximately 700 people. We're not exactly talking an intimate camping experience. Call for RV or riverfront reservations. Others are available on a first-come, first-served basis. 8750 East 26th Avenue 92225; 760/922-8205.

Temecula

If cruising around the area makes you and your dog think it's all just one big subdivision after another, you need a visit to Old Town Temecula, with its attractive storefronts, antique shops, eateries, and host of fun events. While you're at it, take a trip to the area's Wine Country. You can drive while your dog drinks. Wait, your dog can drive while you drink. Hmm. Well, I'm sure you'll work it out between you (see the Diversion Whine Not!).

PARKS, BEACHES, AND RECREATION AREAS

Some people here drive 80 miles round-trip to use Escondido's dog park—one of the closest around at this point. Locals been working for years toward getting their own dog park, and it looks like they're finally going to get their wish: By late 2005, if all goes as planned, there will be a fenced dog park at the Temecula Community Recreation Center, 30875 Rancho Vista Road. Call for updates: 951/694-6410.

16 Duck Pond Park

☙☙ (See Riverside County map on page 208)

Feel like breaking bread? Do it with the ducks! This pretty park has a duck-filled pond as its centerpiece and its raison d'être. They appreciate the bread, but they also appreciate you coming with a dog who isn't a duck-chaser. (Jake,

DIVERSION

Whine Not!: You can visit Temecula's fine wineries with your dogs, so there's no need to cry into your beer. Most of the 18 wineries here allow dogs to join you at their outdoor picnic areas. One of the humans in your party can go inside, do some tasting and touring, and perhaps bring out a bottle fresh from the cellars for your little picnic.

A very dog-friendly winery is **Bella Vista Cilurzo Vineyard & Winery** (41220 Calle Contento; 909/676-5250). "We love dogs!" says a winery rep who has a dog of her own. Equally dog-friendly is **Keyways Vineyard & Winery** (37338 DePortola Road; 909/302-7888). "We allow horses," says a Keyways vintner. "Every week about 20 riders come up, park their horses, drink some wine, and ride away." (Now that's a new twist on drinking and driving.) "So of course we'll allow dogs." **Wilson Creek Winery** also welcomes pooches at its picnic tables (35960 Rancho California Road; 909/699-9463).

You'll find a helpful list and map of all of Temecula's wineries, their websites, and basic info at www.temeculawines.com.

who is a duck dog through and through, would go out of his bird here.) You can bring your calm leashed dog to the pond's edge or walk your normal leashed dog on a path that meanders through willows and other shady arbors.

This park doesn't have great scenery nearby: It's across the street from a big Target store and a slightly less unattractive place, the Tower Plaza shopping center. 28250 Ynez Road, at Rancho California Road; 951/694-6410.

🐾 Lake Skinner County Park

🐾🐾🐾🐾 (See Riverside County map on page 208)

So what if your dog can't swim in the lake or even hang out in your boat with you? Of the 6,040 acres of park, the lake makes up only about 1,200 acres. That means several thousand acres of hilly chaparral country are all yours. Leashed pooches are permitted to peruse the trails and run around the open turf areas.

During the rainy season, the trails may be closed. Call before you visit. The day-use fee is $2 per adult and $1 per child. Campsites are $12–18. Dogs are $2 extra. There are approximately 265 campsites. From I-15, take the Rancho California Avenue exit northeast and drive about nine miles to the park. Call 800/234-PARK (800/234-7275) for reservations. For park information, call 951/926-1541.

PLACES TO STAY

Lake Skinner County Park: See Lake Skinner County Park, above, for camping information.

   Motel 6: Rates are $45–67 for the first adult, $6 for the second. 41900 Moreno Drive 92590; 951/676-7199.

La Quinta

PLACES TO STAY

La Quinta Resort & Club: First, for all of you who have stayed at the La Quinta motel chain with your dog, this isn't one of those motels. Not by a long shot. This La Quinta is the mother of all La Quintas. This internationally famous resort is probably the most legendary of all the posh getaways in the Palm Springs area. The town of La Quinta was named after it, if that tells you anything. Built in 1926, it's the area's oldest resort. It quickly became a favorite retreat for the stars of the Golden Era of Hollywood. (Frank Capra wrote *It Happened One Night* in a casita here, and after its success, he declared it his good luck charm and returned frequently to write other screenplays.)

   Before you read on, you should know that if your dog is more than 25 pounds, he can't accompany you here. Jake Dog cried in his kibble when he heard about this rule. I thought I'd spare you and yours the same disappointment and tell you up front, and not down below. Actually, according to some unidentified sources, bigger dogs have been known to be allowed here. It may be worth a try, if your heart is set on this wonderland and your dog weighs more than his bag of dog food.

   Everything here is top drawer. The 804 guest casitas, each a Spanish-style cottage, are beautifully furnished and offer real privacy and peace. Many have wood-burning fireplaces. The landscaping is lush, with gorgeous flowers and palms everywhere. The restaurants are magnificent (some allow doggies at their patios), and the shops at La Quinta's plaza are some of the finest around. Even the beauty parlor is special—a fun Art Deco style. For humans, there are 41 swimming pools, 34 spas, 23 tennis courts, and 90 famous holes of championship golf. You can get a massage in the sun, work out in the fitness center, and do a zillion other wonderful things. For dogs, there are a few little areas to ramble leash-free on the surrounding 45 acres, but you'll have to ask about those because we're not supposed to tell you where they are.

   Dogs are relegated to the cottages with enclosed private patios. Rates for these are $225–445. Dogs pay a $100 fee for the length of their stay. 49-499 Eisenhower Drive, P.O. Box 69 92253; 760/564-4111 or 800/598-3828; www .laquintaresort.com.

Mecca

PARKS, BEACHES, AND RECREATION AREAS

🔞 Salton Sea State Recreation Area

🐾 🐾 🐾   (See Riverside County map on page 208)

If you ever wanted to explore the Salton Sea, this is a great place to start your observations. The park has 16 miles of shoreline, including five beaches. Dogs must wear the mandatory leash attire, but they manage to have a fabulous time anyway.

Unfortunately, dogs are not allowed on the trails that connect a couple of these areas together, but you can transport your pooch from one area to another by car. Try to spend at least one night. Three of the beaches are primitive, and they have campsites right at the seaside. While dogs must be leashed, they still love dunking their paws in the very buoyant water.

The day-use fee is $4. Camping costs $10–14. There are 149 developed sites available on a first-come, first-served basis. Dogs generally prefer the cheaper, more primitive sites. Take Highway 111 southeast of Mecca about 10 miles, and you'll find the park headquarters and visitor center on the west side of the highway. (About half of the park is in Imperial County. If you're approaching the lake from the southeast side and have a hankering to discover the Imperial section of the park, take Highway 111 to any of several entrances, including the popular Bombay Beach area.) 760/393-3059.

PLACES TO STAY

Salton Sea State Recreation Area: See the Salton Sea State Recreation Area, above, for camping information.

CHAPTER 6
Great Escapes

Yes, dogs, there really is life beyond the L.A. area. And sometimes it can be most spectacular. These dog-friendly places are excerpted from my book, *The Dog Lover's Companion to California,* an award-winning 1,000-page scoop on dog-lovin' places in the Golden State—and these listings are just the tip of the iceberg.

MONO COUNTY

June Lake

PARKS, BEACHES, AND RECREATION AREAS

Silver Lake

Leashed dogs may wag a tail or two when you catch trout after trout here. This 80-acre lake is stocked with many thousands of rainbows each year. But what really sets dogs off is that when you take them for a long hike up the magnificent trail that takes you far, far away from the bait store, the full-service resort, and the boat rental facility, they can be leash free!

The trailhead is near the camping area ($13 per site, dogs must be leashed). Once you start hiking, you and your leash-free dog may never want to return. The trail can loop you into Yosemite National Park, so you have to watch how long you tread, because dogs are banned from Yosemite's trails. But an exciting and not too strenuous hike will take you along the Rush Creek drainage, past Gem Lake and Agnew Lake, and into the pristine Ansel Adams Wilderness. Bring a big lunch and lots of water, and you'll have a vacation your dog will remember into her old age.

The lake is about halfway on the June Lake Loop, so you can exit U.S. 395 at the north or south end of the loop (Highway 158), depending on the direction you're traveling. The campground, which has about 63 sites, is open May–September. All sites are first-come, first-served. 760/647-3045 or 760/647-6595.

PLACES TO STAY

Double Eagle Resort and Spa: So you think you'll be roughing it just because you're staying in the eastern Sierra Nevada? No way. This is not a resort in the classic California lakeside sense of the word. It's a resort in the "ooh" and "aah" sense of the word. The Double Eagle was recently listed by Forbes.com as being one of the top 10 spas in the world. It's an outstanding, upscale place, with amenities that will leave you and your dog drooling.

The two-bedroom cabins are new, luxurious, and exquisitely furnished. Wood-burning fireplaces and stoves, big decks, and fully equipped kitchens make you feel right at home in the quiet forest setting. The resort is on 14 acres and bordered on two sides by National Forest land. This makes for some wonderful hikes. Nanda Devi, a lovely golden retriever, gave us the heads-up about this place. She enjoyed hikes by the lake and swimming, while her mom reveled in spa treatments.

The spa offers more than 50 specialty massages. One involves stones. It's somehow supposed to be pretty relaxing. A few treatment rooms have fireplaces. It's worth the extra money if you want the ultimate in relaxation during winter. Humans love the indoor swimming pool, whirlpool, and excellent fitness center. The resort's restaurant offers healthful, delicious cuisine. None of this interests dogs, but that's OK. It gets you there, which gets them there, and that's what counts.

Dogs are allowed at five of the cottages. Rates are $287–319, with dogs costing $15 extra. 5587 Highway 158 93529; 760/648-7004; www.doubleeagleresort.com.

Fern Creek Lodge: It's kind of like a little village here. You've got 10 cabins (some are like big, two-story houses), four apartment units, a store that sells everything from groceries to fishing gear, and a large barbecue area. All the buildings are arranged in a semicircular fashion, with the main lodge and store in the center. Fern Creek has a very dog-friendly atmosphere, with many people either visiting with dogs or wanting to pet yours.

Rates are $55–130. The biggest cabins sleep up to 16 people and cost $210. Dogs are $10 extra. 4628 Highway 158 93529; 760/648-7722 or 800/621-9146; www.ferncreeklodge.com.

Gull Lake Lodge: You're surrounded by forest at this *very* dog-friendly lodge. Owner Vikki Magee loves dogs and has a great theory about traveling pooches: "No bad dogs make it as far as the car," she says. It's been her experience that dogs who get to vacation with their people must be pretty darned special. And she's right. "Besides," she says, "they don't steal towels." Upon your arrival, you'll likely be greeted by her own two fabulously friendly pooches, Taco and Maggie.

The entire lodge has been remodeled. All units now have kitchens and are looking very nice. Rates are $70–165, and that includes fish-cleaning facilities. The lodge is between June and Gull Lakes. Some rooms have lake views. 132 Leonard Street 93529; 760/648-7516 or 800/631-4081; www.gulllakelodge.com.

Silver Lake: See Silver Lake, above, for camping information.

Mammoth Lakes

This charming resort town is a magical ski haven in the winter and an angler's dream in the summer. It's an excellent base for exploring the 200,000 surrounding acres known as Mammoth Lakes Recreational Area.

The lakes in this region are numerous and abound with great fishing and camping opportunities. The mountains and forests are rife with hiking and cross-country skiing areas for you and the pooch of your dreams. You can ski just about anywhere in the national forest, as long as you keep your dog off the groomed cross-country trails. And once you get away from people, you can unleash your obedient dog and bound through nature together.

Dog-friendly lodgings abound, but if you need extra help watching your dog (should you want to ski with your human traveling partner, for instance), check out Tailwaggers Too, which offers excellent doggy day care and overnight boarding. (It's right upstairs from Tailwaggers dog bakery, at the Sierra Center Mall, 924 Old Mammoth Road; 760/924-2800.) Another place your dog can hang out while you ski or dine or shop is Marta's Doggie Day Care. (See description under Edelweiss Lodge, below.) At either day care, your dog will probably have as a good a time as you will. (And if you ski like I do, a better time.)

DIVERSION

Up, Up, and Away: If the idea of dangling 11,000 feet above sea level doesn't faze you or your dog, hop aboard the **Mammoth Mountain Ski Area gondolas** for a lofty adventure.

Actually, during your 12-minute ascent from 9,000 feet to 11,000 feet on the Scenic Gondola Ride, you'll glide only a few dozen feet above the ground—spectacular views make it seem as though you're higher. You can sniff out a scenic spot less than a quarter mile away or try your paw at descending the mountain. It's rather barren, and the trails aren't for the faint of heart: They're narrow and seem precipitous at times. (One very windy afternoon, I got several hundred yards down and decided that I'd better turn around. I felt like I was going to blow off the mountainside.) The hike all the way down takes about 1.5 to 2 hours, depending on how you handle the trails.

The fee for adults is $16. Older children are $8, and kids six and under go for free. Dogs of all ages go for free, too. Exit U.S. 395 at the Mammoth Junction exit and drive west along Highway 203/Main Street through the town of Mammoth Lakes. Go right on Minaret Summit/Minaret Road. In about four miles you'll see the gondola station on your right. 760/934-2571 or 888/4-MAMMOTH (888/462-6668).

PARKS, BEACHES, AND RECREATION AREAS

Devil's Postpile National Monument
😾😾😾😾

Although Devil's Postpile is actually just over the border in Madera County, it is accessible only via its neighbor, Mammoth Lakes. If you're in the area with your dog, take advantage of this great exception to the national park system—dogs are allowed just about everywhere people can go, as long as they're leashed.

And what a place it is. If the devil ever did have a pile of posts, this would be it. The 60-foot wall of columnar basalt "posts" is truly awe-inspiring. Pick up a brochure and find out the fascinating geology behind these geometric (and geologic) wonders.

In addition to the postpile, this 800-acre park is home to Rainbow Falls, where the Middle Fork of the San Joaquin River drops 101 feet over a cliff of volcanic lava. It's a remarkable sight. You can also get to some great backcountry trails from here: The Pacific Crest Trail and John Muir Trail are among the trails dogs love to sniff out.

Unless you plan on going up very early in the morning or after 8 P.M., or unless you're going to be camping or fishing one of the area's lakes with a boat, you'll have to take a fun shuttle bus a few miles down to the valley. On a recent trip, we met up with a little tiny mutt in a front carrier and a giant German shepherd from San Diego. The shepherd befriended my human child and shared a seat with her. (She said it was the best part of the trip. So much for Mother Nature.)

A great place to catch the shuttle is in front of the Mammoth Mountain Inn. Exit U.S. 395 at Mammoth Junction and drive west along Highway 203/Main Street through the town of Mammoth Lakes. Turn right at Minaret Summit/Minaret Road and drive about four miles. You can buy your ticket in the gondola building. The cost is $7 round-trip for adults, $4 for children. Dogs go free. The road is impassable in the winter, so the park is closed during snowy months (which can sometimes last into June, so call first). Call the U.S. Forest Service at 760/924-5500 for bus schedules and pickup locations. Phone 760/934-2289 for Devil's Postpile information.

Horseshoe Lake
🐾🐾🐾🐾 🐕

Most of the lakes in this part of the eastern Sierra are developed and popular among humankind. But although Horseshoe Lake is just a stick's throw from civilization, it's a refreshing exception. Not only is it breathtaking, it's quiet.

You really can get away from folks here. In summer, it's not as heavily fished as other local lakes, partly because it's not stocked with trout. But if you visit with a dog, chances are you'll have more on your mind than fishing anyway. And that's where this lake is a little piece of dog heaven. While your dog has to be leashed around the lake, he's allowed to romp leashless once he hits the connecting trails.

At the north end of the lake, you'll find a trailhead that leads you through magnificent landscapes, all set around 9,000 feet. The air is so clean you can almost feel yourself getting healthier with each step. Jake thinks it's the cat's pajamas. Eventually, the trail runs into the Pacific Crest Trail, where you can choose to venture off on longer or shorter treks. Consult an Inyo National Forest ranger at 760/934-2505 for maps and guidance.

To reach the lake, exit U.S. 395 at Mammoth Junction and drive west along Highway 203/Main Street, through the town of Mammoth Lakes. The road curves to the left and becomes Lake Mary Road. Follow it about seven miles. It loops by Lake Mary and eventually ends at Horseshoe Lake. 760/924-5500.

Lake Mary
🐾🐾🐾🐾 🐕

Dogs have to be leashed around developed and heavily used Lake Mary, but they can trot around leashless when they accompany you on the scenic trail that starts on the east side of the lake. Rangers ask that you wait until you're far from the lake to let your dog run free, and to do so only if she's under good control.

Lots of folks like to take their dog on an early morning walk on the trail, then turn around and fish for dinner. The trout are planted, and it's hard not to catch one while trolling, or even fishing from shore. Most dogs seem to enjoy watching people fish, even if nothing is being caught. Some people don't even mind just walking around the lake with a leashed dog. There's also a gold mine at the very end of Coldwater Campground, next to the trailhead parking. You'll see the signs.

Other folks come here just for the off-leash hiking. The trail takes you many miles away. If your dog is a water dog, she'll love it. You pass by several quiet little lakes and one big one on the way to the Pacific Crest Trail. Consult an Inyo National Forest ranger at 760/873-2400 for maps and guidance.

June–November, 48 campsites are available here for $16 a night, first-come, first-served. Dogs must be leashed, but with the great views of the lake they get, they just don't seem to mind.

To reach the lake, exit U.S. 395 at Mammoth Junction and drive west along Highway 203/Main Street, through the town of Mammoth Lakes. The road curves to the left and becomes Lake Mary Road. Follow it about three miles to the lake. 760/924-5500.

Shady Rest Trail
😺 😺 😺

This national forest trail is on the edge of the town of Mammoth Lakes, making it as convenient as it is splendid. Unfortunately, since the city officially runs this trail, leashes are the law.

During the summer, you and your pooch can walk or run on the six-mile forested trail that loops around Shady Rest Park (a Mammoth Lakes recreation park, where leashes are also the law).

In winter, it's a stunning place to take your dog on a little cross-country ski trip. Leashes can come in handy here. We've seen some people leash their dog to their belt while skiing. When there's a little uphill slope, guess who's the engine? Most dogs wouldn't appreciate this and are happier gamboling through the woods than playing mush dog. Dogs aren't allowed on the groomed trails (there's nothing like paw holes to dampen a smooth cross-country adventure), but they can usually trot along on the left side of the trail.

From U.S. 395, exit at Mammoth Junction and drive west along Highway 203/Main Street until the U.S. Forest Service Visitors Center, which will be before town on your right. You can stop in here and ask for additional trail information or proceed west on Highway 203 another quarter mile to Old Sawmill Road. Turn right and follow the road to Shady Rest Park. You'll see parts of the trail weaving around the park's perimeter and even along the entry road. Call 760/924-5500 for more information.

PLACES TO EAT

Giovanni's Restaurant & Lounge: Order a pizza to go and bring it to the outdoor tables to share with your dog. One of our favorite combos is the Gio special, with pesto, artichokes, mushrooms, and feta cheese. (Jake spits out the veggies oh so delicately but wolfs down the cheese and crust.) 437 Old Mammoth Road; 760/934-7563.

Schat's Bakery: This is a great place to grab a coffee and warm pastry before a morning hike. Relax at the outdoor chairs here. 3305 Main Street; 760/934-6055.

Tailwaggers: Here's a dog's ideal alternative to Schat's Bakery. Tailwaggers is a gourmet dog bakery, with cookies featuring items like beef puree. Hmm, I think I'll still get my cookies at Schat's. Dogs love visiting here when they come for treats and dog boutique items, but they're not always so keen on visiting the other part of the Tailwaggers business: the self-service dog bath. The tubs are a great place to come after a messy day at a lake or on a muddy trail.

In addition, Tailwaggers now offers wonderful pooch massages. The massage therapist, Andrea Baldwin, is known for her wonderful human massages at a nearby highly acclaimed spa. The dogs we've spoken with tell us she also has a magic touch with canines. Call for her hours, fees, or to book an appointment. Tailwaggers is at the Sierra Center Mall, at 924 Old Mammoth Road; 760/924-3400; www.tailwaggersbakery.com.

PLACES TO STAY

Convict Lake Resort: Dogs love coming to this terrific resort. Jake Dog thinks it's because they feel so welcome. Says the owner: "We love all pets, even ostriches and tarantulas." Psst: They even take cats.

Pets can stay at several deluxe cabins. The owners recently built four super-luxurious cabins, which come with fireplaces, double spa baths, and even steam showers. (A steam shower, should you be in the dark ages of pampery bathroom fixtures as I am, is a regular shower with a control that makes steam billow out any time you want. You don't even have to take a shower to get a steam. It's kind of like a spa steambath in your own cabin. Take that, Davy Crockett.)

In summer, dogs and their people can go out on the lake in a boat, help fish for supper, watch you ride a horse, or just hike around the wilderness on the other side of the lake. Dogs like Jake have plenty of swimming options. The resort also has a wonderful restaurant, but you'll have to get takeout if you want your dog to partake.

The regular cabins are cute, and they cost only $99. The new cabins are $210–250. There's even a cabin that sleeps up to 34 people. That's $960. Dogs are $15 for the length of their stay. Route 1, Box 204 93546; 760/934-3800 or 800/992-2260; www.convictlake.com.

Crystal Crag Lodge: Stay at this charming mountain resort on the shores of Lake Mary and you can wander around many acres of beautiful land with your leashed dog. But you'd better visit from May to mid-October, because the lodge is closed in the winter.

The rustic wood cabins are attractive and have full kitchens and baths. Most come with living rooms and fireplaces, too. Dogs like all that, but water dogs think it's truly the cat's meow that you can rent a small aluminum boat and meander around the lake.

Rates are $85–170. Dogs are $9 extra. 307 Crystal Crag Drive 93546; 760/934-2436; www.mammothweb.com.

Edelweiss Lodge: Has your dog been very good this year? If so, she deserves a visit to the rustic, cozy, super-dog-friendly cabins and apartments that comprise the Edelweiss Lodge. The lodgings all have kitchenettes, wood-burning stoves, and access to a Jacuzzi.

"Yada, yada, yada," your dog may be saying right about now. OK, we'll cut to the chase: Edelweiss has everything a dog could dream of (except cats). Dog-adoring managers Keith and Marta want to make every dog feel at home, and start out by providing pooches with a Doggie Welcome Basket. This includes a dog bed/pad, blankets to protect the human bedding, gourmet dog biscuits, temporary ID tags, water and food bowls, and poop bags. "We even provide a dumpster to put the poop bags in, but you can't take it to your room," says Keith. (Whew!)

Marta even has her own doggy side business, Marta's Doggie Day Care. She'll walk your dog for you if you're off for a while and need to leave your dog in a kennel in your room. (This is allowed here.) If you want complete day care, your lucky dog gets to go to her home, where day care dogs cavort about as if it's their home. She takes the dogs for walks and hikes, and brings them on errands with her. She also houses dogs overnight, but that's probably not necessary given the breadth of dog-friendly lodgings here. Sometimes guests ask Marta and Keith if their dog can just hang out with them at the lodge office for a while, and that can be worked out, too. Rates are about $25 daily for full day care, $15 for a good walk.

Lodging rates are $115–325. Dogs are $10 extra. 1872 Old Mammoth Road 93546; 760/934-2445 or 877/233-3593; www.edelweiss-lodge.com.

Lake Mary: See Lake Mary, above, for camping information.

Rockcreek Lodge: If you like modern cabins, they've got some attractive small and large ones. If you like your cabins rustic and old, they've got those, too. And if you like your rustic cabins with only cold running water, you can even get a couple of those here (from the 1920s!).

Dogs love coming here because the lodge is set on seven acres of lodgepole pines, with several trails leading out from the property. The trails can take you on some magnificent hikes to lakes, remote forests, and peaceful meadows. A fishable creek is a quick walk from the lodge. (Come in the summer for a stunning wildflower display.) Stay here and you're on the edge of the John Muir Wilderness. After a long day of outdoor fun, settle back in with a delicious meal from the lodge's restaurant.

Rates are $85–150. Dogs are $15 extra. Route 1, Box 12 93546; 877/935-4170; www.rockcreeklodge.com.

Shilo Inn: Don't worry about your large dog being allowed to stay here— the manager *prefers* big dogs! All the rooms are mini suites, and they're air-conditioned, which is a rare feature up here. Unnecessary in the winter, but it can be a real blessing in August.

The very sweet dog-friendly owners ask to know ahead of time if you'll be bringing a dog so they can plan a room strategy (perhaps to avoid having a cat as your next-door neighbor). They also work with a nearby veterinarian who boards pets for people who will be skiing during the day and don't know what to do with the pooch. They'll be happy to give you the info you need.

Rates are $89–150. Dogs pay a $10 fee for the length of their stay. The motel is a half block east of Old Mammoth Road, on Highway 203. 2963 Main Street 93546; 760/934-4500; www.shiloinns.com.

SAN LUIS OBISPO COUNTY

San Simeon

Dogs aren't trusted anywhere near the gilded towers of William Randolph Hearst's castle, so if you're thinking of visiting while your dog is with you, forget it. He'll have to wait in the car for at least three hours while you tour the castle, and that's a very bad idea.

But that doesn't mean you have to forgo this spectacular attraction. The Tail Wag's Inn, about nine miles south in Cambria, will board your dog for as long as your tour takes. With all the frills they provide your pet, she may come back thinking she should be living in Hearst Castle (see the Cambria section).

Unfortunately, dogs are no longer allowed to amble on San Simeon State Beach (although you can still camp there), so your romping room here is rather limited. But if you stay at the wonderful Best Western Cavalier (see Places to Stay), you'll be staying at the only beach around here where dogs are allowed. They have to wear leashes, but at least they get to enjoy themselves. (You can access the beach even if you don't stay there, but it's sure nice to stay at a place where you can play on the beach.)

PLACES TO EAT

San Simeon Beach Bar & Grill: The panoramic ocean views from the outdoor tables (where dogs are allowed) make this a real destination restaurant for hungry dogs and their people. It can get windy here, though. Enjoy clam chowder, pizzas, and good grilled grub. 9520 Castillo Drive; 805/927-4604.

PLACES TO STAY

Best Western Cavalier Oceanfront Resort: This is San Simeon's only ocean-front hotel, and it's one of the most attractive and well-run Best Westerns we've ever checked out. (But don't let its brochure get your hopes up: The picture on the cover is not of the Best Western. It's Hearst Castle.) Many of the 90 rooms have a wood-burning fireplace, a stocked minibar, close-up ocean views, and a private patio. There's even room service, so you and your dog can dine together in the comfort of your own seaside abode. The humans in your party can keep in shape in the fitness room or at the two outdoor pools (with ocean views to drool for). And if you stay here, you and your leashed pooch will have easy access to the long beach that backs up to the lodging. This is a huge deal right now, because no other beach in the area permits pooches.

Sunny Dog, a canine reader from Dayton, Ohio, had his person, Peggy, describe what they love most about their visits here: "It is quite delightful to sit on your patio and drink in that fabulous ocean view. The firepits (surrounded by chairs) are lit at sunset and left burning through the night for those folks that want to enjoy the fire, the sound of the ocean, and the distant light from the Piedras Blancas Lighthouse." Nice writing, Sunny.

Many people are tempted to leave their dogs in their rooms when they go explore magnificent Hearst Castle, but this is a big no-no. The Cavalier makes it easy for you to do the right thing: It provides numbers for dog sitters and for a wonderful kennel (see the Cambria section for kennel info). Be forewarned, though: At busy times, you need to make dog-care reservations well ahead of your visit.

Rates are $119–279. 9415 Hearst Drive 93452; 805/927-4688 or 800/826-8168; www.cavalierresort.com.

Motel 6: A Motel 6 in the same town as Hearst Castle? Go figure. This one started as a Holiday Inn, so it's a cut above many other Motel 6 facilities. Rates are $38–47 for one adult, $6 for the second adult. The size limit of the past is history: "Just no horses," says a manager. 9070 Castillo Drive 93452; 805/927-8691.

Cambria

A stroll through this charming village can be fun for you and your dog, but Cambria serves a more important purpose: It's the home of the Tail Wag's Inn, a quality kennel where you can board your dog for part of a day while you visit Hearst Castle about nine miles north in San Simeon.

Laura, the owner of this kennel, heard of too many dogs who had been left unattended in sweltering cars as their caretakers sauntered around the magnificent castle for hours. So she created a relatively inexpensive, yet luxurious package to encourage people not to risk the lives of their dogs. For $11 (she has upped the price only $1 in 14 years), your kenneled dog gets a "continental breakfast" of dog treats, takes at least two good walks, and drinks Crystal Springs bottled water. Hey, what the heck, if you're spending the day among opulence, why shouldn't your pup? And the walks aren't just to the corner and back. Laura takes the dogs' needs to heart and strolls them to a nearby grassy area with a creek, trees, "and god knows, lots of smells," she says.

The **Tail Wag's Inn** is a boarding kennel (overnight boarding is the mainstay), but it's the kind of kennel a dog doesn't seem to mind. One regular boarder escaped from her house during a thunderstorm and her owner was frantically looking everywhere for her. Where did she run? To the Tail Wag's Inn, in fact, to the kennel she normally uses. "She was just there barking at her kennel as if to say, OK, let me in, and where's my blanket and some food?" says Laura.

Day-boarding dogs can arrive 8 A.M.–1 P.M. and have to leave by 5 P.M. Reservations are required. This is important, because some folks have thought they could just drive here and drop off their pooch. They've been mighty disappointed when they've had to forgo their trip to Hearst Castle because there was no room at the inn. In addition, your dog's shot record is also required. The kennel is at the Village Service Center, 2419-A Village Lane. Call 805/927-1589 for reservations or more information.

Bad news for dogs who like sand and surf: Moonstone Beach and Shamel County Park's beach no longer permit pooches. Fortunately, the boardwalk at Moonstone does. It's a very pleasant little 1.5-mile jaunt each way. There are even poop bags along the way (for your dog, in case you were wondering).

PARKS, BEACHES, AND RECREATION AREAS

See above for a tip on where you can take your dog for a decent stroll over-looking the ocean. The pickings are slim here these days, so dogs tend to take what they can get and not complain.

PLACES TO EAT

Main Street Grill: Your dog is sure to love the smells emanating from the barbecue here. It's a meaty place, with decadent fries to boot. It doesn't have outdoor tables, but there's plenty of grass outside for your picnic-style dining pleasure. We've seen many dog folks sharing their meal with their pooches on the grass. (Do you really have any choice other than to share your barbecued meat with your hungry dog when eating it at dog's-mouth level? We think not.) 603 Main Street; 805/927-3194.

Mustache Pete's: Thirsty dogs can get a bowl of water while you order a prime rib sandwich (au jus, no less). Dogs think people have it better here. The gourmet pizzas are delectable. Dine at the patio with your furry friend. 4090 Burton Drive; 805/927-8589.

Pasta Factory: The homemade pastas are delicious. Dine alfresco with your dog at the breezy patio tables. 1316 Tamsen Street; 805/927-5882.

PLACES TO STAY

Cambria Pines Lodge: You and your dog get to stay at one of nine cabins here that permit pooches. The 25-acre property comes with oodles of Mon-terey pines for your dog's perusal. Your stay comes with a full breakfast in the lodge. The cabins are $109–149. Dogs are $25 extra. 2905 Burton Drive 93428; 805/927-4200 or 800/445-6868; www.cambriapineslodge.com.

Cambria Shores Inn: This charming and very dog-friendly little inn is just a bone's throw from the dog-friendly boardwalk at beautiful Moonstone Beach. Literally. You could throw a bone (OK, a tennis ball) from your room, and if you have a good arm, it will cross the street and end up down on the beach. Of course, this won't work if you don't have an ocean-view room, but with three-quarters of the rooms here blessed with ocean views, your chances for a water landing are pretty good.

The innkeepers welcome dogs with open arms and with a VIP dog basket!

The basket includes a beach towel (these can be replenished), a matching green sheet to cover the bed if your dog sleeps there (it matches the decor of the room, too), and dog treats (these are not green). "Dogs are our niche," explains a friendly innkeeper. "We like to make them feel right at home." If only home were like this. Upon check-in, humans get homemade chocolate chip cookies. At "hors d'oeuvres hour" in the late afternoon, guests can relax after a long day of fun, eat all kinds of tasty treats, and, in the future, drink a little wine. (The inn will be going through a remodel soon. After it's done, the owners will go for a liquor license.) A scrumptious continental breakfast, consisting of fresh fruit, croissants with chocolate nut butter, bagels with cream cheese, a carafe of orange juice, and a dog biscuit (for the Very Important Pooch in your party), is delivered to your room in the morning. If you prefer, you can pick up your breakfast in the lobby.

Rates are $95–180. Dogs are $10 extra, with a maximum of two dogs per room. 6276 Moonstone Beach Drive 93428; 805/927-8644 or 800/433-9179; www.cambriashores.com.

Fogcatcher Inn: If your dog has a look of panic on his face while reading this over your shoulder, reassure him you're not taking him to the Dogcatcher Inn. (This is how I first read the sign, and I figure if I can make that mistake, dogs can, too.) In fact, this is one of the most relaxing and lovely places you could stay with a dog in these parts. The inn has a lovely English country style, with vaulted ceilings and gardens that are to drool for almost all year round. The rooms are spacious and well appointed, and each has a fireplace, microwave, and fridge. The heated outdoor pool has a decent ocean view, and a free hot breakfast buffet comes with your stay here. (No beasts at the buffet, please. We know how literally dogs take the phrase "all you can eat.")

What dogs like best is that they get a dog biscuit or two or three upon check-in. As for size limits, don't worry: "Last weekend we had a big German shepherd and a little Pekingese," says Mike, who loves doggy guests. "We take any good dog." Two rooms allow pets. Rates are $119–320. Dogs are $25 extra. 6400 Moonstone Beach Drive 93428; 805/927-1400 or 800/425-4121; www.fogcatcherinn.com.

Pismo Beach

PARKS, BEACHES, AND RECREATION AREAS

Oceano Dunes/Pismo State Beach
🐾🐾🐾🐾

It's hard to tell what dogs enjoy more here—exploring the long, wide beach or wandering through the great dunes above. Your leashed dog can get all the exercise he needs by trotting down the miles of trails on the unspoiled dunes. If he likes cold ocean spray, take him down to the beach for a romp among the gulls. (Dogs are allowed at both of these state beaches. This is a huge relief when you've come from the dog-verboten state beaches to the north.)

Camping is available at a couple of sections of the beach. Fees are $10 for the on-beach camping area south of the Grand Avenue entrance (4WD vehicles are recommended) and $20–29 for camping among the trees at the Pismo State Beach North Beach Campground. There is a total of 185 campsites. For more info, call 805/489-1869. Call 800/444-7275 for reservations.

To avoid the $6 day-use fee at the Grand Avenue entrance, drive west from Highway 1 and park on Grand Avenue before the ranger kiosk. Once at the beach, head north. Walking south will put you in the middle of a busy off-highway vehicle area—not the best place for a dog. 805/473-7230.

Pismo Beach City Beach
🐾🐾🐾

Does your dog like watching people in bathing suits play volleyball? Does she enjoy sniffing at bodies slathered with coconut oil? If so, this beach is for her. It's rarely so crowded that it's uncomfortable, but it's rarely so uncrowded that it's a bore for a social butterfly dog.

The farther north you walk, the fewer people you'll encounter. Dogs have to be leashed everywhere, though. But this shouldn't stop the digging breeds from helping you uncover prize Pismo clams (fishing licenses are required for the human half of the team). We once saw a dog who would thrust his entire snout into the wet sand and come up with a clam every time. His owner didn't even have to use his clam fork.

One of the many access points is west of Highway 1, at the foot of Main Avenue near the recreation pier. 805/773-4658.

PLACES TO EAT

Old West Cinnamon Rolls: This little café has some of the best cinnamon rolls we've ever laid teeth on. They're hot, sticky, and absolutely decadent. Enjoy them at the front bench with your pooch at your side. 861 Dolliver Street; 805/773-1428.

The Scoop Ice Cream Parlor: When you say "The Scoop" to most dog people, they tend to think of the plastic bags, newspapers, or little shovels they use for scooping the, well, you get the picture. But this ice-cream parlor is so good that "The Scoop" might hold a whole new meaning to you after you visit with your pooch. Hang out, cone in hand, canine at feet, at the outdoor seating. 607 Dolliver Street; 805/773-4253.

PLACES TO STAY

Cottage Inn by the Sea: Stay here and you get a very attractive, spacious, country-style room with a gas fireplace, a fridge, a microwave. You also get a deluxe continental breakfast. About the only thing you don't get is an ocean view. People without dogs can get the ocean views, but people with dogs have to settle for looking at the Pacific from the terrific pool and spa, which are on a bluff over the ocean. (Pooches can only peep at the Pacific from the beach itself, since they need to stay away from the pool area.)

The best part for dogs is that the pet-friendly rooms are on the ground level, and each has a fenced area in back. This makes dogs smile. So do the biscuits they get at check-in. Rates are $99–179. Dogs are $10 extra. 2351 Price Street 93449; 805/773-4617 or 888/440-8400; www.cottage-inn.com.

Oceano Dunes/Pismo State Beach: See Oceano Dunes/Pismo State Beach, above, for camping information.

Sandcastle Inn: This one's on the beach. Even dogs enjoy an ocean view. Rates are $139–269. Dogs are $10 extra. 100 Stimson Avenue 93449; 805/773-2422; www.sandcastleinn.com.

Sea Gypsy Motel: If you're looking for a reasonably priced room or studio apartment on the beach, pull your caravan over to the Sea Gypsy Motel. It's conveniently located a couple of blocks from "downtown" Pismo Beach and has a heated pool in case the ocean is a little too clammy for you. Rates are $45–145. Dogs are $15 extra. 1020 Cypress Street 93449; 805/773-1801 or 800/592-5923; www.seagypsymotel.com.

SANTA BARBARA COUNTY

Santa Barbara

PARKS, BEACHES, AND RECREATION AREAS

Douglas Family Preserve
🐾🐾🐾🐾🐕

This is one terrific chunk of leash-free land, and thanks to the very hard-working members of the Dog PAC of Santa Barbara and hundreds of dogged volunteers, it looks like it's going to stay that way. In spring 2004, the Santa Barbara City Council voted unanimously to let dogs be their doggy selves and continue to enjoy this big park naked. (Lest any lewd images of dogs not wearing clothes cross your mind, this is dog park parlance for leash-free.)

The preserve is about 70 acres, and it's on a magnificent bluff overlooking the Pacific. Dogs drool over this place, and rightly so. The ocean breeze is cool, relaxing, and must contain some pretty fascinating scents, judging by the looks on dogs' faces as they sniff it in rapture. The park has great unpaved trails for perusing the preserve. It also has quite a few oaks, cypresses, and pines. To the north of the park is oak woodland, to the south is coastal sage scrub. An estuary and wetlands are below. Way below. Two hundred feet down the bluff, to be exact. Dogs have to stay away from there, because that's where some protected species hang out. There's really no access anyway, so it's almost a moot point.

There's still a bone of contention between the preserve's neighbors and the park patrons with dogs, and some buffer-zone issues have yet to be resolved. Dog PAC cofounder Mary Anne Morrison implores dogs and their people to "Please be considerate of the neighbors. We want everyone to be happy with this arrangement." Keep leashes on until you're well within the preserve. For an update, phone the parks department at 805/564-5433, or contact Dog PAC at 805/967-3949 or www.dogpacsb.org.

From northbound or southbound U.S. 101, take Cabrillo Boulevard in the direction that's away from the mountains. Turn right on Cliff Drive. You'll come to two stoplights within a block of each other. Turn left onto Mesa Lane (the second light) and then turn right onto Borton Drive. Turn left onto Linda Road and follow it to the end. There is on-street parking. (You can enter the park at Medcliff Drive, Borton Drive, or Mesa School Lane.)

Hendry's Beach/Arroyo Burro Beach
🐾 🐾 🐾 🐾 🐕

You can throw your good dog's leash to the wind here (don't forget to pick it up, though; they're not cheap these days) and take a little stroll on a sandy, crescent-shaped beach together. It's the only beach in the county that allows leash-free dogs, so enjoy! Along your way you'll see surfers, joggers, and loads of other happy dogs. What you won't see—at least if the beach's current leash-free status remains—is a ranger approaching you with ticket book in hand. (This is too common a sight at most beaches around here.)

But be careful where you tread: If you go in the wrong direction once you hit the sand, you could be in a for a $75 ticket. Here's how you get to the right place: The beach (signs will call it Arroyo Burro) is on Cliff Drive, just west of Las Positas Road. Park in the lot, walk to the beach, and turn left—*not* right! (You'll see the fun beachside restaurant, the Brown Pelican. Go to the left of it. You should also see a sign that points dogs in the right—that is, left—direction.) Dogs who are under voice control can shed their leashes east of the slough. The off-leash section starts there and goes almost to the steps at Mesa Lane.

The off-leash program here could change at any time, so be sure to check up on its status. The city likes to say this is a county beach, and the county likes to say this is a city beach. The leash-free part appears to be a city-controlled portion of a county beach. The city parks department (where some people who answer the phone will tell you dogs aren't even allowed at the beach) number is 805/564-5433, or check the website www.dogpacsb.org for updates.

PLACES TO STAY

Casa del Mar: Guests at this small Spanish-style inn get treated well for a decent price (at least decent for these parts). Stay here and you can partake in an extended continental breakfast in the morning and a relaxing wine and cheese social hour in the evening. The inn is clean, quiet, and attractive, with a lush little garden, a sundeck with Jacuzzi, and cozy rooms. It's just a half block from the beach and two blocks from State Street. If you really want a home away from home, you can stay in a suite with a full kitchen and fireplace. Rates are $99–204. (Most regular rooms fall in the lower price range.) Dogs are $10 extra. 18 Bath Street 93101; 805/963-4418 or 800/433-3097; www.casadelmar.com.

Fess Parker's DoubleTree Resort: At first glance, the name "Fess Parker" and the word "luxury" make strange bedfellows. After all, Fess was the actor who brought American frontiersman Davy Crockett and Daniel Boone into millions of homes in the 1950s and 1960s. But while Fess Parker's characters are synonymous with sweat and grit, the real Fess Parker, a longtime Santa Barbara County resident, is known for his good taste and good business sense. (He also owns a respected winery in the county.)

Fess, who hails from Texas, likes things big. The seaside resort has 337 luxurious guest rooms. It's set on a sprawling 24 acres. Standard rooms are a spacious 450 square feet. He also likes things first-class. The rooms are attractive and comfortable, with feather pillows (unless you're allergic), high-quality bath products, evening turndown service, and excellent views. Suites are especially spacious and attractive. The resort even has its own spa, billed as a "French sea spa."

We think Fess must also like dogs, because dogs get the royal treatment here. Fess Parker's dog guests don't have to watch hungrily as you chow down on your tasty room service meal: They can order their own. The in-room pooch dining menu includes premium ground sirloin, a quality brand wet dog food, and gourmet dog cookies. And if you really want to treat your dog, canine massages are available. For $65, your dog can get a 40-minute in-room massage from a dog-knowledgeable massage therapist from the resort's spa. The massage is supposed to be especially good for arthritic dogs.

Although the resort is across from the beach, it's a beach you can't visit with your dog friend. Try the path that runs along the beach's edge, if being near the water is your wish. Otherwise, the 24-acre resort has ample room for romping with your leashed friend. Be sure to clean up after your dog.

Rates are $269–349. 633 East Cabrillo Boulevard 93103; 805/564-4333 or 800/222-8733; www.fpdtr.com.

Four Seasons Biltmore: This elegant oceanfront resort is renowned for its impeccable style, and its gracious, dog-friendly policy is the epitome of that style. Upon check-in, dogs get two dog bowls, a toy, tasty snacks, and their very own pooch menu. Dog walking is available, but who'd want someone else to walk their dog with nearby parks and the beautiful grounds of the Biltmore beckoning? Dog sitting is also available.

The Biltmore is made up of a gorgeous, top-drawer hotel surrounded by 30 private cottage rooms that are to die for. People with pooches have to stay at the cottages. If your budget is plump, it's well worth the stay. The standard cottage rates are $545–750. Super-deluxe ones go up to $2,750. 1260 Channel Drive 93108; 805/969-2261; www.fourseasons.com/santabarbara.

Rancho Oso Guest Ranch & Stables: Dogs and people who enjoy the Old West love staying at Rancho Oso. It's not historic, but it looks that way. You can stay in one of five rustic one-room cabins with knotty pine walls and bunk beds. Or if you really hanker for your pooch to be a "dawgie," try one of the 10 covered wagons. You bring the sleeping bag, they provide the army cots. They're loads of fun to stay in, and they make for great photo backdrops.

The ranch is on 310 acres of hills with enough trees for decent shade in the summer. You can walk your dog on the many trails, but keep her on a leash, because a lot of horses jog on the trails, too. In fact, if you want to ride a horse yourself, you can set that up back at the ranch office. Guided trail rides are offered year-round. (Lots of folks come here to camp with their horses, but that's through a members-only camping organization, and that's a horse of a different color so we won't go into detail.)

Rates are $79–89 for cabins, $54 for wagons. Dogs are $5 extra. 3750 Paradise Road 93105; 805/683-5686; www.rancho-oso.com.

Secret Garden Inn & Cottages: Six of the nine pretty cottages and rooms here allow dogs. Since the dog ambience doesn't necessarily mix with the flowery romantic feel many guests come here for, dogs are asked not to peruse the pretty gardens and public areas around the inn and cottages. A great choice for a night or two is the Garden room, which has French doors that open up to a private little garden. It's your own little Secret Garden, with no nuzzling couples to annoy.

If you like to eat in a cozy setting, you'll never want to leave the inn. You get a full hot gourmet breakfast in the morning, a light snack with wine and cheese in the afternoon, and homemade brownies, cider, and tea in the evening.

Rates for the dog rooms are $160–231. Dogs require a $50 deposit. 1908 Bath Street 93101; 805/687-2300; www.secretgarden.com.

SAN DIEGO COUNTY

Julian

This entire old gold-mining town is a Designated Historic District. It's full of nifty old storefronts and dog-friendly folks. It's also full of tourists, especially if you visit during October, which is apple month in these parts. People here bake more than 10,000 apple pies a week in October—a fun time to visit if you like autumn leaves and crisp apples. Julian is recovering from the terrible wildfires of 2002 and 2003. The more touristy parts of Julian survived, but businesses could use your business; come and play. Your dog will thank you.

PLACES TO EAT

The Julian Grille: You and your dog can dine on tasty burgers, pastas, steaks, and salads at the restaurant's 15-table patio area. 2224 Main Street; 760/765-0173.

    Romano's Dodge House: The Italian food here is *benissimo*. Dine with your dog at the six outdoor tables. 2718 B Street; 760/765-1003.

PLACES TO STAY

This mountain town has some doggone terrific lodgings for lucky dogs and their people.

    Angel's Landing: Angel's Landing is an appropriate name for this 53-acre chunk of pine-covered paradise. It's beautiful, and so secluded you won't even hear any traffic. The owners are some of the most animal-friendly people you'll ever encounter. They love dogs and even have an animal rescue area on the property, with adopted chickens, bunnies, pigs, goats, and horses.

    The Old Butterfield Stage Coach Route runs through the property and makes for a terrific hike with your leashed dog. (Leashes are a necessity here, because the place is also heaven for many deer and wild turkeys.) If it's a very clear day, you might be able to see the ocean from the meadows above Angel's Landing.

    The rooms and suites at the lodge and smaller buildings are clean and pretty. Rates are $49–149. Dogs are $10 extra on weekends, otherwise there's no doggy fee. 2323 Farmer Road 92036; 888/253-7747; www.angelsresort.com.

    Julian Flat Top Mountain Retreat: This beautiful three-bedroom vacation home on eight acres is very private and secluded, which comes in handy with all the huge windows here. (Your dog can walk around in the buff and no one will care.) And yet it's only 1.6 miles to town.

    The house has a wood-burning stove, three wonderful decks with great views, and a loft bedroom that also sports killer views. (If you like seeing stars while you sleep, stake out that room.) But best of all for dogs is that outside

DIVERSION

Pick a Peck of Apples: What Peter Piper did with pickled peppers, you and your dog can do with apples, thanks to the dog-friendly folks at **Calico Ranch orchards** in Julian. From about mid-September through Thanksgiving, you and your leashed, cleaned-up-after dog can sniff out your favorite apples at the orchard's 30 acres of trees. Then take them home to make a to-drool-for apple pie or two. (Or 10.) 4200 Highway 78; 858/586-0392.

they have their very own 32-by-24-foot dog run enclosed by a four-foot-high wooden fence. Dogs can gallop around leash-free to their hearts' content.

Owner Mary adores dogs and their people. "The dog lovers have been the nicest guests," she says. Being a dog person herself, she knows how to make dogs feel welcome at the house: Dogs get a little variety of biscuits in a little bag tied with a red ribbon upon their arrival. Between this and the dog run, your dog may never want to leave.

Rates are $200–210. Specials are often available. When you make reservations, you'll get the address. 858/454-6733 or 800/810-1170; www.julianflattop.com.

Pine Haven: This sweet, cozy cabin is one of the most pooch-friendly cabins we've come across. The entire 1.25-acre property is completely and securely fenced, so it's one big doggy playground! Not only that, but scattered around the tiered property are hidden "treasures" dogs revel in finding. (They're actually dog toys and tennis balls; no gold bullion or anything. "The dogs love running around and suddenly finding a toy," says cabin owner Teresa, who adores dogs and is very involved with dog rescue groups.) In addition, dogs get a basket of toys they can play with and a doggy treat of their own. Plus they can use the cabin's doggy beds and have a choice of two types of "tables" they can dine on. Jake loves slurping water and munching food from these raised bowl platforms. (He has made me promise to buy him his own.) It really doesn't get more dog friendly than this.

With all these dog amenities, it's easy to brush over the cabin itself, but it's got loads of appeal. The living room is especially wonderful, with a floor-to-ceiling stone fireplace and views of a beautiful meadow. The cabin is on a small lane four miles from town and offers plenty of privacy. Rates are $160–180. Dogs are $30 extra for the length of their stay for the first dog, $10 for the second. You'll get the address when you make your reservation. 760/726-9888; the adorable dog-focused website is www.pinehavencabin.com.

San Diego

PARKS, BEACHES, AND RECREATION AREAS

Balboa Park

This luxuriant semitropical park is one of California's best urban parks for people. Attractions include the San Diego Zoo, an enormous planetarium, several theaters, and a few world-class museums. But with the recent addition of three off-leash areas for dogs, Balboa Park is now one of the best urban parks for pooches, too.

Dogs used to be relegated to the lush, green center and the dirt paths on the east and west sides of this 1,200-acre park. Leashes were—and still are—a necessity in those areas. Dogs who wanted more freedom were out of luck until a kindly park official thought it might be nice to give them a chance to cavort about sans leash in a small area. The dogs all thought this was a mighty good idea, and they've been so well behaved that the park doubled their stomping grounds.

The two dog runs aren't fenced, but they're well marked with signs. The more popular dog area is Morley Field, which is the smaller of the two. It's lined by a grove of eucalyptus trees, so there's plenty of shade on hot days. You'll almost always find gaggles of pooches gallivanting about in high spirits. You can get to Morley Field from Morley Field Drive, off Florida Drive, in the north-central portion of the park (northwest of the tennis courts). The second and larger of the areas is Nate's Point, on the northwest side of the park off Balboa Drive, just south of the Laurel Street Bridge. It's a picturesque place (nice for pooches with a sense of aesthetic beauty), with views of the famous old California Tower, Coronado, and even part of Mexico. It's about 1.5 acres, and like Morley Field, it's unfenced, so keep an eye peeled for signs for its boundaries.

To get to the park from I-5, exit at Park Boulevard and head north. Call the Balboa Park Visitors Center for more information and maps. 619/239-0512.

Dog Beach

"Welcome to Dog Beach!" the sign announces at just about the same place that your dog charges out of the car to meet with all his best buddies. Dogs truly do feel welcome here. They're free to run off leash and to get down to the business of being a dog. As long as they listen when you call and don't get into trouble, they can hang out leashless all day. Many dog people bring a folding chair so they can relax while their dog experiences heaven on earth.

DIVERSION

Whatever Floats Your Boat: If you and your salty dog want to explore beautiful **San Diego Bay** by water, a couple of boat-rental companies are happy to accommodate you. You'll have your choice of sailing or motoring around the bay. The sailboats range from 14 feet to 27 feet, with a price range of about $30–100 per hour. Powerboats come in a variety of sizes and horsepowers, with an hourly rate of $65–150.

Note: If your dog isn't a decent dog paddler, bring a doggy life jacket for her. Even if she's Ester Williams, it's not a bad idea. The smaller the sailboat, the better the chance you'll end up in the drink. Plus it can get busy in the bay, with navy-type ships crossing here and there to make things interesting.

Seaforth Boat Rentals is on the San Diego waterfront at 333 West Harbor Drive (it shares the address with the San Diego Marriott Hotel & Marina, should you be looking for a place to stay on the water); 619/239-BOAT (619/239-2628). Action Sport Rentals is in Coronado and right next to the magnificent Loews Coronado Bay Resort, at 4000 Coronado Bay Road; 619/424-4466.

We've seen several folks visit here because, although they don't have a dog, they get great joy out of watching the footloose creatures tearing around. "They have such innocent happiness when they run about and play so gleefully," said dogless dog lover Maxine Chambers one gray morning. "It makes my day."

There are more dog footprints in the sand than human footprints, and not just because dogs have more feet. People come from many miles around, sometimes bringing their friends' dogs and their neighbors' dogs to participate in the whirlwind of excitement.

Dogs are allowed off leash at the north end of the beach, which is wide enough to be very safe from traffic. It's marked by signs. If you wander onto the other part of the beach, make sure you do so before 9 A.M. or after 6 P.M., and be sure to leash your dog.

Exit I-5 at I-8. Drive west and follow the signs to Sunset Cliffs Boulevard. After several blocks, bear right at Voltaire Street. Follow Voltaire Street to its end and the entrance to Dog Beach. 619/235-1100.

Fiesta Island

Hey, dogs! You're going to find out just why they call this 1.5-mile-long island Fiesta Island. You can have a fabulous fiesta, then take a soothing siesta—and you can do it all off leash.

Yes, pooches, you can meet with friends, swim in the bay, chase your shadow, and catch a stick without ever wearing that pesky old leash. As long as you listen to your people and don't cause any problems, this island is all yours. There's no development (as of this printing, anyway, although there's plenty of talk about it)—just dirt and sand and a little grass.

If you aren't very good at listening to your owners, ask them to take you to the far side of the island, where fewer cars cruise by. The perimeter of the island is a beach, and unfortunately, the road runs right behind the beach. It doesn't give water dogs a whole lot of room to run around, but it's enough for most.

If you choose to stay on the beach, you can avoid annoying little Jet Skis by staying away from the watercraft recreation sections of water, which are clearly marked. The interior of the island is made up of fields of dirt. Since this is a bigger area, you'll be farther from traffic here.

The views of downtown San Diego and Mission Bay Park are really spectacular from the south side of the island. Cameras come in mighty handy. (Fiesta Island is actually part of Mission Bay Park.)

From I-5, take the Sea World Drive/Tecolote Road exit southeast to Fiesta Island Road, which is your first right. The road will take you onto the island. 619/235-1100.

Mission Beach/Pacific Beach
🐾🐾🐾🐾

The great thing about strolling down these two contiguous beaches with a dog is that no one seems to care if you don't have bulging biceps or a bikini-perfect body. Having a dog eliminates the need for physical prowess here. And on beaches that have built a worldwide reputation on how dazzling its bathers look, that's a mighty big plus.

On the downside, dogs are allowed to accompany you here only before 9 A.M. and after 6 P.M. The same hours hold for the paved promenade that runs behind the beaches. It's an understandable law during crowded summer days, but it would be a real boon for dogs if that rule could be eliminated during the winter months. Since the poor pooches have to be leashed anyway, what's the harm? (Joe made me write that.)

To make the best of these restricted hours, try a visit to beautiful Belmont Park. The big attraction at this old-style amusement park is a restored 1925 roller coaster, the Giant Dipper. In addition, there's a quaint old carousel and a historic indoor swimming pool. Dogs are required to be leashed and remain with all four feet planted firmly on the ground, but they can still have a good time watching the kids have fun. The park area is also home to dozens of shops and restaurants. It's at West Mission Bay Drive and Mission Boulevard. Its back faces Mission Beach. Call 619/491-2988 for Belmont Park hours and information.

Pacific Beach is north of Mission Beach. It starts around Tourmaline Street. The beach hooks up with Mission Beach and is one long, never-ending strip all the way down to the Mission Bay Channel. 619/235-1100.

PLACES TO EAT

Boardwalk Bistro: If you and your dog find your tummies rumbling, come and dine together at one of 16 outdoor tables in a scenic garden setting. Try the "low-tide special." 370 Mission Boulevard; 858/488-9484.

K-9 Country Club: This is a doggone fun, casual place to take a pooch. The name alone beckons, but since the owner loves dogs, this deli/café has pictures of dogs and sells all kinds of hot dogs, further adding to the poochy ambience. You and your dog can get sandwiches, gourmet coffees, and, of course, hot dogs. Dine together at the outdoor tables. 202 C Street; 619/239-0304.

The Original Paw Pleasers: Dogs and other four-legged critters are welcome to dine inside (yes, *inside*) at least one restaurant around here. The Original Paw Pleasers is a beautiful little pets-only restaurant with gorgeous murals of a park scene of happy dogs and cats. It's a cozy, uplifting place, with oak cabinets and even a "tree." (OK, it's a post disguised as a tree, but it looks enough like a tree that your boy dog might be tempted—don't let him!) And the food is to die for—if you're a pet. If you're a human, you can use coupons they have in conjunction with eateries nearby and grab yourself a bite to bring here so you can eat beside your dog. Some of the more popular items are "dogolate" chip cookies and "bark-la-va." There's also frozen (lactose-free) yogurt with doggy toppings such as liver (this won't cross over to human ice creameries, I'm quite sure), and a doggy Sunday brunch. Owner Loree will even custom-make birthday cakes for your dog.

I rarely mention cats in this book (it's a four-letter word to some dogs), but this is too good to ignore. Cats can come here and get a chicken or calamari cake with faux cream frosting, or a tuna muffin with a delicious nondairy whipped topping. Mmm, good! By the way, if your dog thinks cats are part of the menu, make sure there are none inside before you venture in.

The restaurant also sells lots of gift items for pets and their people. It's in an upscale shopping center in the Hillcrest area of San Diego. This is a must-visit on any dog's list. 1220 Cleveland Avenue; 619/293-7297; www.pawpleasers.com.

Point Loma Seafood: You want a dog-friendly restaurant? Romp on over to Point Loma Seafood, where the dog-loving attitude is as yummy as the seafood. You and your dog can share a bayside table and the stuff memories are made of (that is, french fries). While you dine on such goodies as a shrimp sandwich or crab Louie, your dog will be eating and drinking his own restaurant food: free biscuits and fresh water. The only thing Joe Dog winced at here was the pickled squid cocktail. As it passed by our table, en route to some less fortunate soul, he sniffed the air and backed up as far as his leash would allow. That boy always had good taste. 2805 Emerson Street; 619/223-1109.

Terra: This warm, sophisticated restaurant in the heart of beautiful Hillcrest serves some simply mouthwatering dishes. To name a few we found in the autumn: pumpkin ravioli (with toasted hazelnuts and roasted corn cream), wasabi-crusted portobello mushroom (over rice noodles with tomato-ginger broth), and honey-roasted chicken (on pearl barley risotto). If you're more into your meat, try the filet mignon or the braised lamb shank (with Chilean red wine sauce and root vegetable puree).

This upscale restaurant doesn't forget your canine companion. Indeed not. In fact, Terra has teamed up with the Original Paw Pleasers pet bakery to provide dogs with some lip-licking choices from their very own menu. You may want to try the Puppy Pizza, followed by a carob-dipped pig's ear (advertised as "same great taste, no hair or veins!"). Dogs can dine alfresco at the lovely patio. (At night, you wouldn't even see the veins anyway.) 3900 Vermont Street; 619/293-7088.

PLACES TO STAY

Best Western Lamplighter Inn & Suites: If you and the pooch like your lodgings peaceful and palmy with plenty of flowering plants and trees, the Lamplighter is for you. The rooms are attractive, too. Suites have a breakfast bar and full kitchen. Some have a separate living area. Rates are $69–165. Dogs are $10 extra. (The dog-friendly folks here call it "pet rent.") 6474 El Cajon Boulevard 92115; 619/582-3088 or 800/545-0778; www.lamplighter-inn.com.

The Bristol Hotel: This is one of the cooler hotels to bring a canine in San Diego. It's contemporary, it's hip, it's a happenin' place. The lobby is jazzy, and the rooms are sleek, colorful, and comfortable. Stay here and you get use of a fluffy terry robe. Your dog will have to be content with her coat. Rates are $190–280. Dogs are restricted to 50 pounds or under and cost $50 for the length of your stay. (If you have the max-sized dog, that's a buck a pound.) 1055 First Avenue 92101; 619/232-6141 or 800/662-4477; www .thebristolsandiego.com.

Crown Point View Suite-Hotel: If you want to feel right at home while staying in a dog-friendly part of town, try the apartments/hotel rooms here. Rates are $125–205. Dogs are $75 extra for the duration of their stay. 4088 Crown Point Drive 92109; 858/272-0676 or 800/338-3331; www .crownpoint-view.com.

Doubletree Hotel San Diego/Mission Valley: Dogs need to stay on the hotel's third or fourth floor. At least you won't be paying for a penthouse. Rates are $109–230. Dogs are $50 for the length of their stay. 7450 Hazard Center Drive 92108; 619/297-5466.

The Hohe House: This two-bedroom, two-bath ocean-view vacation rental (pronounced Hoy, not Hoe-Hee, as I was saying until Steven Hohe himself informed me of my errant ways) comes with everything you need for a fun beachside vacation, including bikes, boogie boards, beach chairs, beach towels, beach umbrellas, and coolers. It's a two-minute walk to Pacific Beach and a bone's throw from La Jolla. Dogs are welcome as long as they're under 80 pounds. The well-appointed house is usually rented by the week, for $1275–1875. There's a $350 security deposit and an $85 cleaning fee. Dogs are $10 extra daily. Off-season there's a four-night minimum at $200 nightly.

Next to the house itself is a very cozy little studio efficiency, where only tiny dogs—20 pounds maximum—are allowed. The Hohe Guest Studio rents for $110–130 a night, with a two-night minimum. You'll get the Hohe address when you make your reservation; 858/273-0324; www.10kvacationrentals .com/hohe/hohehouse.

Horton Grand Hotel: Oh, this grand, exquisite, 1880s-era Gaslamp Quarter hotel is as gorgeous and sumptuous as they come. But since it allows only the most itsy-bitsy of dogs (under 15 pounds), I'm not going to go into more detail. (Horse-sized Jake won't let me.) Rates are $119–209. Dog-ettes are $100 for the length of their stay. 311 Island Avenue 92101; 619/544-1886 or 800/542-1886; www.hortongrand.com.

Ocean Villa Inn: Here's a dog's dream come true: The adored, famed, revered, worshipped Dog Beach is right next door to this motel! It doesn't get any more convenient than this. Rates are $69–159. Dogs are $25 extra (for up to two pets) for the length of their stay and require a $100 deposit. 5142 West Point Loma Boulevard 92107; 619/224-3481 or 800/759-0012; www.oceanvillainn.com.

San Diego Marriott Hotel & Marina: The people who work at this lovely waterfront Marriott have a great attitude about large dogs. Not only do they tolerate them, but they're happy to see them. "The size doesn't matter. It's often the small ones that bark a lot anyway," says one hotelier. (Smart man.) This Marriott is on the water, right next to the dog-unfriendly Seaport Village. At least the views of the bay are to bark about—er, to write home about. The humans in your party can enjoy the heated outdoor pools and the sauna, whirlpool, and exercise room. If you like the boating life, you and your dog can rent a boat from a boat-rental company on the property and have a great day on San Diego Bay (see the Diversion Whatever Floats Your Boat).

It's one of the more expensive Marriotts we've come across. Rates are $350–390. 333 West Harbor Drive 92101; 619/234-1500.

The Westin Horton Plaza: It's modern, it's chic, it's a cool place to stay with a dog who's not too big. (Dogs need to be under 40 pounds.) Lucky dog guests will get use of a Heavenly Dog Bed (a smaller version of the Heavenly Bed human guests rave about) and bowls for water and food. "We like to see dog guests come in," says a friendly front-desk worker. "They are so much fun."

This large, upscale hotel is downtown, right next to the famed Horton Plaza shopping center. Rates are $165–225. 910 Broadway Circle 92101; www.starwood.com/westin; 619/239-2200.

Coronado

Folks traveling with dogs aren't allowed to take the ferry to this island-like destination across the San Diego Bay. But a graceful 2.2-mile bridge will get you there just as fast—which is the speed your dog will want to go when she learns she can run off leash at one of the beaches.

PARKS, BEACHES, AND RECREATION AREAS

Coronado City Beach/Dog Beach

The westernmost part of this beach is a nude beach for dogs, where they can strip off their leashes and revel in their birthday furs. And since few people know about it, even the shyest dog will feel at home running around flaunting her more natural self.

As long as your dog is under voice control, she can be leashless at a small segment of this little beach. Your dog has only a few hundred feet of shoreline to run along, but the area between the beach border and the water is fairly wide.

The off-leash section is marked by signs and runs along Ocean Boulevard from around the foot of Sunset Park (on Ocean Drive) to the border of the U.S. Naval Station. You'll see the doggy litter bags. (Not far down the street is a hose-off station, should you not want to go home with sandy paws.) From the bridge, continue straight. In a few blocks, turn left on Orange Avenue and drive through town all the way down to the traffic circle. Go around the circle to Loma Avenue and follow it south about a block to Ocean Boulevard. Drive northwest a few blocks and park on the street around Sunset Park. 619/522-7380.

PLACES TO EAT

Cafe 1134: Pooches who keep you company at these outdoor tables while you dine on sandwiches and coffee are lucky dogs indeed: The staff provides dog biscuits and a water bowl for your fine furry friend. 1134 Orange Avenue; 619/437-1134.

Crown Bistro: The breakfasts here have won "best breakfast" awards many years in a row. It's a mighty convenient place to dine if you're staying at the Crown City Inn (see Places to Stay), since it's part of the inn's property. Dine with your very good doggy on scrumptious California-style food at the bistro's six small, shaded patio tables. This is an intimate place, and at times when it's busy, you may be asked to come back with your dog when there's a little more space. They're really friendly to dogs here, and even provide water to thirsty pooches, but the space is small enough that the owners ask patrons with pooches to call ahead to see if it's a good time to come. Any size well-behaved dog is welcome, pending adequate space. Regulars here include

DIVERSION

Venice, Shmenice!: When you and your dog share a private gondola that takes you through Coronado Cays' scenic canals and waterways, you'll feel almost as if you've been transported to Italy's famed land of canals. The only difference is that instead of your gondolier singing, he'll use a CD player for the Italian tunes. Oh, and there's no ancient architecture. And no magnificent old-world charm. OK, it may not be just like Italy, but it's still a wonderful excursion, and the gondolas—which are sizable and waterway-worthy—are pretty much guaranteed not to tip over, even if your dog gets a case of the wiggles.

The **Gondola Company** can arrange all kinds of special cruises, some featuring a brunch or dinner excursion. The most popular, the basic Passport Cruise, lasts one hour and includes an hors d'oeuvre or dessert plate. Bring your own vino or bubbly; the gondolier provides the wine glasses and an ice bucket. You'll also get use of a blanket. The Passport Cruise is $70 for two people and a dog. (You can invite your friends for $15 extra each. The boat can hold up to six passengers.) Cruises are offered 11 A.M.–midnight. The Gondola Company is right next to the ultra-dog-friendly Loews Coronado Bay Resort, at 4000 Coronado Bay Road; 619/429-6317; www.gondolacompany.com.

a 170-pound rottweiler and a 15-pound miniature dachshund. 520 Orange Avenue; 619/435-3678.

Viva Nova: The folks at this restaurant love dogs. The vegetarian cuisine includes hot soups and chili, which you can eat at the outdoor tables. There's also a juice bar and a health food store that stocks all-natural pet supplies. 1138 Orange Avenue; 619/435-2124.

PLACES TO STAY

Coronado Victorian House: In this gorgeous 1894 Victorian, all the beds in the seven bedrooms are from the 1800s and are topped with featherbed mattresses. You'll feel as though you're sleeping on a very elegant cloud. The rooms at this bed-and-breakfast all have private bathrooms (some with claw-foot tubs) and are beautifully furnished, reflecting the tastes of Bonni Marie, the inn's dog-loving owner. Bonni Marie will proudly tell you about her three "monkeys," her trio of rescued Cairn terriers. She's a most friendly innkeeper. She may even get you out on the dance floor. It's not what you think; Bonni Marie is a dance instructor. Many guests opt for couples' dance lessons in her large dance studio. Dance lessons come in mighty handy for burning off at least a portion of the inn's bountiful breakfast.

Sadly for dogs who weigh more than a large bag of dog food, 40 pounds is the size limit for pooches here. Don't be surprised when Bonni Marie also inquires about your dog's temperament when you call for reservations. "I just want to make sure everyone will be happy," she says.

Rates are $250–500 nightly, with a two-night minimum stay. Dogs are $25 for the length of their stay. An important piece of information to know when you make your reservation: Your reservation is noncancellable, and your fee is nonrefundable. Ouch! 619/435-2200 or 888/299-2822; www.coronadovictorianhouse.com.

Crown City Inn: This sweet little hotel is as welcoming for dogs as it is for humans. People get free use of bicycles and complimentary iced tea/hot chocolate and cookies every afternoon. Dogs get a food mat, water bowl, a treat bag with a toy, and info on pet sitters and dog-friendly parks and eateries. Everyone who comes here is happy.

Your room comes with a fridge and microwave, but with the Crown Bistro restaurant (see Places to Eat) so close to your room, you may want to give your kitchenette skills a break. Rates are $100–240. Dogs are $8–25. 520 Orange Avenue 92118; 619/435-3116; www.crowncityinn.com.

Loews Coronado Bay Resort: Prepare to be impressed. This modern, luxurious hotel presides over a 15-acre peninsula, with the Pacific on one side and San Diego Bay on the other. The rooms are crisp and clean, yet super comfy, with great waterfront views. The gardens are gorgeous, and the palm-lined three-pool area is to drool for (although no drool or dogs are allowed in the pools; pooches can take their dog paddle to the nearby Coronado City Beach/Dog Beach). If you like the sporting life, you can play tennis at the hotel's three lighted courts or rent a boat and set sail on the bay, with your dog as first mate (see the Diversion Whatever Floats Your Boat). Or you and your dog can hire a gondola for an enchanting cruise through the Coronado Cays (see the Diversion Venice, Shmenice!).

Speaking of dogs, the treatment they get here is nothing short of red carpet, thanks to Loews's Very Important Pet Program. Your dog will be welcome with a note from the hotel's general manager. It includes a list of nearby dog-friendly locales, as well as groomers, pet shops, and vets. In your room you'll find food and water bowls, treats, and toys. A doggy room-service menu is also available, with items that sound so good you might be tempted to share them. If you forgot a leash or your pet's bed, you can borrow these from the concierge's "Did You Forget" closet. Dog walking and pet sitting can be arranged if the staff isn't too busy. If you opt for a pet sitter, you'll get a Puppy Pager, which allows hotel staff to contact you in case of emergency.

Rates are $199–515. 4000 Coronado Bay Road 92118; 619/424-4000; www.loewshotels.com.

RESOURCES

National Forests and Wilderness Areas

Dogs of the Los Angeles area, rejoice! If you really want to stretch those gams, the U.S. Department of Agriculture's Forest Service has a real treat for you. Instead of a walk in your friendly neighborhood park, how does an exhilarating, off-leash hike sound? You'll have your choice of millions of acres of national forests spread over a fascinating variety of terrain.

Most dogs call the forests "dog heaven." Those who don't speak English just pant with joy. There's something for every dog's tastes in national forests. Desert dogs are as happy as dogs who like waterfalls and forests. Most national forests have no entry fees, few leash rules, and plenty of free camping. And they all have some of the most beautiful land in California. (National Forests lay claim to 40 million acres around the state. That's 20 percent of California!)

If your dog is obedient enough to come when she's called, and you trust her not to wander off in pursuit of deer or other wildlife, she's more than welcome to be off leash in most of the forest areas. In the descriptions that follow, I mention the exceptions to the off-leash policies that I'm aware of, but there may well be more. And since rules change frequently, you should call before you visit. Be aware that the frontline personnel at the forests might tell you that dogs must be on leash, but they're not always right. Ask for a supervisor or ranger if you have reason to think the leash laws are more lax.

Always carry a leash with you, just in case. It's a good idea to leash your dog on the trail when you see other hikers, or at least to pull your dog to the side so the others can pass by. "Believe it or not, not everyone loves dogs," says Matt Mathes, a dog-loving, very helpful representative of the U.S.D.A. Forest Service. Dogs must be leashed in developed campgrounds (which usually charge a small fee) and in developed recreation areas. But most areas of the forests are set up so that you can plop down a tent just about anywhere you please (for free). When you find that perfect, cool stream with a flat, soft area on the bank, your dog doesn't have to be leashed. But it's a bad idea to leave your dog leashless and outside your tent at night.

In each listing, I've noted any wilderness areas that fall within the forest I'm describing. Many require permits for hiking and camping. Contact a ranger to find out about the rules in a particular wilderness area.

The Forest Service's California website, www.fs.fed.us/r5, offers excellent guides to every National Forest in the state. Maps of specific national forests and wilderness areas are available for $6–10 each via the website or at local forest headquarters, or you can purchase them at many outdoor stores (but they'll be more expensive). It's always a good idea to contact the forest rangers in the area you'll be visiting and ask if there are any exceptions to the leash-free policy where you're planning to hike, or if your forest destination is charging a small fee for use. Only a few forest areas are charging fees at this point (and they're nominal), and at least 80 percent of the fee goes back into upkeep and improvements of those forests.

Now for the obligatory poop paragraph. As far as bathroom etiquette goes, it's not necessary to pack out the poop. If you don't mind it squishing along in your backpack, that's great. But if you bury it, as you should bury your own, that's OK. Leave the forest as you found it. And please don't let your dog go to the bathroom near a stream. It can be a health hazard to anyone drinking the water later.

And dogs, if you come to really love your national forests, tell your people that because of severely reduced budgets, trail maintenance is suffering. Tell them that the trails could sure use a hand. Tell them that rangers would be thrilled to have teams of dog owners working together to help keep up the trails they use. Your people can contact a ranger to see how they can volunteer.

What follows is a very brief description of each forest that's within this book's territory. Again, be sure to contact a ranger before setting out so you can check on changed rules and portions of forests or trails that might be closed.

ANGELES NATIONAL FOREST

This 693,000-acre forest covers about one-quarter of Los Angeles County and most of the San Gabriel Mountains. With more than 620 miles of trails, the forest provides an essential recreational outlet for millions of Southern Californians and their city-weary dogs.

Highlights include waterfalls, out-of-the-way canyons and streams, wild-flower-covered slopes, and thousands of acres of bighorn sheep territory. (Leash your dog if you go sheep-watching.)

The Cucamonga, San Gabriel, and Sheep Mountain Wilderness Areas are all part of Angeles National Forest.

For more information, contact Forest Headquarters, 701 North Santa Anita Avenue, Arcadia, CA 91006; 626/574-5200.

CLEVELAND NATIONAL FOREST

Cleveland National Forest takes you and your *perro* within five miles of the Mexican border. This 566,000-acre chaparral- and conifer-covered land has 331 miles of trails, including a section of the Pacific Crest Trail that runs between the Anza-Borrego Desert and Mexico.

Because of high fire danger, due in part to strong Santa Ana winds, rangers prefer that campers stay at developed sites.

The Agua Tibia, Hauser, Pine Creek, and San Mateo Canyon Wilderness Areas are within the forest.

For more information, contact Forest Headquarters, 10845 Rancho Bernardo Road, Suite 200, Rancho Bernardo, CA 92127-2107; 858/673-6180.

LOS PADRES NATIONAL FOREST

Ranging in elevation from sea level at Big Sur to nearly 9,000 feet at the crest of Mount Pinos, this spectacular forest is one of the most rugged and beautiful in the West.

It's also the second-largest forest in California, with much of its 1.9 million acres encompassing the Big Sur area. Some of the forest's trails crisscross cool streams, where you can set up a tent and sleep deeply as the sound of the rushing water blocks out those oh-so-appealing sounds of your dog chewing and scratching himself.

The Dick Smith, Machesna Mountain, San Rafael, Santa Lucia, and Ventana Wilderness Areas are all part of the forest. Joe Dog loved hiking in the Ventana Wilderness on easy trails shaded by coast redwood and the spire-like Santa Lucia fir.

For more information, contact Forest Headquarters, 6755 Hollister Avenue, Suite 150, Goleta, CA 93117; 805/968-6640.

SAN BERNARDINO NATIONAL FOREST

This forest is home to famed Big Bear Lake and Lake Arrowhead, popular Southern California resorts. It comprises 810,000 acres of land ranging from thick pine woods to rocky, cactus-filled desert.

A favorite activity here is cross-country skiing. Leashless dogs love to lope beside their skiing people in the winter. About 700 miles of trails are open to hikers and skiers. Because of recent complaints about dogs, they could soon have to be leashed throughout the forest. Check with a ranger before setting out. And dogs are not permitted in much of the San Jacinto Wilderness because it runs into Mount San Jacinto State Park (which bans dogs from its trails and backcountry).

The Cucamonga, San Gorgonio, San Jacinto, and Santa Rosa Wilderness Areas are part of the forest.

For more information, contact Forest Headquarters, 1824 Commercenter Circle, San Bernardino, CA 92408; 909/382-2600.

Emergency Veterinary Clinics

If your dog needs veterinary care at night or on weekends, when other veterinary hospitals are closed, here's a list of emergency clinics in the five-county L.A. metro area. All are open at night, and most open Saturday afternoon (some Saturday morning) through the wee hours on Monday morning.

VENTURA COUNTY

Pet Emergency Clinic: 2967 North Moorpark Road, Thousand Oaks; 805/492-2436.

Pet Emergency Clinic: 2301 South Victoria Avenue, Ventura; 805/642-8562.

LOS ANGELES COUNTY

Affordable Animal Emergency Clinic: 16907 San Fernando Mission Boulevard, Granada Hills; 818/636-8143.

Animal Emergency Care Center: 20051 Ventura Boulevard, Suite D, Woodland Hills; 818/887-2262.

Animal Emergency Centre: 11740 Ventura Boulevard, Studio City; 818/760-3882.

Animal Emergency Clinic: 1055 West Avenue M, Suite 101, Lancaster; 661/723-3959.

Animal Emergency Clinic of Pasadena: 2121 East Foothill Boulevard, Pasadena; 626/564-0704.

Animal Surgical & Emergency Center: 1535 South Sepulveda Boulevard, West Los Angeles; 310/473-1561.

Beverly Oaks Emergency Animal Clinic: 14302 Ventura Boulevard, Sherman Oaks; 818/788-7860.

Crossroads Animal Emergency & Referral Center: 11057 East Rosencrans Avenue, Norwalk; 562/863-2522.

Culver City Dog and Cat Hospital: 5558 Sepulveda Boulevard, Culver City; 818/636-8143.

Eagle Rock Emergency Pet Clinic: 4254 Eagle Rock Boulevard, Los Angeles; 323/254-7382.

East Valley Emergency Pet Clinic: 938 North Diamond Bar Boulevard, Diamond Bar; 909/861-5737.

Emergency Pet Clinic of San Gabriel Valley: 3254 Santa Anita Avenue, El Monte; 626/579-4550.

Emergency Pet Clinic of South Bay: 2325 Torrance Boulevard, Torrance; 310/320-8300.

North Bay Animal Emergency Hospital: 1304 Wilshire Boulevard, Santa Monica; 310/451-8962.

Pet Medical Center Chatoak: 17659 Chatsworth Street, Granada Hills; 818/368-5150.

VCA West Los Angeles Animal Hospital: 1818 South Sepulveda Boulevard, West Los Angeles; 310/473-1561.

ORANGE COUNTY

Central Orange County Emergency Animal Clinic: 3720 Campus Drive, Newport Beach; 949/261-7979.

North Orange County Emergency Pet Clinic: 1474 South Harbor Boulevard, La Habra; 714/441-2925.

Orange County Emergency Pet Clinic: 12750 Garden Grove Boulevard, Garden Grove; 714/537-3032.

SAN BERNARDINO COUNTY

Animal Emergency Clinic: 12022 La Crosse Avenue, Grand Terrace; 909/783-1300.

Animal Emergency Clinic: 15532 Bear Valley Road, Victorville; 760/962-1122.

Inland Valley Emergency Pet Clinic: 10 West 7th Street, Upland; 909/931-7871.

VCA Central Animal Hospital: 281 North Central Avenue, Upland; 909/981-1051.

RIVERSIDE COUNTY

Animal Emergency Clinic of the Desert: 72374 Ramon Road, Thousand Palms; 760/343-3438.

Emergency Pet Clinic: 27443 Jefferson Avenue, Temecula; 909/695-5044.

INDEXES

Accommodations Index

Camping

Restaurant Index

General Index

Acknowledgments

Many tailwags to...

My crackerjack fact-checkers, especially my four-paw hubby, Craig Hanson (who once again came through in a pinch); Denise Selleck (so did she); Nellie Fong (ditto); and Nathan Arbuckle.

Annie Dransfeldt and her dogs for scoping out some great places in Ventura County when time was of the essence.

The intrepid "Three-Dog-Dave" Hepperly and his ever-traveling canine crew for their innumerable and invaluable tips and photos.

Sheryl Smith and her dear dog Molly, for her continued suggestions of dog-gone great places.

Johanna Lack and Alec Brewster, for helping me sniff out dog-friendly restaurants.

And to the legions of terrific California dogs who had their humans write to tell me about their wonderful dog-friendly finds around the state. Wherever possible, I've noted you in the text, doggies. (I can be reached at www .caldogtravel.com.)

Keeping Current

Note to All Dog Lovers

While our information is as current as possible, changes to fees, regulations, parks, roads, and trails sometimes are made after we go to press. Businesses can close, change their ownership, or change their rules. Earthquakes, fires, rainstorms, and other natural phenomena can radically change the condition of parks, hiking trails, and wilderness areas. Before you and your dog begin your travels, please be certain to call the phone numbers for each listing for updated information.

Attention, Dogs of Los Angeles

Our readers mean everything to us. We explore Los Angeles and the surrounding areas so that you and your people can spend true quality time together. Your input to this book is very important. In the last few years, we've heard from many wonderful dogs and their humans about new dog-friendly places, or old dog-friendly places we didn't know about. If we've missed your favorite park, beach, outdoor restaurant, hotel, or dog-friendly activity, please let us know. We'll check out the tip, and if it turns out to be a good one, we'll include it in the next edition, giving a thank-you to the dog and/or person who sent in the suggestion. Please write us—we always welcome comments and suggestions.

The Dog Lover's Companion to Los Angeles
Avalon Travel Publishing
1400 65th Street, Suite 250
Emeryville, CA 94608, USA
email: atpfeedback@avalonpub.com